THE POLITICAL
THOUGHT OF
JOHN HENRY
NEWMAN

THE POLITICAL THOUGHT OF JOHN HENRY NEWMAN

TERENCE KENNY

GREENWOOD PRESS, PUBLISHERS
WESTPORT, CONNECTICUT

Library of Congress Cataloging in Publication Data

Kenny, Terence.
　　The political thought of John Henry Newman.

　　Reprint of the 1957 ed. published by Longmans, Green, London, New York.
　　Bibliography: p.
　　1. Newman, John Henry, Cardinal, 1801-1890--Political science.　I. Title.
JC223.N5K4　1974　　　　320.5'092'4　　　73-16741
ISBN 0-8371-7226-8

MAR 18 '74

All rights reserved

First published in 1957 by Longmans, Green and Co., London

Reprinted with the permission of Longman Group Ltd.

Reprinted in 1974 by Greenwood Press,
a division of Williamhouse-Regency Inc.

Library of Congress Catalogue Card Number 73-16741

ISBN 0-8371-7226-8

Printed in the United States of America

TO
**MY FATHER
AND MOTHER**

PREFACE

So many books have already been written about Cardinal Newman that some word of explanation, if not of apology, seems necessary for the publication of this work. This book finds its justification in tackling an aspect of Newman's thought which has never before been adequately treated; an aspect, indeed, of which many have doubted the very existence. Yet Newman did have much to say on politics, as this book will show, and it is hoped that the following pages will contribute to that fuller understanding of Newman's thought which is now rapidly emerging, as well as be found of interest and importance to those whose primary concern is not with Newman but with political thought itself. It is necessary to apologise for the predominance of exposition in the text, but this is a fault which it is very hard to eradicate, since it is not so much the correct interpretation of Newman's political thought which needs to be made public, but the very substance of that thought itself.

For permission to use the great collection of material—letters, journals, etc., at the Birmingham Oratory, I am very greatly indebted to the Father Superior and the Fathers of the Oratory. Like most who have written on Newman I am particularly grateful to the late Father Henry Tristram for much kindness and help.

I was helped in some researches by my friend Gerald Hermolle, and my wife gave me much valuable criticism and encouragement.

CONTENTS

	Page
Note on MSS. and Abbreviations	ix
Introduction	1

Chapter

I. **CONSERVATISM** — 24
   1. The Religious and Intellectual Basis — 29
   2. The Philosophy of History — 36
   3. The True Conservatism of Cardinal Newman — 47

II. **THE STATE** — 63
   1. The World's Evil — 63
   2. The Making of the State — 74
   3. The Maintenance of the State — 79
   4. Justice and the State: Some conclusions — 93

III. **CHURCH AND STATE** — 108
   1. The Church as a State — 108
   2. The Church as an Establishment — 118

IV. **LIBERALISM** — 127
   1. Newman's Opposition to Liberalism — 127
   2. How Liberal was Newman? — 145

V. **NEWMAN AND THE MODERN DEMOCRATIC STATE** — 166
   1. Had Newman a Social Conscience? — 166
   2. Was Newman a Democrat? — 173
   3. Newman's Political Influence Today — 187

A Select Bibliography — 194
Index — 203

NOTE ON MANUSCRIPT MATERIAL

THE manuscript material consulted, with the exception of a few letters in the Gladstone Collection at the British Museum, is that held at the Birmingham Oratory. This material is divided broadly into two—letters and other material. The letters are in five collections—*Personal, Special Subject, Oratory, Miscellaneous* and *Copied*. The *Copied Letters* have been accepted as accurate copies, and where the originals have come to hand I have found them to be so. The other material is mainly the collection of journals, notebooks, jottings, etc., kept in Newman's room, and catalogued under *Cardinal's Cupboards*. In addition, however, over a hundred of Newman's early sermons have recently come to light, which are not yet properly catalogued. Except in the case of these sermons, all the references to manuscript material will be very readily verifiable.

ABBREVIATIONS

MSS.
C.C. *Cardinal's Cupboards* (followed by catalogue number, e.g. A.46).
C.L. *Copied Letters* (followed by name of recipient of letter, then its date).
P.C. *Personal Collection* (followed by the person under whose name the correspondence is filed, then the date of letter).
P.C., Nb. Two notebooks, kept with the *Personal Collection*.
S.S. *Special Subject* (followed by name of subject, name of recipient of letter, then date).

Newman's Published Works[1]
Add. *Addresses and Replies.* Ed. Neville, London, 1905.
Apo. *Apologia Pro Vita Sua.* O.U.P., 1913.
Ari. *Arians of the Fourth Century.*

[1] The standard edition of Newman's collected works is that published by Longmans Green and Co., 40 volumes, 1874–1921 (index by J. Rickaby). Where not otherwise indicated, references are to this edition.

D.A.	Discussions and Arguments. 2nd ed., London, 1873.
Dev.	Development of Christian Doctrine.
Diff., i, ii.	Difficulties of Anglicans.
Ess., i, ii.	Essays: Critical and Historical. 3rd ed., London, 1871.
G.A.	Grammar of Assent. New ed., London and New York, 1947.
H.S., i, iii.	Historical Sketches.
Idea.	Idea of a University.
L.G.	Loss and Gain.
Mir.	Two Essays on Miracles.
Mix.	Discourses to Mixed Congregations.
O.S.	Sermons on Various Occasions.
P.S., i to viii.	Parochial and Plain Sermons.
P.P.C.	Present Position of Catholics.
St. Ath., i, ii.	Select Treatises of St. Athanasius.
S.D.	Sermons on Subjects of the Day.
S.E.	Stray Essays on Controversial Points. Private Print, 1890.
Tracts.	Tracts for the Times. Oxford, 1833–1841.
U.S.	Oxford University Sermons
V.M., i, ii.	Via Media.
V.V.	Verses on Various Occasions. London, 1868.

Other Works

Keble Corr.	Correspondence of J. H. Newman with J. Keble and Others. London, 1917.
M., i, ii.	Letters of J. H. Newman. Ed. A. Mozley, London, 1891.
Ward, Life, i, ii.	W. Ward, Life of John Henry Cardinal Newman. London, 1912.

INTRODUCTION

No attempt at a full-length study of Newman's politics has until now been made, but it is true that many writers have found something to say on this subject. Unfortunately, much that has been written has been rather misleading, where not simply false, so that a serious effort at the exposition and criticism of Newman's political thought is now long overdue.[1] And in the first place, let there be no doubt that Newman had much to contribute to political thought. Perhaps, in the future, he will always find a place in the textbooks, if only because of his profound conservatism, harking back, on the one hand, to Burke, and, on the other hand, pointing to the future, to an anticipation of Sorel's celebrated doctrine of the 'myth', and to much else of interest and importance. Yet this is only one aspect of Newman's contribution, and his views on the State, on the vexed question of its relation to the Church, and on many associated problems, are views which will amply repay investigation.

No sensational claim is made here that Newman is an undiscovered genius of nineteenth-century political thought. He will never be ranked along with, for example, J. S. Mill and T. H. Green. Neither in the extent of his influence, nor in the quality and quantity of his political writings, can he be claimed to rank with these. But, though his precise stature can later be determined, it may confidently be asserted that Newman is entitled to a more honourable place in the history of political thought than has hitherto been generally supposed. However, many seem to have thought that Newman had little or nothing to say on politics, and so, before examining more closely the nature of Newman's contribution, it will be instructive to glance at a few of the reasons for its past neglect.

Nor are reasons hard to find. In the first place Newman wrote

---

[1] The best work on this subject is to be found in Professor Crane Brinton's chapter on Newman in his *English Political Thought in the Nineteenth Century* (London, 1933), and in the late Professor Laski's *Problem of Sovereignty* (London, 1917).

no political treatise, nor did he anywhere set out the main corpus of his political ideas in a form in which they could be readily grasped, and seen in relation to one another. Thus, to discover Newman's politics, it has formerly been necessary to search his works widely for scattered arguments and reflexions, to examine his letters and conversations in print, and then, to gain the complete picture, examine his unpublished papers. All this has been too much for most; but even so, perhaps more would have made the attempt had it not seemed likely in advance that a minute search would reveal little, since it was strongly suspected that there was little to reveal.

One reason for supposing that Newman might be discovered in the end as having nothing to say on politics is that it is undeniable that the major interest in his life was certainly not politics, but religion. But it is quite false to suppose, because Newman was quite unworldly in the sense that he thought the next world immeasurably more important than the present, that he was uninterested in the affairs of this world. Far from it being the case that Newman's religion kept him from an interest in politics, it is much nearer the truth to say that it was his religion which forced him to think about politics. Newman's religion was a social religion, 'for man never stands alone here, though he will stand by himself one day hereafter; but here he is a social being, and goes forward to his long home as one of a large company'.[1] Newman's Church was a visible society, and the question of its relation with the State was bound to arise for him, as it did, both theoretically and practically. This was the starting-point of a body of political thought which was to range far wider than its original object.

Perhaps as potent a factor in the general neglect of Newman's politics has been the wide belief that Newman, while displaying some political interest, went no further than a sentimental and reactionary Toryism. This is very far from the mark. Newman was a conservative indeed, but only with great caution can he be called a Tory, and then it must be admitted that he generally

[1] *G.A.*, p. 308.

disclaimed the label altogether. To imagine that Newman's main political ideas can be called 'reactionary' is to make the very mistake that makes the writing of this book necessary. It will be seen that it was precisely because he was not reactionary in certain important questions, that Newman caused great antagonism towards himself in both the Anglican and Catholic Churches. Finally, it will not now, perhaps, be necessary to spend time dispelling 'the sentimental myth'[1] which has been woven round Newman's name. Far from displaying sentimentality, it was 'a fierce realism' in politics which characterised Newman, as Mr. Keith Feiling has observed;[2] and if Newman, in revolting against the eighteenth-century deification of reason, gave full allowance to non-rational factors and unconscious drives, he was in this none the less realistic, and quite rational, though certainly not rationalistic.

It is now time to prepare for an examination and criticism of Newman's political ideas, and to leave speculation about why they have been ignored.[3] And first, it will be necessary to glance at Newman's personal history and background, since, no more than with any other thinker, did Newman's opinions appear in the void.

Newman was born in February 1801, and died in August 1890. Thus his life spanned a century of great social and political changes, which changes, in their broadest aspect, affected Newman more than is sometimes thought. The circumstances of the very month of Newman's birth may not have been without some effect on him. This was that unhappy period of the Napoleonic Wars known as the 'Armed Neutrality', when England, in her war with France, found Russia, Denmark, Prussia and Sweden combined threateningly against her. Though better fortune was soon to come, it is not surprising that one born at such a time

---

[1] F. V. Reade, 'The Sentimental Myth', *Newman Centenary Essays* (London, 1945), pp. 139–154.
[2] *Sketches in Nineteenth Century Biography* (London, 1930), p. 111.
[3] Perhaps it would be too cynical to submit as one reason for failure to appreciate the extent of Newman's political thought the surprising absence, in the published *Index* to his works, of political references.

should, until very late in life, continue to look with suspicion and dislike across the Channel, and at the ideas radiating from France and transforming Europe. But the war with France at least helped to secure the position in life of Newman's father, to enable him to become a prosperous young banker, and marry a wife of wealth and breeding. In those war years small banks flourished, and John Newman, senior, managed to leave very far behind him those six Cambridgeshire acres, bought by a tailor forbear, from which his own father had not long before set out to London.[1] It is a curious fact that Newman made as much effort to conceal the humble origins of his family, and the eventual business failures of his father, as many prominent men might now attempt to boast of them.

There was little in John Henry's family background which was likely to influence him politically in any particular direction. John Newman, the father, seems to have been of no flaming political zeal, and exerted a steady, sane, tolerant, middle-of-the-road influence on his six children. Ironically enough, his children, and in particular his boys, were by no means content with humdrum opinions, in politics or in anything else. To say nothing of John Henry, whose dramatic defection from the English Church is well enough known, both Frank and Charles, his brothers, were far from the commonplace. Frank, the youngest, 'became a Plymouth Brother, and went to Bagdad to convert the Muslims to Darbyism'.[2] On the unaccountable failure of this mission he became a Unitarian, and fought with great vigour for rational and enlightened views on vegetarianism, teetotalism, mixed bathing and sundry other burning issues. Charles, between his brothers in age, became a convert to the ideas of Robert Owen, and became so convinced that he was the helpless plaything of his environment that he had little heart left for the never-ending struggle to earn a living. Luckily for him his family, and not the least John Henry, was usually ready to assume the onerous burden.

John Newman, senior, can hardly be held directly responsible

[1] The best work on Newman's origins is to be seen in Sean O'Faolain's *Newman's Way* (London, 1952).   [2] *ibid.*, p. 88.

for Charles' Owenite Socialism, nor Frank's various outbursts on social and political matters, but he can be held responsible for John's eventual political ideas at least in so far as he provided the money to send this his eldest son to Oxford. It is as the leader of the Oxford Movement—that great movement in the Anglican Church which did so much to throw back the hostile forces ranged against her—that John Henry Newman is most generally known today. This movement was seen by one intelligent observer, Dean Stanley,[1] to be entirely political in origin, while J. A. Froude found himself able to announce that it was nothing more than 'Toryism in ecclesiastical costume'.[2] It is clear that some examination of Newman's career in Oxford must be made here.

When Newman came to Trinity College, Oxford, in the year 1817, religious questions were, as they always remained, of paramount importance for him, and there is little evidence at this time of an awareness on his part of contemporary political affairs. Yet much had happened in the sixteen years between Newman's birth and his admission to Trinity College. The very month of his birth had seen the violently anti-Catholic Addington replace Pitt as Prime Minister, after the latter's unfortunate embroilment with George III on the question of Catholic Emancipation. Curiously enough, Newman was twenty-eight years later to oppose Sir Robert Peel for his temerity in assisting the introduction of this long-deferred measure, while yet another sixteen years later, he was himself to leave the Church of England for the Church of Rome. There was, of course, more than changes of Prime Minister, even such more dramatic ones as that caused by the murder of one of them—Perceval—to engage the attention of the young Newman during this time. A period which saw the madness of King George III, the scandal of the Queen Caroline affair, besides the varying fortunes and triumphant close of the Napoleonic Wars, was no political vacuum. But it was not so much the great political and military events of which Newman

---

[1] Church, *Oxford Movement* (London, 1894), p. 1.
[2] *Short Studies* (London, 1909), iv, 249.

seemed relatively unaware, so much as of the grave social situation which was indicated in the very year of Newman's arrival at Oxford by the repeal of the Habeas Corpus Act, and by Cobbett's flight to America.

Oxford was then no place to gain a clear and steady view of the country's serious social problems. The isolated and insulated nature of Oxford life at this time has often been stressed. Much of the feverish agitation and movement elsewhere in England showed as no more than a ripple on the quiet surface of Oxford life. College and University affairs might seem starkly real in Oxford, and might later have forced themselves on to the national stage, but many urgent national questions seem to have found little entrance into Oxford consciousness. It is a curious example of this that Tom Mozley, Newman's brother-in-law, could mention quite casually that soldiers quelling riots at Otmoor, after enclosures there, dined later at Oriel.[1] It is hard to realise that this is the same Otmoor, the same enclosures, whose tragic history is so graphically reported by the Hammonds.[2] Newman's early withdrawal from a world of social and political unrest into the more tranquil atmosphere of Oxford may go some way to explain a lifelong obtuseness to the vexing social problems of his age which has puzzled and annoyed many writers.

Yet the unrest was real enough. Of course, it may well have been that nothing would have eliminated much suffering and hardship for a great mass of the people in the rapid industrialisation which was then still taking place. But a succession of bad harvests, coupled with the interference with the importation of corn resulting from the French wars had brought food to famine prices; nor did the Corn Law of 1815 indicate that the landlords were very anxious ever to see cheap corn again. The high price of food, the growing pauperisation of agricultural England through the 'Speenhamland Act', the remorseless extensions of the enclosure movement, and the varied and partially inevitable evils of the unregulated growth of the factory system, made the years

[1] T. Mozley, *Reminiscences of Oriel* (2nd ed., London, 1882), ii, 60.
[2] J. L. and Barbara Hammond, *The Village Labourer* (4th ed., London, 1927), pp. 64 ff.

Introduction

following 1815 bristle with problems with which any government might have found it difficult to cope. For the man it may be still permissible to call the 'archmediocrity', Lord Liverpool, especially before the advent of Huskisson and Canning into his Cabinet, the difficulties must have seemed quite overwhelming.

Although Newman's lack of concern with social problems will always be contrasted with the different attitude of such another as his fellow Roman Catholic and contemporary, Cardinal Manning, it is none the less true that Newman was never long without some important, more narrowly political ideas. Thus, on arrival at Oxford, whatever his exact political allegiance before he came, Newman soon declared himself a Tory. The reason given is characteristic and revealing. 'Toryism was the creed of Oxford' and so Newman took up what he found established because he was already a 'good conservative'.[1] That Newman always remained a good conservative, through temperament and philosophic conviction, will be maintained, but that he remained for long a Tory, in any important sense, will soon be shown to be a mistaken opinion.

Newman's Oxford was a Tory stronghold partly because it was at that time a Church of England stronghold. It has been remarked that the origins of the Tory party are to be found in the Church party of Elizabeth's reign, and in the early years of the nineteenth century there is little doubt that the bulk of the clergy, and certainly the bishops, were Tories, intent on safeguarding the prerogatives of the Church and the general welfare of the Establishment. But besides this, there were certain other elements in the Oxford resistance to Whiggery and liberalism. Oxford had been one of the last strongholds of Jacobitism, and also of the Non-Jurors, those bishops, clergy and laity of the Church of England who would not abandon their hereditary monarch, nor swear allegiance to William of Orange. Both of these groups had disappeared from Oxford, but they had helped to leave their mark on its Toryism, and Newman was later to revive there some of the doctrines of the Non-Jurors.

[1] *Apo.*, p. 492.

There was also much, no doubt, in the Toryism of Oxford of what Dicey has called 'Old Toryism', the last years of the ascendancy of which coincided with Newman's first years at Oxford. This Toryism, incarnate, for example, in Lord Eldon, held the British constitution, as expounded by Blackstone, in a degree of reverence which might almost be called worship. The idea of its deficiency in any respect was, when not sacrilegious, positively dangerous, since such was the unique nature of the constitution that any adjustments to rectify apparent injustices or inefficiencies must of necessity fail of their effect, and bring worse evil in consequence. Something of this spirit no doubt Newman imbibed, but such was far from being the most important element in the Toryism he came to adopt. Indeed, despite the fact that Newman's eventual Toryism while at Oxford seems now, given his particular temperament and the influences to which he was subjected, almost inevitable, it is nevertheless true that during an earlier period of his university career he was drifting in a very different direction. The approach of a kind of liberalism in the later Newman is not unrelated to the profound impressions gained in this early period.

Newman had entered Trinity College while only sixteen, but at the age of twenty-one he succeeded in being elected as a Fellow of Oriel. Thus he achieved a great academic and personal distinction, for Oriel was an intellectual and reforming college in those days of unreformed Oxford, and chose its Fellows with exceeding shrewdness from those persons who combined mere academic ability with those other qualities of mind and character which no examination paper can bring properly to light. It was some of these brilliant members of the Oriel Common Room who were to exercise on the young don a strong 'liberal' influence. The Common Room then, it was reputed, 'stank of logic', but it was not so much the reliance on formal logic as a general exuberant confidence in conscious reason, and an accompanying contempt for tradition and authority, which Newman found there. These Oriel 'Noetics', so called, probably, because they claimed to exercise their highest faculties, where others left them dormant, led Newman, not indeed to call all in question, as they were ready to do, but at least to place what he later found to be an excessive reliance on intellect, to the neglect of moral considerations. Such a mistake, Newman came to think, lay at the root of much that went under the name of 'liberalism'.

Although Newman was not long under the Noetic influence before his arrival in the Tory camp, he had gained much which he was never later to lose. Perhaps Richard, later Archbishop, Whately, together with another Fellow, Hawkins, later Provost of Oriel, had most to do with the sharpening of Newman's intellectual powers which then took place. Newman helped considerably in preparing Whately's *Elements of Logic*, and seems to have been used as an anvil for Whately to hammer out his ideas, while Hawkins took especial care to criticise any looseness of thought or expression in his younger colleague. For the rest of his days Newman was an enemy to all vagueness of thought, and though far from thinking that every idea could be clearly presented within a few words, was remarkably careful to make sure that what words were in fact used to represent an idea did so as clearly as words could present it. Thus on politics as on religion, Newman is very clear that he is the master of words, and not they of him, and for many this has been in some sort a reproach against him. But it is in connexion with the Noetic readiness to question established ideas and institutions that the liberal influence in question is most pronounced. Though there was far more to the life of political and religious institutions than these men were quite aware, they had a quick eye for the indefensible, and they assuredly brought Newman to contemplate without shocked horror the trial of some of these institutions at the bar of reason. Of course with Newman it was not so much a case of condemning the institution for any alleged deficiencies, as the careful attempt to distinguish the essential from the inessential elements in it, the permanent from the impermanent. But Newman had been brought to think deeply by this stimulus, and in fact vindicated triumphantly much that, in his age, was increasingly being questioned: yet at the same time he was more ready for change and the alteration of established things than many conservatively minded people could bring themselves to be. Two examples of this readiness which will be discussed in this book are to be found in the coolness with which Newman as an Anglican was prepared to face the disestablishment of the Anglican Church, and in his later desire, despite bitter Catholic opposition, to see the end of the Temporal Power of the Papacy.

A readiness to change established institutions was a prime example of liberalism for Newman, and it is clear that to some extent he had been brought to share it, but this is far from denying that his general position was to stress the need for continuity and organic life, rather than for change, or to deny that he reserved his liberalism for particular cases. There was, however, another sort of liberalism which began to affect Newman at this time.

The Calvinistic Evangelicalism with which Newman had come to Oxford was rapidly rubbed away in his contacts with Hawkins and the other Oriel Fellows, and in its place appeared an attitude, perhaps better called humanistic, which was prepared to give much more value than formerly to the result of purely human endeavour, in thought and action. Thus, as a Catholic, Newman could extol the virtues of a 'liberal education', and though some have thought that it was only as a Catholic that Newman displayed this liberal outlook, in fact it is to this first period in the Oriel Common Room that one must go to find its origins. Whatever the changes in Newman's political and religious beliefs in 1845, it seems certain that there was no fundamental change in this respect.

But real though this liberal influence was, it was not inconsistent with a simultaneous Tory influence from other sources. From Newman's earliest days at Oriel, and, indeed, before then, he had been enormously impressed by his renowned Oriel colleague, John Keble, author of the *Christian Year*; although perhaps Keble was rather wary of Newman with his vestigial evangelicalism and incipient liberalism. Now Keble was far from being an aggressive Tory, he was generally far too quiet and gentle to be aggressive about anything, but there is little doubt that his calm and unspectacular Toryism was not without effect on his admiring junior colleague. Far more pronounced, however, was the effect on Newman of the more lively personality and more dashing Toryism of another colleague, Richard Hurrell Froude. Newman's description of Froude's politics, that he was 'a high Tory of the Cavalier stamp', is as well known as it is apt, but it should be remembered that it was more a judgement on Froude's manner of attachment to, and expression of, his Tory views, than of their intellectual content. Under the influence of his ardent friend Newman begins to speak of 'our blessed martyr St. Charles, and of King George the Good',[1] and soon went as far in the direction of an avowed and unmistakable Toryism as he ever went. Whether Newman, with his different origins and background, could ever have arrived at a political attitude identical with Froude's is questionable, but it is also a question which it is not necessary to answer. For young as Froude was when he died, he lived long enough to say with Newman, 'Farewell to Toryism'.[2]

Those who have failed to appreciate this fact are often those who look upon the Oxford Movement as primarily a political, a Tory, phenomenon and seem to assume that Newman must therefore still be considered a Tory till his break with the Anglican Church in 1845. But it is most misleading to suggest that all the leaders of this Movement either were Tories to begin with, or were ever animated by precisely the same political ideas, or set of ideas. In fact the politics of some of the leaders of the Oxford Movement were as diverse as their personal backgrounds, and for some of its most prominent leaders, it was in essence hardly a political phenomenon at all. It was not so for Newman. The growth in Newman of the more Catholic view of the Church which he concurrently attempted, through the *Tracts for the Times*, to foist on to the Anglican Church, has been sufficiently illuminated in his *Apologia*. In a relatively uneventful life as

[1] *H.S.*, i, 340.
[2] Froude, *Remains* (London, 1838), i, 429. The precise significance of this title will emerge in subsequent chapters.

Fellow of Oriel, and later, Vicar of St. Mary's, Newman had had time to pursue his religious studies according to his own particular bent. He had also had time to make a special study of political constitutions, though that is not here the important point.[1] These religious studies had been much concerned with the early Church, and much concerned also with certain British seventeenth-century theologians. A picture of the Church as it was, as it could be, might be, and an appreciation of the value of dogma were derived from these studies, and a very unflattering comparison resulted between the Church of Newman's researches and the actual, empirical English Church. The Church for Newman had to be an authoritative and dogmatic Church, and if the English Church were not this, and could not be persuaded to be this, then it was necessary for him to find a Church which was conscious of its God-given authority, which was dogmatic because it had truths to guard and to teach, and which was not only ready to point out the truth, but to single out and condemn error. No doubt a scientific proof of the contention made here, that for Newman the Oxford Movement was nothing more than a religious movement, will have to await a truly scientific history; but, as many have pointed out, from G. K. Chesterton to Mr. Christopher Dawson, the Oxford Movement can surely never be understood unless it is seen as a desperate attempt to uphold the idea of objective religious truth, of dogma, against a rising tide of subjectivism and relativism.

It is true, of course, that the Oxford Movement was begun before all its distinctive religious positions were worked out. The elaboration of Newman's *Via Media* between Protestantism and the Church of Rome was not completed till many years after Keble's famous sermon on 'National Apostasy' in 1833 had served as a point of departure for the Movement. But by 1833 Newman, under the influence of Froude and Keble, and as a result of his own thought, had quite a high enough view of the Church and its role to react violently to its many assailants. There is no doubt that a very genuine fear for the Church and

[1] T. Mozley, *Reminiscences of Oriel*, i, 34.

Establishment was widespread at this time, and it is not difficult to appreciate why this was so.

Apart from the general legacy of torpor and worldliness from the previous century, from which the Church of the new century had not yet shaken itself free, the growth of church-less industrial towns, the strength of the Dissenters, and their malevolence towards the Church, and the uncompromising hostility of an increasingly powerful group of philosophic radicals, as well as radicals of an older type, all helped to make the lovers of the Establishment tremble for its safety. Newman had no especial love for the Establishment, though he loved the Church, but at first he defended the interests of both to the best of his power.

The first *Tracts for the Times* did in fact give a most vigorous defence, and all those who were fearful of a coming onslaught could take courage and rejoice in the sight of such powerful support for the Anglican Church. Not all those fearful for the Church were oblivious of the strong doctrine which was contained in the *Tracts*, but undoubtedly many whose interests were not primarily religious were at first satisfied with what they took as a timely defence of the Establishment. Indeed, some of the very leaders of the Movement were perhaps as concerned with the political issue of the Establishment as they were with more religious or doctrinal points. Yet the dangers and difficulties of the Established Church provided the occasion, and not the whole *raison d'être* of the Movement, though many Tories undoubtedly flocked to its support. It is instructive to notice that William Palmer, of Worcester College, one of the original leaders of the Tractarian Movement, complacently ascribes the Tory return to power in the autumn of 1834 to the success of the revival initiated by the *Tracts*.[1] But Newman at least was prepared to leave the Establishment and its Tory supporters behind in his quest for the true Church; and in 1845 he left the Anglican Church to join the Catholic Church, the Church of liberals such as Daniel O'Connell, to whom he had had such an 'unspeakable aversion'.[2]

[1] *Narrative of Events* (2nd ed., Oxford, 1843), p. 17.   [2] *Apo.*, p. 221.

Of course there were many who thought that Newman had all along been a crypto-Catholic, or at least since the storm over *Tract 90* in 1841, when Newman had tried to reconcile the Catholic ideas and practices of the *Via Media* with the Thirty-nine Articles. Since Newman's justly celebrated autobiography—*Apologia Pro Vita Sua*—there will scarcely now be many willing to reproach his general character. Far from there being duplicity, there was no hint of worldliness or self-seeking in Newman's University career as Vicar of St. Mary's, and he remained always a dutiful son to his eventually widowed mother, and a generous brother to his brothers and sisters. His career, though in some ways uneventful, was far from quiet, surrounded as he was increasingly by the bitter storms of religious controversy. Even at Littlemore, the little village only a few miles from Oxford to which he had retired to spend the last two years of his life in the Anglican Church, he was pursued by the noise of the controversy he had done so much to stir up. How far, in the discussions on politics that Newman had with his fellow recluses at Littlemore, he learnt to look with less anger on the political bearing of the Catholic body in England, cannot be determined, but at least he may well have begun to see a little more clearly the precise nature of their predicament. One fact is certain, and is attested by Newman himself, though unfortunately in a letter which has never before been made public, and that is that not only did Newman's religious position alter greatly in this Littlemore period, but so also did his political views. The nature of this important change in Newman's political outlook, foreshadowed already in his changing views on the Established Church while the Tractarian Movement was in full swing, will later need careful analysis.

It was also during this period at Littlemore that Newman wrote his *Development of Christian Doctrine*, one of the few of his many volumes which must be considered as of crucial importance for gaining a knowledge of his political thought. Although the scope of this book was primarily intended to be confined to religion, in fact the general principles which it involves are obviously capable of much wider application, and throughout the book Newman is constantly illustrating his thesis with examples from the field of politics. Newman's argument—that ideas do not remain static but develop, and that there are certain tests to distinguish the true from a false development of a certain idea—was argued with force and originality. The book was not particularly well received at its publication, since non-Catholics were highly suspicious of an argument which had led the author to such a drastic conclusion, and Catholics were a little puzzled by an originality which they were not quite sure could be distinguished from heterodoxy. Even half a century after the publication of the *Development* it was stated in a prominent Catholic journal that this book was little more than 'the product of a jaded mind'.[1]

Cardinal Wiseman, whom Newman visited at Oscott shortly after his conversion, anticipated the verdict of posterity by having complete faith in Newman, and persuading him to publish his book as a Catholic without any revision or amendment. But Wiseman's confidence in Newman was not shared by all in the now rapidly reviving Catholic Church in England. The growth of the Church at this time was by no means uniform, nor was it without its incidental squabbles, and jealousies, and misunderstandings. Catholic Emancipation had been passed in 1829 largely because of the Irish political situation, and though it benefited English Catholics it could scarcely have been credited to their efforts. The gratitude of a certain section of the English Catholics was soon shown when the 'Liberator', Daniel O'Connell, was blackballed in his attempt at membership of the Cisalpine Club, a society containing men with names honoured for centuries by the Church in England. But the English Catholics themselves were far from united. There could not but be great differences in outlook between Old Catholics, with actual or inherited memories of penal days, and recent converts, with the romantic notions of Kenelm Digby, the broad vision and extravagant hopes of Ambrose Phillips de Lisle, the exuberance of a

[1] *Dublin Review* (1905), vol. 137, p. 270.

Gothic-crazy Pugin, to mention only a few of the pre-Faber and Manning converts. Quite apart from such questions as Ultramontanism, it is not surprising that Old Catholics looked with mixed feelings on these new converts, rushing in with the zeal of neophytes, often in too much of a hurry to come to any very close understanding of those whom they had joined. Newman himself was even regarded by some at first as a potential Judas, but it could be claimed that he rapidly came to have a more balanced and tolerant view of the matters and parties in dispute than any of his contemporaries, and his first critics soon lost their exaggerated fears.

It was the existence of perpetual divisions in the Church which went far to cause a certain reticence on Newman's part with regard to certain political questions which might involve fruitless quarrels. He kept his opinions none the less firmly, however, and at times, and by devious routes, they became public. One important topic on which Newman came to have definite views was the vexed question of the Temporal Power of the Papacy. It is of interest to note that Newman had special qualifications for making a judgement on this issue since he was sent to Rome in 1846 for more than a year, where he formed certain judgements on Pio Nono, the Italian Liberals, and the whole question of the Temporal Power, as can be seen from his later writings. Newman's talent for seeing, through a welter of controversy, the whole background of a problem and the underlying issues of it, as well as divining the ultimate verdict of posterity, is seldom to be better seen than in his conclusions against the necessity of the Temporal Power.

But when Newman returned to England at the end of 1847 the bitter arguments on this and other topics were still in the future. He proceeded to establish his Oratory in Birmingham, convinced, in a prophetic vision of the palmy days of Joseph Chamberlain, that the city was to be a future centre of political power.[1] But there was little in the early years of the Oratory in Birmingham which had any great political significance for

[1] *Oratory Letters*, 25 February 1849.

Newman. It is in the years between 1853 and 1857 that one might look for such matters, for this was the period of Newman's stay in Ireland as Rector of the ill-fated Catholic University. No doubt Newman's general political views developed while he was here, and it is on record that the new Rector was nothing loath to employ Young Ireland men as lecturers for him, but it was possibly the frustration he experienced when confronted by a reactionary clergy, in particular Cardinal Cullen, which had the deepest effect on Newman, as far as his eventual political outlook was concerned.

The events of the passing years, both at home and abroad, were not lost on Newman, though there was little call on him, retired as he was from the public eye, to advertise his opinions. Nor would many have sought them. His numerous published works sold steadily enough, but there is no doubt that Newman was worried about the first period of fifteen years as a Catholic, which had been for him a succession of failures, and reduced his influence greatly among his co-religionists and the country at large. An opportunity to express himself publicly on current affairs came with his editorship of the *Rambler* in 1859. The history of Newman's connexion with this brilliant Catholic journal, in association with Acton and Simpson, is well known, and there is little that further research on the question can bring to light. Suffice it to say here that the journal caused endless irritation among Catholics, not least under Newman's editorship, which lasted only for two issues. This journal, like its successor, the *Home and Foreign Review*, was permeated by a form of Liberal Catholicism. The period of these reviews, 1858–1864, was a period of a great struggle in the Church between Liberal Catholicism and Ultramontanism, a struggle which in 1864, with the celebrated *Syllabus of Modern Errors*, could be seen to be tending to the final Ultramontane victory in the Declaration of Papal Infallibility in 1870.

The battle between Liberal Catholicism and Ultramontanism rent the Catholic Church in the middle decades of the nineteenth century. There is no doubt that Newman was on the side of the Liberal Catholics, however much he disagreed with the manner in which they often acted or expressed themselves. But in stating that Newman was an opponent of Ultramontanism it must be remembered that the Ultramontanism of the decade 1860–1870 was not that of the early days of the nineteenth century. Gallicanism, in all its forms, was a dead and irrelevant issue by this time, and Ultramontanism went beyond its original assertion of the papal prerogatives to an almost unlimited claim for the personal authority of the Pope. The violence and arrogant presumption of some of its leading exponents helped to condemn the new Ultramontanism in the eyes of the whole world, as well as enraging the Liberal Catholics who were themselves mainly Ultramontanes of an earlier sort. Neither was the Liberal Catholicism of this period quite the same as that of Lamennais in 1830, but it resembled it in many respects, particularly in its acceptance of the general plea of liberty in the modern State. It has long been clear that Newman strongly supported the Liberal Catholics on account of their special emphasis on the need for an intellectual reawakening amongst Catholics, but it was not only here that he supported them. Newman insisted as strongly as any Liberal Catholic that the modern State must not attempt in any way to enforce a particular religion or its doctrines on its members. He was a positive enthusiast for the secular State, not passively admitting its present regrettable necessity. There is no possibility of accusing Newman of wanting to claim a freedom for his Church in the modern State which he would not be prepared to extend to others if his Church were in a position to deny it. The tolerant State, neutral on religious questions, was not something which had merely come about; it ought to have come about, and Newman found a justification for it in accordance with the political ideas he had long held.

The general sympathy with Liberal Catholicism which Newman displayed in public, which was less than that which he has recorded privately, did not endear him to many of his fellow Catholics at a time when Ultramontanism was in the ascendancy, and even many of the more middle-of-the-road Catholics were puzzled by his position. But his *Apologia Pro Vita Sua*, written in 1864, had brought Newman out of the obscurity in which he was beginning to fall, and placed him securely enough in the good opinion of Catholics as a whole. This was a factor which helped Newman to surmount some of the unpopularity to which his views naturally gave rise, but before long there was no need to draw on this moral credit. Passions soon cooled after the Declaration of Papal Infallibility in 1870. Both sides were able to claim a victory after this declaration, since its terms were by no means that for which the Ultramontanes had been pressing, while the very fact of a declaration at all was a mortal blow to the Liberal Catholics who had been campaigning against any declaration of any sort at that particular time. Again, although feeling had run high amongst Catholics about the necessity of the Temporal Power of the Pope, opinion soon veered round to that of Newman after its eventual loss. Even Manning, for whom the Temporal Power had been 'the keystone of the Arch of Christendom', and who had been all the more antagonistic to Newman because of the great Oratorian's failure to endorse this point of view, even he 'in the end decided that Providence had placed the Italians in Rome'.[1]

The seal was set on Newman's career when he was made a Cardinal in 1879. Henceforth he was not involved in any further controversies, devoting himself till his death in 1890 to his work at the Oratory and his vast private correspondence. This period of his life does not lack a special interest for the student of his politics, however, as many of his letters about this time contribute much to an understanding of his political thought. Newman had lived a long life, and had seen many changes. An account of these changes would involve nothing less than a history of the nineteenth century. But although in Newman's later letters a lively interest is apparent in such subjects as the development of democracy, the position and prospects of our colonies and kindred topics, it is clear that the events of these days in some

[1] Shane Leslie, 'Manning and Newman', *Manning: Anglican and Catholic* (London, 1951), p. 80.

sense passed him by. They did not lead him to modify very much or reject views which were largely formed and set before the middle of the century was reached. It would be miraculous were this not so, but it must be stressed that although Newman's basic ideas appear at an early stage in his writings, they were capable of, and in fact received, a great deal of development throughout his life.

It is possible to summarise briefly some of Newman's leading political ideas. Some have seen the unity in his life and thought in his attack on liberalism, but it would be unwise to accept this judgement here, if for no other reason than that liberalism, where it means anything definite at all, does not necessarily have a political reference. But Newman's religious beliefs led him to be very critical of the optimism about human nature which is associated with a sort of liberalism, and by the same token he can be designated a conservative. It is in his contribution to conservative political thinking that Newman is most likely to be remembered by those interested in politics today. The particular philosophical and religious views which he held led him to broaden and deepen this conservatism by a remarkable theory of the development of ideas, which theory, while buttressing the conservative notion of the value of tradition, nevertheless did not prevent an adequate conception of the need for change. This theory was a powerful support to conservatism, yet it made a particular form of rigid and intransigent conservatism impossible.

It was in the elaboration of this theory of development that Newman gives expression to the notion of 'myth', which since the day of Sorel has become so well known and widely used, and it is interesting to observe that Sorel himself saw that Newman had preceded him in grasping this notion. That Newman should have been led to discuss this idea was due very largely to an astonishing realism in Newman which should never be forgotten or ignored. He was concerned with how men actually thought and acted, not how they ought to think and act according to the rules of formal logic.

Men lived and died for dogmas, but he had never heard of a martyr for a syllogism. It is now better realised that an appreciation of the idea of myths is necessary to penetrate to various social realities, but at the time Newman wrote his true originality was obscured, largely because of the particular religious service into which his theories were pressed.

Newman's conservatism involves a preference for collective wisdom rather than for that of the individual, but it would be a grave error to go on from here to assert that Newman was a collectivist rather than an individualist. Few can have stated more strongly and eloquently than Newman the claims of the individual, based ultimately on the individuality of the human soul.

This individualism is a basic factor in his whole political outlook, so that it comes as no surprise, for instance, to find Newman putting forward a contract theory of the State. The State for Newman was of limited functions and it had a service character. It has even been sometimes thought that Newman was far from giving the State any legitimacy at all, that he thought it, in its essence, evil and an instrument of evil, but this is to go beyond what can safely be maintained. When Newman's views on all this are examined, it will prove that neither of the terms 'individualist' or 'collectivist' are capable of describing Newman's position, though it may well be claimed that he kept a sound and judicious balance between the two.

If Newman often complained about the evil of States, it is also certain that he had a very high view of the nature and position of the Church. There are times when he speaks in such a way of the Church that it becomes very much a question of how the State can co-exist with such a Church. It is on this question of the position of Church and State that Newman's thought underwent some changes, but it is noteworthy that the theory of the sovereignty of the State is very much involved here. Newman's treatment of this question gained very high praise from the late Professor Laski, and does indeed merit close consideration. But the important point here, for present purposes, is that Newman's ideas on the general subject of Church and State changed considerably during his life. At one time he could assert the positive duty of the State to uphold the Church, but quite early in middle age he was writing scornfully of 'the medieval system' of Church and State, which whatever use it was to the State was of positive harm to the Church, and particularly so if applied in his own day.

Apart from his acceptance of the religiously neutral State, which was a complete acceptance, Newman advanced much farther than has generally been realised towards an acceptance of the democracy of which he had once been highly suspicious. There are many reasons why this has not always been realised, but one reason which should be mentioned here is that Newman's notorious lack of a social conscience would seem to suggest that he was no democrat. Could a democrat be unaware of the many serious social problems which vexed so many of the British people in the nineteenth century? There is much which has to be said on Newman's lack of a social conscience, and though it may not be thought that what shall be brought forward can acquit Newman of all the charges made against him, it will be seen that there is nothing in all this to make necessary any retraction of what has been asserted here, nor to call in question the value of his contribution to political thought in general.

There is much about Newman's political thought that can still be usefully examined, since this book must touch on things which there is no space here to develop. The origins of some of Newman's political ideas would repay some investigation, which investigation will reveal how close Newman was to Locke in a surprising number of details. There is no doubt that Newman owed a great deal to Locke, while it is also clear that Newman did not owe so much directly to St. Augustine, despite some obvious similarities. But the essential aim of this book is to present clearly what Newman's political ideas actually were, without considering closely from whom they were ultimately derived, nor tracing very far what followed from these views. In presenting these ideas, however, the fact has not been lost sight of that it is not only the definite political ideas which must be grasped, but also the manner in which he held them, and the language too in which he expressed them has a special significance. It may well be that the smack of thoroughly British empiricism which hangs about Newman, and his rejection of Thomist terminology and of a Thomist political approach, will be an important factor in inclining others than his own co-religionists to examine what Newman has to offer. How much Newman has to contribute to political thought can now for the first time be decided from the evidence which this book will adduce.

I

CONSERVATISM

THERE has been a good deal of confusion about the political ideas of Cardinal Newman, and not a little of it has been caused by the looseness with which such terms as 'liberal', or 'conservative', or 'Tory', have been applied to him. Thus, although few have doubted that Newman was in some sense a conservative in politics, no one has yet made clear how far this is incompatible with describing him, in another important sense, as a liberal, nor shown whether his undoubted conservatism was of such a nature that it entitles one to label him also as a Tory. It has not helped to clarify matters, indeed it has not always been taken into account, that Newman had his own special uses of the terms 'liberal' and 'Tory', so that even if all the world agreed to call him a Tory, he might still, on his own definition, have to disclaim the title.

Now in the present examination of Newman's conservatism any question of his Toryism or liberalism will be put aside for later discussion. It will be seen that in so far as these terms can be applied to him, they form merely a superstructure on the ideas which form the basis of Newman's political thought. The phenomenon of Toryism, for Newman or for any other writer, has perforce prominent features which are historical, local, accidental and temporary; it is concerned with a certain type of social order, and with us its mention immediately calls to mind questions of an Established Church, of an hereditary monarchy, and other ideas and institutions which have never been exactly reproduced in societies other than our own.

But Newman was a conservative in the deepest meaning of the word, in a sense which would also be applicable to grave and patient thinkers in very different kinds of States from that with which Newman was best acquainted. For this reason, even though there is much of interest and importance to investigate concerning the nature of Newman's Toryism, and the extent of the influence on him in this direction by his Oxford association with John Keble and Hurrell Froude, nevertheless this particular investigation must be delayed. Likewise the question of political liberalism. This has such a special meaning for Newman—it is in fact closely connected with the same set of ideas which account for his own personal conception of Toryism—that it calls for special treatment. But no adequate appreciation of any sense at all in which Newman appears to take a liberal attitude can be expected without a prior understanding of his basic conservatism.

It is important to begin by eliminating certain possible, but false, notions about the origins of this conservatism. In the first place it must be emphasised that Newman was not conservative in the sense that he was comfortably situated in the world, and was therefore anxious to preserve the state of affairs which had brought about such a happy arrangement. Perhaps in any age there will always be those whose conservatism rises little above this level; but the easy conservatism of the rich was in fact bitterly resented by Newman, and by no means something which he himself displayed.[1] Yet it may well be argued that a temperamental conservatism underlies an early statement that 'dislike of change is not only the characteristic of a virtuous mind, but in some sense a virtue itself'.[2] It would be a mistake to put much stress on this. Newman showed no undue conservatism in the habits of his private life, and his mind remained to the end flexible and receptive. He makes it clear enough that he is not one of those 'sober men' who 'are indisposed to change in civil matters'.[3] Rather was it one of the glories of his own age that it showed great changes; that it swept away some of the fictions and sophistries, the 'shams'[4] of the past, recognising that the form of institutions might remain unaltered, while their original nature and purpose were frustrated or destroyed. Yet if Newman's conservatism can be ascribed neither to a narrow self-interest,

[1] *H.S.*, iii, 131–132. [2] *P.S.*, ii, 60. [3] *Dev.*, p. 203. [4] *Diff.*, i, 212.

nor to a conviction rooted in a certain kind of temperament, neither again can it be related to that wider form of self-interest which will naturally affect a Churchman. For to the member of a Church which has, perhaps with great difficulty, achieved a satisfactory position for itself in a stable society, a careful conservatism on grave social questions which might involve this position must seem not inappropriate. But it was on the very question of the relation of Church and State that Newman was least conservative, with his dislike of the Establishment in his later Anglican days, and his dislike, as a Catholic, of the Temporal Power of the Papacy, at a time when such a good liberal as Lord Acton was still in favour of it.

It would be more rewarding to search for the origins of Newman's conservatism in his connexion with the Romantic Revival of his age, for there is little doubt that a fairly convincing picture of Newman as one of the great Romantics might easily be drawn. This revival had two separate aspects which may profitably be isolated, and each had its separate effect on Newman. Romanticism, narrowly defined, might be described as a literary movement, heralding a return to the Middle Ages, which movement 'met and mingled with that other movement of return to nature and sentiment which has its origins with Rousseau'.[1] The undeniable influence on Newman of these movements needs to be examined with care. In the first place, it is clear enough that a growing interest in the Middle Ages, so long despised as a dark night of Gothic ignorance and superstition, might well be expected to foster conservative influences as a deeper sympathy with, and attempt to understand the roots of our past became more common. But all the evidence goes to show that Newman knew little of, and cared little about, the Middle Ages. He never studied this period of history, nor showed any sympathy for it, whatever his friends may have done. Nor if attention is turned to those who are often thought of as Romantics, and who might be expected to have influenced Newman, is it possible to find any direct or substantial evidence of this. Since, apart from vague

[1] Dawson, 'The Romantic Tradition', *Medieval Essays* (London, 1953), p. 212.

generalisations, few verifiable claims have ever been made for the influence on Newman of particular Romantics, a detailed answer on this question is perhaps a work of supererogation, but at least the cases of Coleridge and Sir Walter Scott should be considered. A resemblance between Coleridge and Newman has very often been discerned, and this resemblance is nowhere closer than on the subject of politics; yet even here there was no direct influence, and it is curious to observe that it was not until his own thought was quite mature that Newman even read Coleridge's work.[1]

It is much more hopeful to look for influence on the Oxford Movement in general and also on Newman in particular from Scott, whose name occurs repeatedly in his pages. It was not so much a general doctrine or particular idea which Newman gained from Scott, but rather an attitude which the often maligned Romanticism of the age did much to create. For Scott reflected and aroused an increased interest in history,[2] and even though for too many writers of the early nineteenth century this interest showed itself in the exaltation of one period of history above the rest, yet there can be little doubt that it gave an impetus to historical research, and besides increasing our knowledge of the past, led to a better understanding of the very process of historical inquiry. John Stuart Mill bears witness to the fact that a deeper insight into the play of cause and effect in history was becoming general in his early days.[3] Newman's approach was thoroughly historical, and was conservative because it was historical. He did not isolate one period of history as a golden age. There was no golden age for Newman—neither in the past nor in the future. When brought up against a specific problem, Newman strove always to place it in its historical context, and it was because, as a Catholic, that he was able to look at every hotly disputed point

---

[1] Davis, 'Was Newman a Disciple of Coleridge?' *Dublin Review* (1945), vol. 435, pp. 165–173.
See R. J. White, *Coleridge's Political Thought* (London, 1938), pp. 11–28, for a summary of Coleridge's thought which is almost applicable to Newman.

[2] As Newman pointed out at an early age. See C.C., B.7. 'Essay on Modern History' (1821). For the influence of Scott on the Oxford Movement see, e.g. Keble, *Occasional Papers* (London, 1887), pp. 1–80.

[3] *Mill on Bentham and Coleridge* (ed. F. R. Leavis, London, 1950), p. 131.

through the long vista of the centuries that he was generally able to take the most balanced view in the current controversies, and often enough that view proved correct by subsequent events. It is noteworthy that, as an Anglican, Newman had given a measured and temperate criticism of the reformers eager to lay hands on his Church, on the grounds, not that they were necessarily ill-disposed to the Church, but that they were simply ignorant of its history, and could not therefore reform it in a way consistent with its particular genius.[1]

Thus this aspect of the Romantic Revival can truthfully be said to have had its effect on Newman, although it must be admitted that a knowledge of, and a love for, history need not always be a factor inclining anyone to conservatism. That other aspect of Romanticism, which is concerned with the return to nature and to sentiment usually associated with Rousseau, perhaps affected Newman, though the direct influence of particular writers cannot be discerned. Newman has never been supposed to exalt the 'natural man', in fact the exact reverse must be asserted, and it would not be true to say that Newman actually opposed sentiment to reason, but there is no doubt that Newman shared in a general reaction to the aridity of much eighteenth-century rationalism. Without disparaging conscious reason, Newman saw that the part it formed of the total personality of man was smaller than had earlier been supposed, and that in fact men's actions were seldom explicable in terms of it. But the defence of unconscious against conscious reasoning to which this led may well have had conservative implications, for this sort of argument can well be turned by a conservative to explain his hostility to certain reforms and changes which may be in question. Reformers may have a clear and rational case to present, but the conservative may oppose change on the grounds of what might before have been called instinct or feeling, and now can be called unconscious reasoning. This has the great benefit for the conservative of making less necessary the tiresome task of refuting an opponent's rational arguments, and the need for finding better

[1] *V.M.*, ii, 53.

ones. This chapter will contain at least one passage of Newman's earlier work which could be interpreted on these lines.

The fact of a connexion between Newman's writings and the Romantic Revival may seem the more likely in that Newman himself thought that the Oxford Movement was part of a larger European movement. This movement was united by a common spirit, rather than a common doctrine, but its effect was great for the 'old Benthamism' was 'shrivelling up' and a richer and warmer philosophy was succeeding.[1] This 'spirit afloat' in Europe was specifically connected by Newman with the Oxford Movement and with Scott and some English Romantics. There may be involved here some confusion on Newman's part between the Romantic and the Catholic Revivals, which despite their interaction may better be considered apart, but it is only necessary to point out here that Newman was not alone in asserting this connexion, though he did not emphasise its conservative and reactionary implications as much as some have done.

It is clear that Newman's conservatism was at least affected by Romanticism, but it is not necessary, for any other than purely literary purposes, to determine the exact limits of this influence. It would not even be possible, so vague are the terms which such an inquiry would have to employ. As long as the general climate of thought and opinion to which Newman was exposed is not forgotten, it will be much more instructive to examine the positive bases of this conservatism. For it was based on certain fundamental ideas which, when grasped, hold the key to his whole political position, and these ideas were not simply annexed by him from any thinker or set of thinkers, nor were they especially characteristic of his own age. It is time to examine these ideas.

I. THE RELIGIOUS AND INTELLECTUAL BASIS

There is an immediate and obvious religious basis for Newman's conservatism, a basis which is common to all those sharing the same broad outlook on religion. It has sometimes been

[1] *Ess.*, i, 303–304.

bluntly said that the basis of political conservatism lies in a belief in the inevitable insufficiency and wickedness of man, whereas progressive politicians are perpetually haunted by the idea of his perfectibility, not in some far off heaven, but here on earth. Without discussing the exact limitations to the truth of this contention—and its general truth can hardly be doubted—it is at once clear that if such is the case, Newman's type of religious belief must bring him very definitely into the conservative camp.

It is not simply that Newman accepts the traditional Christian doctrine of the Fall, of original sin. For there are many varieties of emphasis which can be placed on a dogma which is widely held, and the force and clarity with which it is expounded may also vary considerably. Now Newman could hardly have stressed more strongly the disastrous results of the Fall. As a result of it, 'all our daily pursuits and doings need not be proved evil, but are certainly evil without proof, unless they can be proved to be good'.[1] The infection of sin was everywhere, so that Newman thought it the very distinguishing mark of a Christian that he should hold 'a melancholy view of the world'.[2] It is sometimes thought that the gloomy picture of the human lot which Newman painted in his early days seemed to brighten for him in later life,[3] but in fact no fundamental change of attitude is visible.

But this is not all. It was not only that Newman emphasised so very strongly this one dogma, with its obvious conservative political implications. Newman was distinguished by his extraordinary insistence on the very idea of dogma itself. Dogma was necessary since religious truth must be taught, and the truths of religion were eternally true, and remained true whether or not any human mind was aware of them. In this Newman was reacting violently against that current of thought and feeling which was flowing ever more strongly in his own lifetime, a religious trend which stemmed in some part from the great

[1] S.D., p. 108.   [2] Dev., p. 228.
[3] See, e.g. M. C. D'Arcy, 'The Parochial and Plain Sermons', *Newman and Littlemore* (Oxford, 1945), p. 58.

Schleiermacher, and which seemed to him to replace the old objective and eternal truths of dogma by the shifting sands of subjective religious experience. As far as religion was concerned, Newman took his stand on conservatism and dogma, and took as his especial foe 'liberalism', by which he 'meant the anti-dogmatic principle'.[1] If violent opposition to any form of liberalism is sufficient to make one a conservative, then Newman was conservative indeed, and it is the tone and temper of this opposition of Newman's which has been largely responsible for the widely received picture of him as an ultra-conservative cleric. Unfortunately, the connexion between liberalism in politics and liberalism in religion, either in Newman's terminology or anyone else's, is by no means clear, and something must soon be said about this point. It will be shown that Newman's opposition to political liberalism was not as great as is often thought, where this opposition existed at all, but it is nevertheless true that some of this hostility to religious liberalism was also brought over against the political variety. Liberalism was a term of reproach, and Newman seemed to think it had certain root errors which could be found in many of its forms.

But although a hatred of the very word 'liberal' may have some practical tendency—more perhaps in Newman's day, when the two great parties were the Liberals and the Conservatives, than in our own—to incline one to some form of conservatism, it does not seem necessarily and inevitably to have any such effect, and so it is well not to dwell too long on this aspect of Newman's thought. Nor does the mere love of dogma, and its use, make anyone a conservative. Liberals have their dogmas, and conservatives notoriously wallow about in a welter of unsorted emotions and instincts. A conservative, where he does indeed admit to a dogma, may sometimes hold fast to one which has not altered in any way, despite vast external changes, and may refuse to listen to any plea for the modification or re-interpretation of its expression. Newman can by no means be accused of this sort of rigidity. It was his very insistence on the *Development*

[1] *Apo.*, p. 150.

of Doctrine that was to embroil his name in the Modernist controversies of the early twentieth century, and to cause momentary doubts among some pious Catholics whether Newman might not turn out to have been a religious liberal after all.

Thus the immediate and obvious religious basis for Newman's conservatism must be sought rather in his adherence to one particular doctrine—that of the Fall—rather than in his advocacy of the idea of dogma as such, though this did have the effect of embittering him towards the very term 'liberal', and of recommending to him the general label 'conservative'. Yet to find the ultimate religious basis of Newman's conservatism it is necessary to go right back to his belief in the very fact of the existence of God. The existence of God was not a matter for argument and proof: it was the most obvious and overwhelming fact. It was not that Newman denied that proofs were impossible, rather was it that they were not his concern. It is doubtful how far he could even envisage the state of mind which could entertain a doubt on this subject. So staggeringly clear and self-evident for Newman was the fact of God's existence that it had the effect of throwing all else into the realms of shadow and unreality. He could attain certainty about his own existence—in common with most sane people—and so was led to declare that he was aware of only two supreme and luminously self-evident beings—himself and God.[1] From here appears an individualist strain in Newman's thought which cannot be neglected when evidence of certain apparently collectivist notions is brought forward. That is not the important point here. It is rather that Newman was led by the vividness of this awareness to embrace certain particular intellectual positions, which might be called vaguely Platonic, and which must be grasped if Newman is to be properly understood. For all but God was in shadow for him. Persons were not unreal— they alone were fully real in an unreal world[2]—but they were ultimately unknowable. Matter was a mystery. Men had a false but harmless belief in matter as distinct from impressions on their

---

[1] *Apo.*, p. 108.
[2] 'Individuals are the only facts.' C.C., A.46.3, p. 1. This is an unpublished philosophical note-book of some importance to an understanding of Newman's philosophy.

senses—'If I could', said Newman, 'I would consider matter simply incommunicable, like spirit.'[1] The most that human beings can attain to is of 'shadowy representations of realities which are incomprehensible to creatures such as ourselves'.[2] Newman as a child had been convinced of 'the unreality of material phenomena',[3] and it comes as no surprise to learn that he was soon to be irresistibly attracted to the Christian Platonism of Clement and Origen. They taught him the existence of a real world beyond the senses, of which this world is but an instrument and veil. This idea Newman found also in the *Analogy* of his great master Butler, and it is very clear that Newman owes a great deal to that work.

But it is not necessary to determine exactly the source of Newman's philosophy, nor even to inquire too closely into the epistemological suppositions underlying it. Newman had no time for philosophy. His turn of mind was, he considered, logical, ethical and practical. Above all practical. It was even a point in favour of the Neo-Platonists that their philosophy was aimed at the practical result of destroying Christianity.[4] What he wanted from philosophy was results. Why, he asks, should one read such writers as Fichte, Schelling and Hegel for oneself, 'for notoriously they have come to no conclusion'.[5] But while avoiding the necessarily difficult task of examining minutely the philosophy of this despiser of philosophers, his general position must be established.

At first sight, thought Newman, the visible world seemed quite sufficient to account for itself. It was one vast system with its own laws and principles, with a minute web of cause and effect, such that any event could be traced back to a preceding cause without any need to postulate another and higher system to explain its existence. Yet since Newman not only believed in a God, but in the traditional Christian idea of a particular Providence, he could not regard this world as self-sufficient. Thus he regarded it as 'the instrument, yet the veil, of the world invisible—the veil, yet

---

[1] *ibid.*, p. 60.   [2] *Ari.*, p. 75.   [3] *Apo.*, p. 113.
[4] *H.S.*, iii, 98.   [5] *C.C.*, A.46.3, p. 43.

still partially the symbol and index: so that all that exists or happens visibly, conceals and yet suggests, and above all subserves, a system of persons, facts and events beyond itself'.[1] This invisible world lay all about us: it was the hidden Kingdom of God, eternal and unchangeable. In the same way that St. Augustine's City of God has been linked with the concept of the Intelligible World of Plotinus, so it would be possible to link what Newman says of the real and invisible world with his concept of the Kingdom of God. But the all-important point here is that these two worlds, visible and invisible, both lay under the general plan of Divine Providence. Both were systems, or schemes, as Newman sometimes spoke of them. Much of the working of the visible system could be seen. Events could be isolated for examination and their causes traced. General laws were discoverable not only in the physical life of the visible world, but in its moral, social and political life. Yet the whole consequences and causes of any given thing in this natural order was finally beyond us. If this were so in the visible world, still less would the system of the invisible world, which was not so open to inspection, be perfectly comprehended. Butler had tried to show that Christianity, a particular scheme under the general moral government of God, was itself an intricate system, and was carried on by general laws in a manner analogous to the natural system.

Newman used these ideas for the same religious purposes as Butler, but in the political importance which attaches to them the name of Burke comes more readily into view. For Newman's tremendous insistence on system, on the ubiquity of general law throughout the whole visible and invisible worlds, brings him very close to Burke's profound sense of the 'divine concordance of the Universe', to use a phrase which goes back to Nicholas of Cusa. As with Burke, this concordance for Newman included the State in its scheme, and perhaps few words could indicate the latter's position more aptly than those of Burke which speak of the 'eternal society . . . connecting the visible and invisible world,

[1] *Ess.*, ii, 192.

according to a fixed compact sanctioned by the inviolable oath which holds all physical and all moral natures, each in their appointed place'.[1] This conception of order was not mechanical for Newman, any more than it had been for Burke, and it is possible to argue that Newman reflected to some extent the increased interest in biology which the nineteenth century witnessed. Indeed, the celebrated theory of the development of ideas which Newman put forward in 1845 has sometimes been condemned as depending on too biological a notion of development.

It is a short step from ideas of order such as these to a view of society in which each of its members has his own unique position and unique role to fill, his special niche in society, perhaps occupied through a fixed and hereditary status. If Newman did not quite represent an ultra-conservative point of view here, there is no doubt that he had a vision of a society with a stable class structure. He had also a strong sense of the interdependence of social ranks and classes, and though he found the terms 'high' and 'low' invidious in this connexion, he found it necessary to assert this interdependence by the use of such terms as 'right hand' and 'left hand' ranks.[2]

It is not yet time to examine the details of Newman's political position, but the basis of his fundamental conservatism is beginning to appear. His profound sense of order and of law is apparent in all his writings, and it will be seen that a typical conservative position is at length reached when bad and unjust laws are defended on conservative grounds. But Newman's conservatism is on the whole far from typical, and it is necessary to probe a little further this idea of system and law on which so much depends. This will involve some consideration of the philosophy of history which Newman possessed, and it will be necessary to examine whether Newman's concern for such a subject is prejudicial to the claim for his historical feeling, already asserted as a factor inclining him towards conservatism.

[1] *Reflections on French Revolution* (Everyman ed.), pp. 93–94.
[2] Letter of 7 September 1834. Quoted M. Ward, *Young Mr. Newman* (London, 1948), pp. 268–269.

2. THE PHILOSOPHY OF HISTORY

Newman was not only convinced of the reign of law over the physical universe, but equally conscious of its sway over the moral, social and political world. There were laws on which States rose and fell, and these laws, as all the laws at work in society, could be discovered in history. Their presence was even shown, so Newman at one time appears to think, by the fact that the course of human events moves in cycles.[1] Further, these laws were not merely generalisations from the past, for the purpose of explaining the past, but were on occasion used by him to predict the future.[2] This is at first sight perplexing. It has been the very point on which Newman has been congratulated that he shared with St. Augustine that Christian interpretation of history which is different 'from any other in its combination of universalism with a sense of the uniqueness and irreversibility of the historic process'.[3] Yet Newman specifically condemns the philosophy of history of St. Augustine, on the same grounds that many do so today, i.e. that it was too theological, that St. Augustine erred in introducing the concept of final cause into history.[4] Newman might seem to have the worst of two worlds, for with his historical laws and cycles he appears to miss that uniqueness of the historic process which Christian and liberal historians alike have emphasised, while at the same time he seems to miss that universalism which the Christian interpretation of history can afford. He lays claim to a sort of universalism, in so far as he insists that the web of cause and effect is all embracing and universal, but this is not the sort of universalism which can group together apparently widely separated movements and events, where the direct link of cause and effect may be hard to demonstrate, and can find a meaning in events which is exterior to these events themselves, in virtue of, and to illustrate, a prior thesis which itself has not been derived from history.

[1] *V.M.*, ii, 54; *Dev.*, p. 199; *H.S.*, i, 173–174; *V.V.*, p. 137.
[2] *H.S.*, i, 228–229.
[3] C. Dawson, *Religion and the Modern State* (London, 1936), p. 80.
[4] P.C., Allies, 11 November 1854.

The truth is that Newman thought that he could simultaneously and without contradiction hold two different types of a philosophy of history. It is in fact true, as many have been aware, that he gives classic expression to the Augustinian type, but he does so at times almost unconsciously, since he considered its use of value only to the converted, and thought time better spent on an approach which could be shared by all, and which he was confident would not yield results inconsistent with those of the theological approach. Yet undoubtedly Newman put forward the former type when he stressed that the Incarnation stands at the centre of history, after which event history is seen to be meaningful, and to have a goal.

> Christ came to make a new world [he said]. He came into the world to regenerate it in Himself, to make a new beginning, to be the beginning of the creation of God, to gather together in one, and recapitulate all things in Himself. . . . The world was like some fair mirror, broken in pieces and giving back no one uniform image of its maker. But he came to combine what was dissipated, to recast what was shattered in Himself. He began all excellence, and of His fulness have all we received.[1]

So the history of the world shows a Divine purpose and plan: the empires before Christianity, the literature of Greece, the organisation of Rome, all were 'economies' of God ministering to Christianity;[2] all history is now a preparation for the coming of the Kingdom of God, displaying the ever new forms of the struggle between the Church and the World.

All this certainly entitles anyone to talk of Newman's 'Augustinian' philosophy of history, but the actual words Newman uses are more reminiscent of a writer much nearer his own day—Friedrich Schlegel—than of St. Augustine. It is very curious that Newman, whose resemblance to St. Augustine is so strong, nevertheless betrays very slight evidence of having

[1] S.D., p. 61.
[2] P.C., Allies, 3 September 1854. Much of what Allies gained in this correspondence reappears in a paper, 'The Philosophy of History', which is printed as the first section of the first volume of his *Formation of Christendom* (London, 1865).

been especially influenced by him. He quotes him very infrequently, and rarely in all his vast range of published and unpublished work has occasion to mention that great Doctor of the Church. At first sight a comparison between Schlegel and Newman would seem more promising, particularly with reference to this question of the philosophy of history. It has been seen that Newman said that Christ had come to combine the scattered pieces of the mirror which should reflect His image. Schlegel says that the philosophy of history is concerned with 'the restoration in man of the lost image of God: so far as this relates to science'.[1] Yet although this parallel reveals a fundamental similarity of outlook, there was little discernible influence on Newman in any direction, despite some obvious and striking similarities of ideas, and despite the fact that Newman was acquainted with his work.[2]

But Schlegel's view that the philosophy of history should have a scientific character is echoed by Newman, who does not seem to be aware, when doing so, that he himself could already be described as a leading exponent of the non-scientific type. 'My notion of the Philosophy of History', he says, 'is the science of which historical facts are the basis' and its object was to discover laws of the social and political world. These laws were not to be assumed in advance, and then illustrated by reference to particular historical events. 'For myself,' he says, 'I cannot help thinking that laws are a sort of fact in the subject matter which is in question.' The introduction of the idea of final causes would be as disastrous here as in physics—'First let us ascertain the fact, and then theologise on it.'[3]

Here is an approach to the philosophy of history very different from the Augustinian one which he has before now been recognised to display. Yet one should not be misled about this. Newman could well admit to holding two different types of a philosophy of history, as a result of two opposite approaches to it, but he would not admit to any inconsistency therein. Nor was it necessary for him to do so. He professed to observe the world

---

[1] F. Schlegel, *Philosophy of History* (revised ed., London, 1846), p. ix.
[2] See especially here P.C., Allies, 3 September 1854.
[3] P.C., Allies, 16 November 1854.

of history, and to discover there facts. But laws were facts in the world, and were capable of observation. These laws, particularly those of the social and political world, were not rigid and inflexible, nor associated with any *a priori* necessity. They were simply generalisations from the past, and could give greater or lesser conviction of their future fulfilment according to the nature of the material used for the generalisation. But the laws could never be seen as necessary in their operation. A law, Newman emphasised, was not a cause, but a fact, and he insisted that we have no experience of any other cause but will.[1]

The idea of the relation of cause and effect which is involved here is an individual one. It might have seemed from what was said about his views at the beginning of this section, that Newman's remarks on the minute web of cause and effect which covers the universe, would qualify to rank him with those such as Herbert Spencer, who postulated a 'natural causation' in human affairs, without which 'government and legislation are absurd'.[2] But the intricate, universal system of cause and effect of which Newman spoke, was not all it seemed. 'What is called, and seems to be, cause and effect, is rather an order of sequence, and does not preclude, nay, perhaps implies, the presence of unseen spiritual agency as its real author.'[3]

It can now be seen why Newman thought there was no inconsistency between his two philosophies of history. It is true that he hoped to look out, without religious preconceptions, on the facts of the world as they were presented to any honest inquirer, but the laws discovered, whatsoever they were, would be the very laws on which Divine Providence guided the world. 'Depend on it,' he says, 'when once the laws of human affairs are drawn out, and the philosophy into which they combine, it will be a movement worthy of the Law-giver.'[4] Thus laws were there, whether their ultimate origin in God were accepted or not, they were there to explain the past and the present, and to some extent to predict the future too. But the philosophy to which

---

[1] *G.A.*, p. 55. [2] *Study of Sociology* (3rd ed., London, 1874), p. 46.
[3] *Ess.*, ii, 193. [4] P.C., Allies, 16 November 1854.

Newman refers is that which held that God was the real upholder of the entire visible and invisible worlds, and that he worked not by isolated and particular action but by general laws in accordance with a general plan. 'The course of events, the revolution of empires, the rise and fall of states, the periods and eras, the progresses and the retrogressions of the world's history, the great outlines and results of human affairs, are from His disposition,'[1] said Newman.

It appears from this that, granted his original assumptions, Newman had no reason to doubt that the laws of the social and political world, whoever they were discovered by, would prove in any way inconsistent with a theological interpretation of history. This is not to say that this position does not involve very great philosophical difficulties, not all of which Newman was concerned to answer, or even to recognise. A consideration of some of these difficulties would take this discussion too far from its starting-point and purpose, and considerable risk attaches to the venture of explaining not what Newman meant to say but what the author thinks Newman meant to say. But Newman is not so much likely to be attacked for the religious basis and background to his philosophy of history, as for the allegedly scientific character of it. It is this apparent conviction of his that historical laws can in fact be scientifically established which will lead many to discount that thorough-going historicism which has earlier been put forward as an important factor in his conservatism.

Newman's practical excursion into the philosophy of history is best seen in his *Lectures on the History of the Turks* (1853). His reading of Turkish history, from the sources which a well educated man with a taste for history might be expected to use, seems to have convinced Newman of his ability to discover certain historical laws which were operative in the history of the Ottoman Empire. In his lectures there is a galaxy of them. 'Barbarism is ever pending over the civilised world', we learn; 'cupidity is stronger than conservatism'; it is 'a natural law' that 'empires are sudden manifestations of power which are as short

[1] *Idea*, pp. 64–65.

lived as they are sudden';[1] all these and many more such reflexions Newman feels entitled to make. Of course, there was nothing rigid about these laws. Newman was aware of certain obvious criticisms to which he might be subject, and so he stresses that he is 'but attempting to lay down general rules, to which there may be exceptions, explicable or not'.[2] And if Newman was careful at this time to avoid the reproach of being too sanguine about the universal validity of his historical laws, later in life he became much more suspicious of philosophical views of history. Many of them, he now thought, were 'mere exhibitions of ingenuity',[3] though he seems here to have been thinking primarily of the type which interprets history by means of some particular principle, as, for example, historical materialism. Newman came, indeed, much nearer to that critical philosophy of history to which even historians cannot reasonably object, when we find him criticising the very idea of 'facts' in history. Facts in history were not quite of the same nature as facts in physical science, as Newman had once assumed, and he went on to analyse the working of different assumptions in certain historians which led them to very different conclusions.

But after all it must be admitted that Newman never went far enough with the purely critical philosophy of history and never quite realised the difficulties of his own position. As far as the establishment of laws is concerned, there is no need to look beyond Newman's *Lectures on the Turks* for a salutary lesson on that subject. Newman was here laying down laws which he denied were more than general rules, and he was displaying much caution in doing so. Yet despite his caution, Newman thought that one clear rule emerged from history, which he could safely put forward without the doubts and reservations which other rules required. This was that any change from barbarism to civilisation can only be achieved by a very gradual process—and on this point Newman has proved to be wrong in the case of the very people he had in mind.

Of course the speed of the actual changes in Turkey can

[1] *H.S.*, i, 12, 76, 160.   [2] *ibid.*, p. 178.   [3] *G.A.* (1870), p. 280.

be exaggerated. As Sir Harry Luke says, 'The moribund appearance which the Ottoman Empire presented to the outside world at the beginning of the nineteenth century was to a certain extent deceptive.'[1] Again, Newman was unaware of the changes which were taking place there even as he wrote; he did not foresee that the ideas of the French Revolution would find their way to, and a lodging ground in, of all places, this barbarian Power. The young Turks; Yeni Turan; the speed at which a national and cultural consciousness could grow, were all outside his range of vision. Thus Newman's own attempt at a philosophical history, despite the caution of his theorising, and apart from the merits of the lectures in themselves, has been subject to the fate which time alone perhaps can bring to anticipations of the future based on philosophical views of the past.[2]

There is more of interest here than the mere fact that the 'laws' which Newman put forward proved in the event to be unreliable. Rather is it instructive to observe that here, in his *History of the Turks*, at the very moment and place where Newman has the chance to attempt a scientific assessment of historical evidence, without religious or other preconceptions, he suggests the fruitlessness of such attempts by falling back on an earlier and more respectable type of a philosophy of history. He surveys the evidence and formulates general rules thereon, but the eye which selected the material was all along prepared to be closed to an 'external' view of the history of the Turks, in order that it might examine more closely its inner and essential moral aspects.[3] In the contest between two great hostile forces Newman takes leave of the scientific historian in seeing behind it the whole history of the warfare between good and evil.[4] It is in this realm of ideas that Newman is most at home, and has most to offer. Any science of history is bound to be unsatisfactory, but there will always be room for a philosophy of history of the frankly theological type.

[1] *Making of Modern Turkey* (London, 1936), p. 44.
[2] But as late as 1919 it could still be claimed that Newman had been conclusively and emphatically proved right in his main points. See Canon William Barry's article, 'The Turks, Cardinal Newman and the Council of Ten', *Nineteenth Century*, August 1919.
[3] *H.S.*, i, 104.   [4] *ibid.*, p. 158.

There will always be those who will demand this, else 'the whole history of the world would be nought else than an insoluble enigma—an inextricable labyrinth—a huge pile of the blocks and fragments of an unfinished edifice—and the great tragedy of humanity would be devoid of all proper result'.[1]

Though Newman's 'scientific' approach to the philosophy of history has most important implications and results for this study, there is little doubt that admirers of Newman will not wish to put a great deal of stress on it. Newman was well equipped to portray the whole course of the world's history as the struggle between the Church and the World, in something like the way St. Augustine had seen the warfare of the City of God and the Earthly City, and it is on these lines that many will think Newman had most to offer. Newman had indeed much to say of the Church and the World, but it might be more rewarding to look for other terms when discussing his philosophy of history. It might be possible, as long as no Manichaean dualism is conjured up, to hold that Newman saw history as the eternal warfare of good and evil, that he was keenly aware of the mystery of iniquity, working itself out in time. Perhaps the final result of a more adequate treatment of Newman's philosophy of history, when that task is ever completed, would be to see it as concerned with the development of moral consciousness in history. M. Guitton has already put forward a view of this sort.[2] Unfortunately M. Guitton's work seems to have been marred by an absorption in the theory of the development of ideas, which is admittedly at the centre of much of Newman's thought, so that he does not seem to see the full implications of some of Newman's remarks. Yet it is true that Newman's view of history was powerfully affected by his theory of development.

This theory has yet to be examined, but suffice it to say now that Newman thought ideas were reflexions of objects in the real world, and that in the various developments which these ideas underwent in the visible world, they were capable of a

---

[1] Schlegel, *Philosophy of History*, p. 279.
[2] J. Guitton, *Philosophie de Newman* (Paris, 1933), pp. 136 ff.

normative test by reference to a transcendent and intemporal reality outside history.

Such a view clearly rules out at once a certain type of conservatism. As M. Guitton has pointed out, if Newman had to choose between slogans current in Germany about the time he was writing, he would have to affirm that 'only the rational was real', and deny that only 'the real is rational'. That is, if Newman is to speak of a spiritual and transcendent reality outside history, of such a nature that it becomes possible to speak of relations between truths outside the world of time and history, and ideas which represent it in time, and moreover to judge which ideas do adequately represent this truth, then it becomes impossible to consecrate the mere movement of history, to 'divinise' it, as some theories of development are accused of doing.

To this extent Newman is not conservative, although his fundamental conservatism remains. His fondness for a philosophy of history may raise doubts about the strong historical sense which was asserted to be a factor in this conservatism, but even if this historical feeling is altogether denied his basic conservatism will be indisputable. This examination has helped to clarify some of those ideas, quite unconnected with any historical sense, or lack of it, which lie at the basis of Newman's conservatism, and has made it possible now to see more precisely wherein his conservatism exists. The ideas discussed also make it possible to answer first a question which naturally arises out of what has gone before, and which deserves to receive an early answer in any discussion of a writer's politics.

It may well be asked of a religious writer who ventures into the field of politics, how far he conceives that politics can be studied apart from theology, or, for that matter, from certain other subjects. Whether or not an autonomous political science lies at the end of the writer's reflexions, it is well that something should be known of his views on the aims and scope of the subject with which he has come to occupy himself.

Now Newman has said that there is a visible system of things, and of this system the State is a part. But the visible world is, after all, only a veil and instrument of the real world, so that the State perforce becomes a 'type',[1] a representative or organ of this real, invisible world. Yet this does not mean that the State becomes an unsubstantial wraith, about which accurate knowledge is neither possible nor desirable. The whole world is subject to law, the social and political world no less than the physical. This view of law can have its difficulties but from one point of view the idea of their presence makes the study of politics open to all, on the same terms, and opens the way for a true political science. In fact a true political science was certainly envisaged by Newman in his determination to start from the facts of the political world, and if he himself found that it was impossible in practice to view the world without certain sometimes unrecognised preconceptions and values, he was in this not unlike many another who professes to study political science.

Even though the laws which Newman thought a scientific study of facts could establish were all no more than generalisations from experience, and therefore not necessary and immutable, yet there was in fact a great difference between two different sorts of law. The laws of physical nature could not be assimilated to those of the social and political world. Physical nature did in fact remain fixed in its laws, whereas moral and social nature was self-governed, man's free will prevented the possibility of undeviating laws. Thus any social study could hope for no more than a limited exactitude. There was no lack of realism here. The fact of free will did not mean that any historical law or trend could easily be reversed. Even at the time when Newman was most hostile to the growth of popular power in the country, he was quite ready to agree to the practical inevitability of historical development in that direction. There might be a general law in accordance with which a society seems necessarily to develop, but in face of any practically inevitable law the individual can still take no other guide than conscience.[2]

It is in this setting that one should consider Newman's frequent references to cycles in history. These cycles were not so much a

[1] *Ess.*, ii, 193.   [2] *U.S.*, p. 152.

restraint on human freedom as a result of it. Reason brought progress in history, but sin brought the 'same bad round again'.[1] Nor, when Newman's ideas are more closely examined, was it literally the same bad round again, for 'the past never returns; the course of events, old in its texture is ever new in its colouring and fashion',[2]—Newman was a Guiccardini rather than a Machiavelli. Thus Newman clearly recognises that a social study on the model of the physical sciences is not possible, but this is not enough for him to despair of a scientific social study. The phenomena with which such a subject must deal are not simply submitted to the senses and verified by them, but still, evidence is not taken at random, 'but, like the evidence of the senses, sifted and scrutinised'.[3] The question is, does theology slip in at this point? Must Newman in the end subordinate his politics to theology, where the empirical evidence alone is useless or inconclusive and the need for some principle of selection, if not scale of values, becomes necessary?

The truth seems to be this. As Newman could take part with others in a common search for the empirical facts of the political world, so he could hold with many others the same general principles and values, which were not a direct consequence of, or in an obviously direct relationship with, his theological views. Little that he says on the subject of politics is invalidated for others because of his avowed theological beliefs. Of course, theology for Newman was still the queen of the sciences, but he did not think of theology in the way which it has sometimes been placed in Thomist textbooks. He did not emphasise the role of theology as a regulator of other studies, but rather contented himself with the observation that if a thing was true for theology, it was so for any other study, and vice versa. He was tolerant of apparent contradictions between theology and another science, and looked forward to the future thought and research which would eventually remove them. Yet theology could not simply be ignored by other sciences if they were to develop to the full. No science was self-contained. All the social sciences took an abstract and a

---

[1] *V.V.*, p. 137.   [2] *Idea*, pp. 17–18.   [3] *Dev.*, p. 111.

partial view of man, and the conclusions they reached were useless for proper action or understanding unless the boundaries of the particular science could in the end be transgressed. It is interesting to note, however, that Newman explicitly states that politics will suffer less than many other subjects if it does ignore theology.[1] In an unpublished work the same thought occurs, where it is stated that 'the growth of society is distinct from the actions of the Church, showing that society rests on elements independent of the Church'.[2]

It seems that this study can go forward with no further doubts that what Newman has to say is of practical importance only to those of the same religious beliefs. It is of interest and importance to all, though perhaps it may well be of particular importance to those of his own communion, if it persuades them by force of his powerful example to face the facts of the political world and to see them as they are, and not so much as they ought to be according to the categories of a political philosophy which many find in the last resort to be inseparable from theological and metaphysical assumptions far from universally held.

3. THE TRUE CONSERVATISM OF CARDINAL NEWMAN

Something of the views which lie at the basis of Newman's conservatism has now been seen. A general pessimism about man and his capabilities has been noted, as also a great sympathy for the past which owes much to the Romantic Revival. Newman's profound conviction of the order and harmony of the Universe has been mentioned, an order which extends throughout the visible and invisible worlds, which embraces all forms of life. The State itself is a part of this order, and so likewise is every individual, the least significant of whom has his own particular niche in society, his own part in the general plan of the Universe. It is the tremendous sense of law which Newman gained from a world permeated by law that brought him to the position that any law, even if unjust, was preferable to disorder. In the same

---

[1] *Idea*, p. 72.   [2] C.C., A.46.3, p. 85.

realm of ideas can be found what is called here the true conservatism of Cardinal Newman. For on the basis of these ideas Newman erected a theory of development which has a very powerful conservative application.

It has been seen that there is little ground for supposing that Newman was a fanatical opposer of change as such, but there is no doubt that he was keenly aware how often 'projected innovations turn out, if not nugatory, nothing short of destructive'.[1] It was not so much a question of the wrong-headedness of reformers, or the pig-headedness of conservatives, but that 'novelty is often error to those who are unprepared for it, from the refraction with which it enters into their conceptions'.[2] This refraction is explained by Newman's theory of development. And to some such theory Newman was impelled, for though he was so conscious of 'the philosophical bond which connects one age with another',[3] so vividly impressed by 'the strength of a political establishment which has been the slow birth of time',[4] nevertheless he was equally conscious of the danger of 'a slow corruption'.[5] The problem of permanence and change in history could not be avoided.

Newman's theory is based on the Alexandrian philosophy which had swept him away at the outset of his career, reinforcing as it did the impressions of his childhood and the ideas he had gained from Butler and Keble. He was led to suppose that the greatest knowledge which was possible for us in the visible world was of 'shadowy representations of realities which are incomprehensible to creatures such as ourselves'.[6] The real world beyond the senses was ultimately unknowable, though a deepening insight into it was possible. But if the human mind could hope for little more than a knowledge of shadows, it could at least grasp more than it could actually express. The ideas which language sought to express were infinite, and capable of infinite modification and combination, whereas language was definite and limited, confined largely to an arbitrary selection of some part of this vast quantity: it was 'a sort of analysis of thought'.[7]

---

[1] *H.S.*, i, 180. [2] *V.M.*, i, p. lii. [3] *ibid.*, ii, 54. [4] *H.S.*, iii, 106–107.
[5] *Dev.*, p. 203. [6] *Ari.*, p. 75. [7] *U.S.*, p. 341.

Not only could the mind grasp more than it could express: it could grasp more than it was conscious of holding. This is the origin of that implicit reason, appearing later in the *Grammar of Assent* as the 'Illative Sense', which Newman contrasts with explicit reason. That all men commonly reason by some inward faculty, rather than by some explicit rule, seemed to him a plain psychological fact. It was hardly possible to reproduce this process in its entirety, for

> the mind ranges to and fro, and spreads out, and advances forward with a quickness which has become a proverb, and a subtlety and versatility which baffle investigation. It passes from point to point, gaining one by some indication, another on a probability; then availing itself of an association; then falling back on some received law; next seizing on testimony; then committing itself to some popular impression or some inward instinct, or some obscure memory.[1]

Such was the process of implicit reason, while explicit reason arises from the mind's attempts to analyse and put in order this complex process. But, Newman insists, 'The exercise of analysis is not necessary to the integrity of the process analysed. The process of reasoning is complete in itself, and independent. The analysis is but an account of it; it does not make the conclusion correct; it does not make the inference rational.'[2]

It seems to follow from this that it is not possible, for instance, to dismiss myths merely after an examination of their precise historical truth, since, in accordance with the ideas just indicated,

> if the alleged facts did not occur, they ought to have occurred...; they are such as might have occurred, and would have occurred, under circumstances;... Many a theory, or view of things, on which an institution is founded, or a party held together, is of the same kind. Many an argument used by zealous and earnest men, has this economical character, being not the very ground on which they act (for they continue in the same course though it be refuted), yet, in a certain sense, a representation of it, a proximate description of their feelings in the shape of argument, on which they can rest, to which they can recur when perplexed, and appeal when questioned.[3]

[1] *ibid.*, p. 257.   [2] *ibid.*, p. 259.   [3] *ibid.*, p. 343.

It comes with some surprise to see Newman, more than sixty years in advance, putting forward something so very like Sorel's conception of the myth; and since the name of Sorel conjures up also the names of Marx on the one hand, and Mussolini on the other, it seems to bring Newman very suddenly out of the dead theological atmosphere of early Victorian Oxford into the arena of modern politics, away from remote arguments about the doctrines of the primitive Church, on to the argument about whether Marx's celebrated theory of increasing misery can now be treated as a myth.[1]

That Newman is in fact putting forward something very like Sorel's notion of myths is obvious enough from a preliminary superficial examination of what the two writers are actually saying, but in any case the matter is put beyond reasonable doubt by Sorel himself laying claim to a resemblance between them on this point. And yet there might appear to be some need for explanation here, in that in the midst of an exposition of the ideas which are supposed to form the basis of his conservatism, it has emerged that these ideas seem capable of supporting so revolutionary a doctrine as Sorel's myth of the general strike. It must be stressed at once, however, that it does not appear that Sorel derived his idea of myths directly from Newman. In his *Introduction à l'économie moderne*, where the idea of the myth is introduced, though not developed in the more assured form which it takes in *Réflexions sur la violence*, although, as one might expect, the names of Vico, Croce and Bergson appear, there is no mention of Newman. In the *Réflexions* the name of Newman now appears, and it is interesting to note that, after quoting a typical passage from the *Grammar of Assent*, Sorel says, 'It may be seen from this that the illustrious thinker adopts an attitude which strongly resembles that of the theory of myths.'[2] Thus, if the

---

[1] G. Sorel, *Introduction à l'économie moderne* (10th ed., Paris, 1922), pp. 394–395.

[2] English translation (T. E. Hulme), London, 1916, p. 32; (3rd ed., Paris, 1912), p. 45.

The passage continues 'It is impossible to read Newman without being struck by the analogies between his thought and that of Bergson: people who like to make the history of ideas depend on ethnical traditions will observe that Newman was descended from the Israelites.' Unfortunately, the story of Newman's Jewish descent is now itself recognised as a myth, though not of the specifically Sorel type.

The *Réflexions* were first published in 1906, the *Introduction à l'économie moderne* in 1903.

theory does not come from Newman, at least Sorel found striking confirmation from him; and, indeed, it would have been possible for Sorel to cite more confirmatory evidence than in fact he does.[1]

For Sorel, 'anticipations of the future take the form of myths, which enclose all the strongest inclinations of a people, of a party or of a class, inclinations which recur to the mind with the insistence of instincts in the circumstances of life',[2] and so 'a myth cannot be refuted, since it is, at bottom, identical with the convictions of a group, being the expression of these convictions in the language of movement; it is, in consequence, unanalysable into parts which could be placed on the plane of historical descriptions'.[3] What was of fundamental importance for this great French thinker was that the passage from principles to action could not be understood without employing the theory of myths.

Now Newman was as certain as Sorel that 'Life is for action',[4] and this belief forms as much a part of his theory as Sorel's, but he sees, nevertheless, that the conservatives, the fanatical resisters of change of any sort, are often acting on these mythical grounds. In an interesting passage in one of his note-books,[5] which, since it is not published it is well to include *in extenso*, Newman makes this clear.

> Nothing is so frivolous and so unphilosophical [he says] as the ridicule bestowed on the contest for retaining or surrendering a rite or an observance, such as the use of the Cross in Baptism or the posture of kneeling at the Lord's Table. As well might satire be directed against the manœuvre of two generals concerning some apparently small portion of ground. The Rubicon was a narrow stream. A slight advantage gained is often at once an omen and a measure of ultimate victory. Political parties, to place/look at the matter on the lowest ground, are held together by what are the veriest trifles. An accidental badge, or an inconsistency may embody

[1] Sorel cites passages from Newman at pages 5, 32 and 156 (trans., Hulme). Among many other passages which he might have adduced are those to be found in the following places: *U.S.*, p. 343; *Apo.*, p. 431; *D.A.*, pp. 292–297.
[2] *Reflections*, p. 133.   [3] *ibid.*, p. 33.   [4] *D.A.*, p. 295.
[5] C.C., D.5; 13. A paper on the Church of England and the Revolution of 1688, written about 1834. It is endorsed by the Cardinal as 'not worth anything', but this one may take leave to doubt.

the principle and be the seat of life of a party. A system must be looked at as a whole; and may as little admit of mending or altering as an individual. We cannot change one joint of our body for a better; nor can we with impunity open one vein. These analogies must not of course be pressed too far; but they apply far more to morals and politics than theorists of this day are willing to believe. It is remarkable how hidden, as well as insignificant, are these depositaries and treasure houses of our most important habits. . . . [Here follows some illustration of this thesis.] Not to search into history, how fully is this principle exemplified in the late history of the Catholic question. The political feelings of large masses of our population in various ranks of life were bound up in a resistance of the so-called claims of the Papists. Men of reasoning minds were perplexed, perhaps scandalised, at the diversity of grounds on which the resistance was defended; men of true Catholic views might consider it unworthily based on the mere Protestant and (in their origin) latitudinarian principles of 1688. But the genius of Toryism had gradually (as it were) fossilised the base material which at first existed. Every practical man saw clearly that it was the dogma or measure which united a large and powerful party; the keystone, small in itself, momentous from its position, the bond of great doctrines, the thread upon which a row of costly beads was strung.[1]

It seems to follow from all this that there need be no initial revolutionary bias in the theory which underlies Sorel's notion of the myth, nor in Newman's similar theory, which latter is itself the basis of his theory of the development of ideas. Sorel, granted his general views and his own political circumstances, could consistently apply the theory for a revolutionary purpose, while Newman almost equally consistently could apply it for preventing change. Almost, but not quite, since the legitimate deductions from Newman's theory make a certain form of conservatism impossible; in other words, he finds that he cannot deny that 'in a higher world it is otherwise, but here below to live is to change, and to be perfect is to have changed often'.[2]

It is now possible to see the form the notion of development

[1] C.C., D.5; 13. 'The Church of England and the Revolution of 1688.'
[2] *Dev.*, p. 40. cf. *Ess.*, i, 123–124.

took for Newman. The human mind embraced more than it was conscious of, or could express. Ideas, images of objects in the real world, impressed themselves on the human mind, but they could not be defined in any comprehensive formula, and had to be indicated by a series of partial propositions. This was because an idea, though whole and individual, could only be seen in its aspects and relations. The idea was commensurate with the sum total of its possible aspects. Newman's description of the process of the development of the idea, too long to quote here, is very striking.[1] Such ideas as that of the rights of man, or of utilitarianism, are not, he thinks, passively received by men, but become an active principle in them, leading them to propagate and apply the idea, and to reflect upon it. All may not be clear on what it is that moves them, and a period of confusion in the various groping expressions of the idea will take place. However, judgements and aspects of the idea accumulate, a definite teaching emerges, which modifies, or is modified by other views of it, so that all the various aspects of the idea which have come to light are seen by the separate individual where before they were seen in their entirety only by the aggregate of minds. Newman then goes on to describe how the idea, once it has received coherent expression, works its way into the intellectual and institutional life of a country, and modifies, and is modified by the existing social and intellectual framework.

There are many difficulties which spring at once to mind. Must the development of the idea be seen as merely psychological, or is it an ontological development which Newman postulates? A thorough examination of difficulties of this sort is not in place here, where a broad picture is sought of all that Newman's idea of development meant for his politics in general, and his conservatism in particular. Neither is it necessary to spend much time on the different types of development which Newman distinguishes, although it is clear that, besides strictly political developments, the logical, historical and metaphysical developments which he distinguishes all have some political importance.

[1] *Dev.*, p. 34.

Indeed the very notion of the development of ideas could have political significance whether or not Newman distinguished a peculiarly political kind. When Newman discusses political developments he reveals one of his most characteristic positions. A barbarian and a civilised society were distinguished by the role of reason in them.[1] The barbarian society was not really capable of development, but in the civilised State reason was always the incentive or at least the pretence of development. These developments were difficult to exhibit in a scientific analysis, since they were capricious and irregular. Newman points out a fact that is widely recognised today when he says that the intellectual process which attempts to justify a political development is often posterior to the development itself. It will be seen that Newman was looking forward at that very moment to some theory of Church and State which would justify the actual practical position which was by then achieved in England. This intellectual process which followed the practical was the conscious process, though men had been moved to alter the existing political framework from reasons of which they were not fully conscious. Sometimes, however, the dialectic through which the idea is developed can take place in one individual thinker, and thus the actual development of the idea outside him is anticipated. Not only is it anticipated temporally, but this anticipation can be a real aid to its eventual development, and Newman cites Locke's philosophy, which was much more than a mere defence of the Revolution, and had a vast influence which long survived his death.

More interesting than any examples of political developments is the fact that Newman thought he was able to provide a method for deciding which were faithful developments, and which not.

He did this by providing seven notes of genuine developments, the first of which consisted in 'preservation of type'. Many writers in the hundred years since the book was written have claimed that Newman was here assuming that he knew what the genuine idea really was, which on his own theory he could not

---

[1] This distinction is discussed in the next chapter.

possibly know, in order to see if it be preserved; but this is an undeserved stricture.[1] He was talking of a preservation not of the idea, but of the type, and he illustrates his meaning in various ways, pointing out, for example, that 'the political doctrines of the modern Tory resemble those of the primitive Whig; yet few will deny that the Whig and Tory characters have each a discriminating type'.[2]

The second note of the true development of an idea was that the principles which it embodies should maintain continuity during the development. The principles themselves are abstract and general, and so incapable of development, but the doctrine, which owes its life and vigour to these principles, relates to facts, and grows in a given fashion according to the individual or social mind into which it is received. Yet Newman did not think it always possible to distinguish between a principle and an idea or doctrine, for what is a doctrine in one system may be a principle in another. Again, as with infallibility in the Catholic Church, it is sometimes difficult to see in a particular case whether a principle or a doctrine is in question.[3] From much that Newman says on principles it seems that they are often identical with what he usually calls first principles, those postulates which are necessary if thought is to exist at all, and which at one time Newman treated simply as assumptions, later as a sort of intuition.[4]

There were five other tests for deciding on the faithfulness of a development. A truly developed idea should display an assimilating, unitive power; it must develop in a logical sequence; in early days it should have shown, perhaps only in one isolated thinker, some definite anticipation of what it was to become; it should be

---

[1] This objection seems first to have been raised by W. Palmer of Worcester College in his *Doctrine of Development and Conscience* (London, 1846), p. 121. By the end of the century Newman was being taken to task for precisely not doing what others had accused him of. See A. M. Fairbairn, *Catholicism: Roman and Anglican* (London, 1889), pp. 165-166. Newman was ably defended on this point by W. G. Williams. See *Newman, Pascal, Loisy and the Catholic Church* (London, 1906), p. 99.

[2] *Dev.*, p. 175.

[3] *ibid.*, p. 179. Newman came to think of papal infallibility as a principle, rather than a doctrine. Ward, *Life*, ii, 218.

[4] On these two senses of first principles see Ward, *Life*, ii, 507-508.

conservative of what has gone before it; finally, it should display chronic vigour.¹ It does not need much reflexion to show that there is something rather arbitrary about the devising of these seven tests, and there is a great deal to be said for M. Guitton's reduction of the seven into three groups, so that one group is founded on permanence, the second illustrates this permanence by appealing to structure, while the third shows how the element of permanence survives the obstacles in its way.² But, even though these tests may have something of an arbitrary nature about them, they at least deserve careful consideration on their own ground, which they have not always received. Indeed Newman's own candid admission that his whole story was 'undoubtedly an hypothesis to account for a difficulty', has been turned against him as almost sufficient refutation in itself.³ This is hardly fair, but it was understandable at the time the theory saw expression. The whole theory was novel;⁴ Newman was felt on all sides to be a wanton breaker of the ecclesiastical peace, and in the theological climate of Oxford in 1845 it was not likely to be judged, as a theory, on its own merits; now, with the complete change in this atmosphere, it is, as being concerned with theology, not often judged at all.

The sense of continuity in things which this theory inspired in Newman is readily apparent. The development of ideas was an eminently social process, which involved a partnership of the living and the dead, and to which those yet unborn would be able to make their specific contribution. It can be no surprise that a sane and balanced conservatism is so typical of Newman. For

---

¹ *Dev.*, pp. 171–206.
² The revised arrangement would thus be as follows: 1, Preservation of Type; Anticipation of Future; Conservative Action on Past. 2, Continuity of Principles and Logical Sequence. 3, Power of Assimilation and Chronic Vigour.
    For reasons extraneous to the subject on hand which led Newman to lay down seven tests, see Guitton, *Philosophie de Newman*, pp. 93–94 n. Cf. Ward, *Life*, ii, 343.
³ The foregoing admission is at *Dev.*, p. 30. Typical of those who take the hypothetical nature of the theory as evidence against it is W. A. Butler, in *Letters on the Development of Christian Doctrine* (Dublin, 1850), pp. 50 ff.
⁴ For a summing-up of the question of Newman's debt to Moehler, see H. Tristram, 'J. A. Moehler et Newman', *Revue des sciences philosophiques et théologiques*, xxvii (1938), pp. 184–204.

him, as for Burke, 'the private stock of reason' of a given individual at a given time is necessarily severely limited, and for two reasons. Firstly the moral and intellectual shortcomings of individuals do much to diminish this stock, while, secondly, according to Newman's theory of development, the individual thinker does not grasp an idea as a whole, but breaks it up into aspects and relations. Time, and the co-operation of many minds, is therefore necessary for the adequate comprehension of ideas, and for all these reasons it becomes only common sense for individuals to take a stand with Burke, and 'avail themselves of the general bank and capital of nations and of ages'.[1] This is what Newman advises, and recognising that the individual may sometimes encounter difficulties in appropriating ideas which come to him in an abstract form, he praises especially 'a wisdom, safe from the excess and vagaries of individuals, embodied in institutions which have stood the trial and received the sanction of ages'.[2]

Newman is no more afraid than Burke to glorify 'prejudice' but as with Burke, it is prejudice in favour of 'the wisdom of our ancestors'[3] which he vindicates. This must be emphasised, in order to place in perspective what has been said about the process of implicit thought. It might be thought from Newman's account of it that the individual has successfully freed himself from any objective test of the truth of the results of his own internal thought processes, and that he can rest content with the subjective truth which emerges from the lazy and prejudiced thinking which he can dignify with the name of 'illative sense'. That judgement will not stand. In dealing with the so-called illative sense Newman was dealing with very real and important facts about how people commonly think which were largely ignored in his day, and are not always recognised today.

And further, in the end, corporate reason transcends that of the

[1] *Reflections on the French Revolution* (Everyman ed.), p. 84. Great similarities between Newman and Burke are obvious, but most have been best catalogued by Wilfrid Ward in his various works. See 'Functions of Prejudice', *Dublin Review* (January, 1906), vol. 138, pp. 99–118.
[2] *Idea*, p. xxii.
[3] *M.*, i, 205. This letter, dated 1829, contains Newman's best-known early statement on the value of tradition.

individual. This is the burden of the theory of development, the glorification of prejudice and tradition, of prejudice in favour of tradition. As with so many other things, Newman does not reconcile the difficulties which arise on a consideration of the roles he assigns to corporate and to individual reason.

But despite any of these difficulties, it remains clear that Newman had good grounds for his stressing of the value of tradition, and it is here that many will find his most important contribution to political thought. Yet the idea of tradition is not isolated in Newman's thought, but a part of a large and complex system of ideas. Tradition itself should not be conceived of too narrowly. It should be noted, for instance, that though it may be thought of as the transmission from age to age of 'the wisdom of our ancestors', tradition is not merely the handing down of intellectual doctrines, or of ideas embodied in institutions. For tradition, 'in its fulness is necessarily unwritten; it is the mode in which a society has felt or acted during a certain period, and it cannot be circumscribed any more than man's countenance and manner can be conveyed to strangers in any set of propositions'.[1]

Thus the idea of tradition is closely linked with that of national character, an idea which finds such very frequent illustration in Newman's writings. This connexion has been exposed, in words which apply exactly to Newman, by Sir Ernest Barker, in his book *National Character*. He explains that the nation 'is one, and has a character of its own, by virtue of the unity of its tradition, which is the deposit and crystallisation, in an objective form, of the seething and moving thought of human minds'.[2] In fact, national character 'is tradition, socially created and socially transmitted tradition'.[3] It is not easy to trace the source of this concept of national character, which so gripped Newman. Few clues are available in the numerous references to this idea which Newman makes,[4] but if any one name must be singled out as indicating an important source, it must perhaps be that of Moehler.[5] From

---

[1] *V.M.*, i, 32. [2] *National Character* (London, 1927), p. 7. [3] *ibid.*, p. 9.
[4] See e.g. *Idea*, p. 308; *H.S.*, i, 60; iii, 300 ff.; and the brilliant sketch of the English national character, *D.A.*, pp. 334 ff.
[5] See *Diff.*, i, 54–55.

Moehler, and possibly also from Schlegel, Newman was subject to that influence which stemmed from Herder, and which helped spread far and wide the idea of separate national characters, of different civilisations rather than of a single undifferentiated civilisation set against barbarism. Though the idea of national character is essential to Newman, to his theory of the State, and to his conservatism, nevertheless he might still at times appear to be talking in pre-Herder terms about barbarism and civilisation. It could be argued, however, that Newman is rather looking forward to the twentieth century, to a position akin to Collingwood's, than looking back to the eighteenth century.[1]

It must be emphasised that, despite the enormous importance which Newman placed on national character, this in no way led him to the growing nationalism of his age. In fact he abhorred nationalism, and did not hesitate to say so.[2] But Newman realised more clearly than many at his own time, how divergent are the main streams of tradition in different countries, and the different national characters which are partly the cause and partly the effect of this divergence. Every national character has its strong points and its weak, and many neither weak nor strong, good nor bad, but purely idiosyncratic. Growing from these is a mass of custom, beliefs, traditions and the like, and these tend to a certain definite form of government for their complete expression. If the national character of a people calls for a particular type of government with which it may be in harmony, it is obvious that it is ludicrous to imagine that the British constitution, for example, can be exported round the world. Newman pours scorn on those who seem to think it possible.[3] Even today, in the middle of the twentieth century, it cannot be said that so firm a grasp as this on the importance of national character is everywhere and always displayed. Newman's dislike of nationalism is now shared by many in the West, but not all those who decry nationalism still

---

[1] Besides certain similarities between Newman's and Collingwood's idea of development in history, there are some resemblances between their accounts of the nature of barbarism. *The New Leviathan* (London, 1942), 36.92; H.S., i, 166.
[2] See e.g. H.S., i, 200; *Diff.*, i, 303; ii, 236.
[3] P.P.C., p. 247; H.S., i, 180.

retain a clear hold on the enduring realities of national character. Newman's position is a useful one for the present time and if it were shared by more today, then perhaps the prospects for advance in international co-operation would be increased.

Important as this idea of national character is for Newman, it is possible to be misled as to the exact significance of it in his thought. Too much stress, for instance, must not be laid on an early belief on this topic, which Newman, while later reporting it, is not concerned to reaffirm, and in fact declines even to defend. The passage in question is none the less significant.

> Besides the hosts of evil spirits, I considered there was a middle race, δαιμόνια, neither in heaven, nor hell [he says]; partially fallen, capricious, wayward; noble or crafty, benevolent or malicious, as the case might be. These things gave a sort of inspiration or intelligence to races, nations and classes of men. Hence the action of bodies politic and associations, which is often so different from that of the individuals who compose them. Hence the character and the instinct of states and governments, of religious communities and communions.[1]

Mr. Werner Stark comments that this passage shows that 'Newman strove to win a clear vision of the national character, the individual character of a multitude of men—to comprehend it as an ideal type; and in this endeavour he grappled, perhaps unwittingly, with the central problem of every descriptive sociology.'[2]

Perhaps: but what the passage indubitably shows, however, is the connexion of another of Newman's favourite ideas, the *genius loci*, with national character.

Just as an individual had his own peculiar character, so had the nation, and so also had a particular society within the nation, and the character or spirit of such a society he called its *genius loci*. It is not altogether clear whether the society, to be possessed of such a spirit, must rest on a territorial basis, or whether it could be said to inhabit institutions unconfined to particular buildings, or even

---

[1] *Apo.*, pp. 129–130. [2] *Newman Centenary Essays*, p. 159.

geographical areas. The influence of place, alone, on men's feelings and imaginations Newman would be inclined to place very highly, and so it would seem an essential element in the idea, but in the last resort one is taken back once more to tradition. Thus Newman sums up his notion in his *Idea of a University*, speaking of 'a self-perpetuating tradition, or a *genius loci*, as it is sometimes called; which haunts the home where it has been born, and which imbues and forms, more or less, and one by one, every individual who is successively brought under its shadow'.[1]

It is impossible to get far away from tradition while reading Newman, and there have been few better apologists for its value.

> By tradition is meant [he tells us] what has ever been held, as far as we know, though we do not know how it came to be held, and for that very reason think it true, because else it would not be held. Now, tradition is of great and legitimate use as an *initial* means of gaining notions about historical and other facts; it is the way in which things first come to us; it is natural and necessary, to trust it; it is an informant we make use of daily. Life is not long enough for proving everything; we are obliged to take a great many things upon the credit of others. Moreover, tradition is really a ground in reason, an argument for believing, to a certain point. . . . Tradition, then, being information, not authentical but immemorial, is a *prima facie* evidence of the facts which it witnesses.[2]

But, in this very place which shows the high value Newman assigned to tradition, is the evidence which goes to show that high though it be placed, it is not after all sufficient in itself. In the last resort it requires 'some ultimate authority to make it trustworthy'.[3]

The place of authority in Newman's thought is so often misrepresented that it will need a special examination in the next chapter, but, at the least, it is undeniable that in both his politics and his religion, authority in some form holds a more important place than tradition. But this does not contradict earlier assertions about the value ascribed to tradition, unless an upholder of this value must give tradition the foremost place in determining

---

[1] p. 147.   [2] *P.P.C.*, pp. 46–47.   [3] *ibid.*, p. 88.

historical or other truth. In politics, it is difficult to see what sort of authority Newman had in mind, and it seems, for reasons soon to be examined, that ultimately the authority in question was of two kinds—firstly, that of the Church on political matters pertaining to faith and morals, and secondly, and in the last resort, that of the individual conscience. This authority needed invoking the less because tradition was, to some extent, the regulator of its own truth. Inasmuch as tradition was the product of the development of ideas, and tests for the genuine development of ideas existed, then tradition was subject to a scrutiny which could be called objective, though in a very real sense internal. Further, a false development will in any case in time become corrupt and die. In the same way, it seems that even a true development of a false idea, i.e. an idea which is not a reflexion of a real object, cannot expect ultimate survival. Newman's whole theory made it possible for him, without leaning on any arbitrary or external authority, to put forward a powerful traditionalism and conservatism, while not failing to observe norms in human development and progress. He thus places himself on the side of the great conservatives like Burke, and avoids the thoroughgoing conservatism to which, for instance, some of Hegel's ideas so easily lend themselves.

The whole subject of the traditionalist element in Newman's conservatism requires more attention than it can here receive, and the remaining references to it in this book by no means exhaust the topic. Yet something of the ideas on which it rested has been brought forward, and these same ideas will now be seen to underlie a great deal of the political thinking which will emerge in the following chapters.

II

THE STATE

1. THE WORLD'S EVIL

In a famous passage of his *City of God*, St. Augustine says that, setting justice aside, kingdoms are no different from robber bands. Newman seems to echo these words when he claims that 'All states of the world, all governments, except so far as they are Christian, except so far as they act on Christian principles, are scarcely more than robbers and men of blood.'[1] Newman is as emphatic as St. Augustine that true justice is only to be found in that commonwealth of which Christ is the founder and ruler. But there has been a great deal of controversy in the past about the correct interpretation of St. Augustine on this whole problem of justice and the State, and it is interesting to note that some of the arguments which have been used in the course of this controversy have a very special relevance when considering the apparently similar position of Newman. It will be useful, therefore, while using this question of justice as a key to open to view Newman's central ideas about the State, to make some extended comparisons between them.

It must be remembered that Newman put a great deal of stress on the doctrine of the Fall, and the corruption with which the world therefore abounded. Nor is there any real evidence to show that this melancholy view of things ever became much more cheerful for him. It was 'a dark world',[2] and it always remained so. In a beautiful and famous passage of the *Apologia* it is said that 'the sight of the world is nothing else than the prophet's scroll, "full of lamentations, and mourning and woe"'.[3] It was essential not to become too attached to the things of the world, which

---

[1] S.D., pp. 263–264. Cf. *De Civ. Dei*, IV, iv. Welldon's edition (London, 1924), i, 155, '*Remota itaque justitia, quid sunt regna nisi magna latrocinia.*'
[2] P.S., i, 328.   [3] p. 334.

would be 'as monstrous and insane . . . as to desire to feed on ashes, or to be chained to a corpse'.[1] But for all this he was well aware of the beauty of the physical world, and was ready to hymn the praises of the earth and the things of the earth.[2] If it is true that in Christianity the world-accepting and the world-renouncing tempers meet, it is also true that this is seen at its clearest in some of its most eminent representatives, and J. N. Figgis had excellent reasons for coupling the names of Newman and St. Augustine in this respect.[3]

The Fall is at the centre of Newman's ideas on politics. In the first place, as already seen, such a doctrine makes impossible a certain type of progressivism. But, secondly, the immediate result or meaning of the Fall is that man is prone to evil, his vision of a higher world than this in which he dwells becomes blurred, he hears only faintly the commands from a higher sphere—and so 'men need a local government on earth'.[4] Hence the Church, a visible channel of invisible grace, a concrete representative of the invisible world. There is a difficulty, however, about Newman's conception of the Church which must be met at once. It is not immediately clear how much, nor for how long he was influenced in his attitude to it by that Calvinism of his youth, which in the first chapter of the *Apologia* Newman shows to be opening out into more Catholic views. The question is important, since the Calvinist doctrine of predestination is closely associated with the idea of a Church of the Elect, of those predestined to eternal glory, a Church in endless conflict with its enemy, the World. Now although it has been accurately stated of the very young Newman that he adopted *'avec une netteté juvenile le schéma Augustinien . . . un conflict irréconciliable entre la Cité de Dieu et la Cité du Malin'*,[5] the truth seems to be that from the time of his first published writings he had given up the belief in a sharp distinction between the Elect and the World. By the time Newman was ordained a priest in the Anglican Church he had left this position behind, though he did not at once lose his evangelical

---
[1] S.D., p. 103.   [2] e.g. H.S., i, 114–115.
[3] *The Political Aspects of St. Augustine's City of God* (London, 1921), p. 67.
[4] *Idea*, p. 515.   [5] L. Bouyer, *Newman* (Paris, 1952), p. 52.

tone and phraseology.¹ There was in fact a great deal which remained constant throughout his adult life in his attitude to the Church. It was ever a visible body for him, the notion of an invisible Church being unscriptural and dangerous.² It was not a body of saints, but, in Bellarmine's words, 'a congregation of men bound by common profession and sacraments, under legitimate pastors'; to which, as a Catholic, Newman would add the missing three words, 'especially the Pope'.³

Not all accept this view. Y. Brilioth thinks that Newman was much more, and much longer influenced by the idea of a Church of the Elect than he himself realised, so that, whereas some of his fellow Tractarians were dominated by a 'static' view of the Church, in Newman himself there was 'nearly the same antithesis between the empirical and the purely spiritual conception of the Church which is at the bottom of St. Augustine's view'.⁴

Now if what has been argued here already is correct, Brilioth is mistaken on this point. But the fact of a resemblance between Newman and St. Augustine on this subject has been pointed out by a writer of a very different background from Brilioth,⁵ and it is important to decide how far this resemblance can legitimately be pressed.

For St. Augustine, then, everyone born into this human life becomes a member of one of two cities, the *civitas Dei* or the *terrena civitas* about which we know that 'Two loves . . . have given origin to these two cities, self-love in contempt of God unto the earthly, love of God in contempt of one's self to the heavenly'.⁶ Now this use of the term *civitas* is interesting here, and it is instructive to follow Sir Ernest Barker's explanation of its use.⁷

---

¹ See entry for 29 May 1825 in 'Copies of Memoranda' (Birmingham Oratory MSS.). These are late copies by Newman from an early unpublished journal. The same point is established from many recently discovered sermons of Newman at the Oratory. From published sources the same fact emerges. See *M.*, i, 119–121; also, e.g. *P.S.*, i, 49; *S.D.*, Appendix.   ² *P.S.*, iii, 221.   ³ *Ess.*, ii, 36.

⁴ *The Anglican Revival* (London, 1925), p. 261. Brilioth's reliance on Harnack's interpretation of St. Augustine must be noted here, since not everyone will follow Harnack on this subject.

⁵ C. Dawson, 'The City of God', *Monument to St. Augustine* (London, 1930), p. 72.

⁶ *City of God*, XIV, xxviii. (Everyman ed., ii, 58.)

⁷ *ibid.* (Everyman ed.), i, pp. xii–xv.

He explains that St. Augustine had gained from the philosophers of antiquity the idea of human society as distinguishable into four grades, or 'concentric rings'. The first is the *domus*, the household; above this is the *civitas*, which passed from its original meaning of 'city' to become applicable to the State in general; above and wider than this is the *orbis terrae* which embraces the whole Earth and all the human society on it. Beyond this, and widest of all, and including all, is *mundus*, including not only human society but spirits as well. But as time went on the term *civitas* came familiarly to be applied to what was properly *mundus*, and in this St. Augustine followed the common practice, so that his two cities must be thought of as covering the whole universe, including angels as well as men, but divided along the lines he has set out. This might be considered as making what might be called a vertical split in the single society of the ancients, but from St. Paul another element enters, which gives cause for making a horizontal split also. St. Paul had taught that there existed in the heavens a commonwealth which was prepared for the righteous, and on earth a polity in which the righteous must stay as pilgrims, along with other men. St. Augustine accepted the view of the supramundane society, but seems to differ from St. Paul in stretching his city of the righteous from earth to heaven, while not allowing any of its members to belong to the earthly polity, his *terrena civitas*. This was bound to be the case for him on his own definitions, from which it is also evident that the *terrena civitas* cannot be identified with any particular society; not, as might seem tempting, with the Roman Empire; and it is impossible to make this identification because it may well have been that in any particular society there were men who loved God. If there were any at all who loved God they would presumably live in some society or other. In the same way it is not possible to identify the *civitas Dei* with the Catholic Church, 'since the Churches are now full of those who are to be hereafter sifted, the corn from the chaff'.[1] Even if St. Augustine did sometimes appear to particularise his earthly city, and even though this may have had

---

[1] *City of God*, xix, xlix (Everyman ed., ii, 223).

far-reaching historical consequences, it is none the less important to recognise the actual distinctions which he himself lays down.

Now there is much in Newman which is parallel to all this. He speaks of an invisible world in which God, the angels and the souls of the dead exist;[1] and that this is the *civitas Dei* of St. Augustine is clearly seen in his statement that this world includes holy and obedient creatures, that it is a Divine Kingdom, eternal and unchangeable.[2] Besides the Divine Kingdom there is a mediatorial kingdom, the actual empirical Church, a kingdom over sinners for the sake of sinners.[3] But however similar this may be to St. Augustine's position, it does not seem possible to go on to say that similarly Newman sometimes speaks of the Church and the Divine Kingdom as one and the same thing. If this limits the resemblance between Newman and St. Augustine, it is even more limited by the fact that when Newman spoke of the 'World', the great antagonist and opponent of the Church, he did not mean quite what St. Augustine meant by his earthly city.

At first sight these conceptions are very similar. 'Is not the world in itself evil?' asks Newman, and it appears from his own answer that the sin of the world is much the same as that which divided the two cities of St. Augustine.[4] But a closer scrutiny reveals the fact that the resemblance is not complete. In his sermon on 'The World Our Enemy',[5] preached on that text of St. John's which forms a recurrent motif in his work—'We know that we are of God, and the whole world lieth in wickedness', a distinction is made between different senses of 'the world'. He thinks that some explanation of the term is necessary because although people knew that the world was in some vague sense harmful, and that it was connected with man in society as contrasted with man in his private life, yet this was more or less all that most people knew about it.

One sense in which it is possible to understand this word is,

---

[1] 'The Invisible World', *P.S.*, iv, 200–213. This world is 'the hidden kingdom of God'. *ibid.*, p. 208.
[2] Sermon at St. Clement's, Oxford, 26.12.1824. (This is one of the recently discovered sermons already mentioned, to which it is impossible as yet to give a more exact reference.)
[3] *ibid.*   [4] *S.D.*, pp. 79–80.   [5] *P.S.*, vii, 27 ff.

then, in its reference to 'the present visible system of things, without taking into consideration whether they are good or bad'.[1] It refers to the vast system of relations which bind men together in human society, relations political, economic, both national and international, familial and the rest, a system binding men together not only in respect of what they have in common, but also in respect of their very differences, by which men are made dependent on each other. This system, as framed by God, must be actually and positively good, but it is all the more dangerous to religion simply because of this goodness, which is after all only a relative and minor one. Since it is not only good, but visibly so, here and now, men are led to prefer the immediate minor good to the *summum bonum* which is far off, and come to rest in the world as an end in itself.[2]

If the world is in this sense a system which is good because of its Creator, there is another sense in which it is the reverse of good, because however the world was actually created, in its infancy,

> while as yet the elements of human society did but lie hid in the nature and condition of the first man. Adam fell; and thus the world, with all its social ranks, and aims, and pursuits, and pleasures, and prizes, has ever from its birth been sinful.[3]

More explicitly:

> the whole visible course of things, nations, empires, states, politics, professions, trades, society, pursuits of all kinds, are, I do not say directly and formally sinful (of course not), but they 'come of evil'; they hold of evil, and they are the instruments of evil; they have in them the nature of evil; they are the progeny of sinful Adam, they have in them the infection of Adam's fall; they never would have been as we see them, but for Adam's fall.[4]

The full implications of these passages will soon be considered, but it is well to stress at once that the evil of which Newman

---
[1] *P.S.*, vii, 28.
[2] Thus 'the science of good government' can be dangerous and sinful. *ibid.*, p. 30.
[3] *ibid.*, p. 31. [4] *S.D.*, p. 105.

complains in the world can be related particularly to the spirit and life within it. About the world viewed in its connexion with the principles and practices which actually direct it, Newman had few illusions. 'When was the face of human society . . . other than evil?'[1] he asks. There was no point in moaning at the especial wickedness of one's own age, for things would always be as bad. The great mass of men remain no better or worse than before, though they have heard the Gospel—the whole world is nothing more than 'a confederacy of evil'.[2]

It might seem that the world in this second sense could be identified with the *terrena civitas*, but this is impossible since Newman refuses to point to any particular man or set of men as being exclusively of the world; or rather, he would not allow any man to be pointed out as not being a member of the world to some extent. Men are a mixture of good and evil; they have 'two sides, a light side and a dark, and . . . the dark happens to be the outermost. Thus we form part of the world to each other, though we be not of the world.'[3] The world then, as was implicit in his definitions already given, is an abstraction referring to principles and practices and not to the men who hold them, at least, not to men in their entirety, and it must be admitted that it is quite possible to view man from a certain aspect like this as long as he is not made into two persons instead of one. It follows from this that though 'in our idea of the two, and in their principles, and in their future prospects, the Church is one thing, and the world is another, yet in present matter of fact, the Church is of the world, not separate from it'.[4] The conclusion must be, then, that the world, in the sense in which it comes in for most denunciation from Newman, is not a definite community of particular men, as might be inferred from certain descriptions of it such as that which calls it a 'vast community permeated by religious error which mocks and rivals the Church',[5] nor any particular men at all, though it is something more than the sum

---

[1] *P.S.*, v, 132. For later views on this whole subject, defending the apparent harshness of expression, see *S.E.*, p. 77. See also H. Tristram, *Living Thoughts of Cardinal Newman* (London, 1948), pp. 146–150.

[2] *S.D.*, p. 80.   [3] *P.S.*, vii, 36.   [4] *ibid.*   [5] *S.E.*, p. 76.

total of the wickedness of individual men—it is the wickedness of men in society, and Newman had a strong sense of the way in which, by mutual sympathies and the like, error was transmitted through the community.[1]

Newman's 'World' is not the same as the 'earthly city', nor are the Church and the World in the same relation to one another as the two cities of St. Augustine. But Newman, in saying strong things about the evils of the world, and often therein appearing to include the State, cannot hope to escape the judgement or reproach that is often made about St. Augustine—that he denied the essential position of justice for the State.

That St. Augustine did deny this, is, to say the least, a very probable interpretation of his thought. It is true that Augustine seemed to feel disposed to argue with the Ciceronian account of the State, since this account did not insist that justice must render to God, as well as to man, his due, but there was more than a quibble here. Augustine was convinced that if God were not given his due there would be little likelihood of man faring much better. With man as he is, and depraved as St. Augustine believed him to be, then if justice were to be an essential element in the State it might be necessary to say that there had never been a State in the past, and there was not likely to be one in the future. To avoid this position, Augustine sought for a definition which would avoid the *juris consensu* which he found in Cicero's definition, and the broad definition at which he arrives accomplishes this, while incidentally allowing him to grant Rome the title of *respublica*. This definition, '*Populus est coetus multitudinis rationalis rerum quas diligit concordi communione sociatus*',[2] broad as it is, testifies to a strong individualism in St. Augustine, to his strong sense of the importance of human purposes in society.

Despite all this, however, it is by no means universally admitted that St. Augustine really intended to do what he appears to be doing in his exclusion of justice from the definition of the State.

[1] *S.E.*, pp. 77–78.
[2] *De Civ. Dei*, xix, xxiv, Welldon, ii, 444. Translated in Everyman ed. as 'A people is a multitude of reasonable creatures conjoined in a general agreement of those things it respects', ii, 264.

The famous phrase, already quoted, which could be interpreted as meaning that robber bands and States are alike in having no necessary connexion with justice, could also be interpreted as meaning that the whole point of the difference between the robber band and a kingdom lies in justice, which is in fact necessarily associated with a kingdom.[1] There are undoubtedly good reasons enough for hesitating to attribute to Augustine this view of the irrelevance of justice to the definition of the State; but it is not only the good reasons which have made some hesitate in this matter, but also the view that it is somehow 'deplorable' for a Christian saint to give utterance to such thoughts.[2] If he were not a Christian saint it may not be too fanciful to suppose that he might have suffered from the same sort of reputation which has for so long, or at least until recently, been attached to the name of Machiavelli. And yet there would be nothing necessarily shocking if such were St. Augustine's views, whether he be right or not. Man was still a moral agent for him. There was no question of the State creating its own justice; it was not a moral organism, at least in any supra-personal sense. Mr. Christopher Dawson has much reason on his side in defending what he supposes to be St. Augustine's view, and it is highly significant that he uses a quotation from Newman to establish his case.[3] He thinks that Newman held that justice was not essential to the State, and that Newman's Church and the World represent the same point of view as St. Augustine's, despite terminological differences. The latter judgement is broadly correct, and it remains to be decided whether the former can be accepted.

The hesitation to ascribe to Augustine a view of the State which

---

[1] The meaning of this famous phrase is, of course, much disputed, but a very sound examination of it is made by R. H. Barrow in his *Introduction to St. Augustine's City of God* (London, 1950). His remarks on the use of the word *'remota'*, and on the translation of *'regna'* (pp. 255–256) are important. This passage can be treated as an exception to Augustine's general view (see note 2).
[2] This attitude appears to be taken in Carlyle, *A History of Medieval Political Theory in the West* (2nd ed., London, 1927), i, 164–168. A. J. Carlyle uses the term 'deplorable' in *Social and Political Ideas of the Middle Ages* (ed. F. J. C. Hearnshaw, London, 1923), p. 51.
[3] *Monument to St. Augustine*, p. 62.

sets aside justice is due to more than a fear of being shocked. To show the manner in which justice was connected with the State for Augustine, it seems best not to argue from the force of certain words in some key passages, though this must also be done, but to develop the discussion along the lines laid down by Sir Ernest Barker in his introduction to the *City of God*.[1] Here he stresses the importance of the terms *pax* and *ordo*, and seeks to show that if *vera justitia* is absent, yet nevertheless the State involves a relative justice, adjusted to the defects of sinful man. Now peace for St. Augustine is certainly a key word; it is for him more than a political concept, it is also a metaphysical one. It is an order, giving like and unlike things their place. Since peace is always the aim, and the aim of all, of the egoist, of the State, of the bloodiest war, and since this peace is a kind of order, it seems undeniable that it is possible to link some form of justice with St. Augustine's theory.

However, all of this would be by no means explicit in what he says, although it is noteworthy that just the same sort of considerations and arguments can, as will later be seen, be used in the attempt to acquit Newman of too cynical an attitude to justice, a fact which must have some tendency to show that such projected interpretation of St. Augustine is not unfounded.

It would be difficult to imagine more sweeping remarks about the evil of States than those which Newman actually makes. The 'world' was evil for him, and many of the passages in which he stresses this show that he intends to include the political community itself within the condemnation.

> Look into the history of the world [he bids his hearers in one of his sermons; and continues] and what do you find there? Revolutions and changes without number, kingdoms rising and falling; and when without crimes? States are established by God's ordinance, they have their existence in the necessity of man's nature; but when was one ever established, nay, or maintained, without war and bloodshed?[2]

[1] Everyman ed., i, pp. xvii–xix. R. H. Barrow argues on the same lines in his Introduction.
[2] *P.S.*, vii, 32.

The fact that Newman uses the expression, 'or maintained', in this passage is important, since it goes some way to showing that he was not merely thinking of the historical origin of States, but was going further. This is seen more clearly in the passage where he insists that

> earthly kingdoms are founded, not in justice, but in injustice. They are created by the sword, by robbery, cruelty, perjury, craft and fraud. There never was a kingdom, except Christ's, which was not conceived and born, nurtured and educated, in sin. There never was a state but was committed to acts and maxims which it is its crime to maintain, and its ruin to abandon.[1]

Unlike the Church, other kingdoms 'spring from evil and depend on evil; they have their life and strength in bold deeds and bad principles' while only the Church has its life imperilled if its members are evil, since only for the Church is its 'original principle abandoned'[2] thereby. There is no doubt that Newman is saying far more here than that the historical origins of most States were often of a morally doubtful nature. Yet, to determine the limits of what he means, it is important to bear in mind that the quotations given have been from sermons, and in his sermons Newman was inclined to strike a more gloomy note than he might have considered necessary in a political treatise. Nor, with his views on the depravity of man, and his distaste for the optimistic type of religion prevalent at the day, is this severity of tone a surprising feature of his sermons.

However, to arrive at a balanced view of what Newman really thought about justice and the nature of the State, it is important to examine what he has to say in places other than his sermons.

Now the State was not a supernatural, but a natural phenomenon for Newman, both before and after the advent of Christianity, and can be studied as such—it is part of the visible system of the things. Yet, starting from a belief in God, Newman concludes that all this visible scheme is ultimately from Him. Nor

[1] S.D., p. 242.   [2] ibid., p. 243.

does this apply merely to the physical world, but, as Newman makes clear, to

> the intellectual, moral, social, and political world. Man, with his motives and works, his languages, his propagation, his diffusion, is from Him. Society, laws, government, He is their sanction. The pageant of earthly royalty has the semblance and benediction of the Eternal King. Peace and Civilization, commerce and adventure, wars when just, conquest when humane and necessary, have his co-operation, and his blessing upon them. The course of events, the revolution of empires, the rise and fall of states, the periods and eras, the progresses and the retrogressions of the world's history, not indeed the incidental sin, over-abundant as it is, but the great outlines and results of human affairs, are from His disposition.[1]

It seems from this that Newman, despite his forceful language elsewhere, does not consider that literally all wars and conquests are unjust, nor all States quite simply instruments of sin. The difficulty at once arises, which Newman does not explicitly face, though he has provided hints towards its solution, that the present visible system of things is from God, and yet so permeated with evil. More particularly, as a Christian Newman must hold that the powers that be are ordained by God, yet he asserts they are much concerned with evil. In face of this apparent inconsistency in the attitude of Newman to the State, it will be necessary to review a wide range of scattered remarks and isolated arguments in order to construct a coherent account of his ideas on this subject, making it possible to decide if any inconsistency must be allowed to remain.

2. THE MAKING OF THE STATE

As all writers on politics have some theory about man, whether explicit or not, which it is wise to grasp if their ideas about the State are to be fully understood, so Newman had certain views, apart from the obviously vitally important religious idea of man. There is no isolated, abstract individual for him, 'because in fact man does not live in isolation, but is everywhere found as a

[1] *Idea*, pp. 64–65.

member of society'.[1] He stresses this often. 'Man is a social being and can hardly exist without society and in matter of fact societies have ever existed all over the habitable earth.'[2] Now this, it is important to realise, means that the social nature of man is an empirical fact more than a metaphysical assertion. It seemed an empirical fact to Newman that man was a rational, progressive and social being, but in saying this he claimed to do no more than to lay down a general rule. 'Since, as a rule, men are rational, progressive, and social, there is a high probability of this rule being true in the case of a particular person; but we must know him to be sure of it.'[3]

Although his terminology may not always have been consistent on these points, it is nevertheless true that this lack of concern with a metaphysical approach to the nature of man, and thence to the State, is a most characteristic and important feature of Newman's thought. Since Catholic political thought is widely considered to be generally neo-Scholastic in approach, it is instructive to note that here at least is one great man who does not share this approach.

The divergence which exists here between Newman's thought and that in the Scholastic tradition is methodological, possibly epistemological in origin. It has sometimes been thought that it stems from a difference on the problem of universals, such that Newman does not admit the possibility of abstractive intuition, which the Thomist requires, and so is consequently very far from allowing the possibility of abstracting a universal from a limited number of particulars, though most Catholic writers would deny this. However, as has just been seen, before he can make a remark about the actual concrete nature of man for which he would believe himself to have full justification, he believes that he must take into account literally all men, that is, he must review the totality of particulars.

[1] *G.A.*, pp. 296–297.   [2] *Idea*, p. 251.
[3] *G.A.*, p. 213. However, Newman's language in certain passages could be interpreted, but for the quoted sentence above, as implying certain necessities which it is hard to see that a purely empirical account of man's nature could establish. See e.g. *P.S.*, vii, 32; *H.S.*, i, 164.

But whatever the basis by which it was established, man was rational, progressive and social for Newman, though these inclinations did not work as a blind instinct in man impelling him to the State. The State is only explicable in the light of consent, and Newman did not shrink from employing the term 'social contract'.[1] In this he was, most probably, not trying to affirm anything about the actual historical origin of social groups or of States, since he admitted that nothing is known of man outside society, but was stressing the element of human purpose which he thought so essentially bound up with the State. For to him at least, it was

> plain that everyone has a power of his own to act this way or that, as he pleases. And, as not one or two, but everyone has it, it is equally plain that, if all exercised it to the full, at least the stronger part of mankind would always be in conflict with each other, and no one would enjoy the benefit of it; so that it is the interest of everyone to give up some portion of his birth-freedom in this or that direction, in order to secure more freedom on the whole; exchanging a freedom which is now large and now narrow, according as the accidents of his conflicts with others are more or less favourable to himself, for a certain definite range of freedom prescribed and guaranteed by settled engagements or laws. In other words, Society is necessary for the well-being of human nature. The result, aimed at and effected by these mutual arrangements, is called a State or Standing; that is, in contrast with the appearance presented by a people before and apart from such arrangements, which is not a standing, but a chronic condition of commotion and disorder.[2]

Newman found nothing mysterious or inexplicable in the very essence of the State, and his strong underlying individualism made any sort of State worship impossible. It is not suggested that Newman was here anything other than representative of the general attitude in the England in which he came to maturity. Locke had triumphed over Filmer, and whatever the wide

---
[1] e.g. *Apo.*, p. 341; *Diff.*, ii, 271.
[2] *D.A.*, p. 312. Cf. *Diff.*, ii, 269–270. 'The very idea of political society is based upon the principle that each member of it gives up a portion of his natural liberty for advantages which are greater than that liberty.'

The State

political differences which existed in the first decades of the nineteenth century, it is fair to say that a form of Lockean liberalism was generally accepted. The importance of Newman's attitude here, however, is that it cuts him off sharply from some of the thinkers of the so-called Romantic reaction, with which he is often considered to have some association. If de Maistre be thought in any way representative of a continental political reaction to some of the ideas of the French Revolution, it must be stressed that it is hard to imagine such as he using or allowing the language about the State or the social contract which Newman has been seen to use. Thus it is possible to say that in some important respects Newman is nearer to Bentham than de Maistre. If for Bentham government was a vast evil, for many in the first half of the last century it was an evil of some sort; and so Newman's sense of the positive importance, though limited purposes of the State, derived initially, perhaps, from Patristic sources, was strengthened by the general climate of the age.

Of course, Newman is not so individualistic as the last few pages taken alone might suggest, nor is his view of the State simply mechanical. He was clear that a State needs much more than a number of discrete individuals coming together in mutual agreement. There is no question, however, of introducing the conception of a common good, as the Scholastics would, but instead Newman brings forward his characteristic idea of a common possession. In words too little known he says

> a state is in its very idea a society, and a society is a collection of many individuals made one by their participation in some common possession, and to the extent of that common possession: the presence of that possession held in common constitutes the life, and the loss of it constitutes the dissolution, of a state. In like manner, whatever avails or tends to withdraw that common possession, is either fatal or prejudicial to the social union.[1]

The common possession, or life, of a State consists in objects of the *imagination*, 'such as religion, true or false. . . , divine mission

[1] *H.S.*, i, 161.

of a sovereign or of a dynasty, and historical fame;' or in 'objects of *sense*, such as secular interests, country, home, protection of person and property'.[1] Now, to set aside for a moment this distinction, it can be seen at once that all this must make Newman's definition of the State very wide, and it must be wide for a similar reason that St. Augustine's is wide, and with similar results. For on Newman's definitions most of what are, and have been, generally considered States will still be so, though the type and value of the State will depend on what its common possession actually is, in the same way that the moral worth of the State for St. Augustine depended on the quality of those things which its members actually loved or sought.

A close inspection of the idea of a common possession must be delayed, but it is necessary to make clear at once that the use of this idea does not entail here any retraction of previous remarks about Newman's individualism. Unfortunately one of the few writers to tackle the subject of Newman's social thought has seized on an expression—where Newman says that a society is 'made one' by a common possession—and thinks this helps to confirm his thesis of the 'idealistic tenor' of Newman's thought.[2] But there is a sense in which all political philosophies must hold the State to be 'one', and Newman's words should not be given more than their due weight here. Of course, the terms 'idealist' or 'collectivist' have some legitimate application to him. Whatever the exact extent of the influence on him of Platonism and Christian Platonism, perhaps few would care to deny that it was at least strong, and Newman was after all the expounder of a theory of the development of ideas which exalted corporate reason above individual reason. But it simply is not possible to hold that Newman's thought was idealist or collectivist in any sense which would make the State more real than the individual. At the base of Newman's whole political thought was an individualism springing from a powerful grasp on the individuality of the human soul. If there were nothing unfathomable in the State, there was so in the individual.

[1] *H.S.*, i, 162.   [2] Werner Stark, *Newman Centenary Essays* (London, 1945), p. 158.

The State

No one outside of him can really touch him, can touch his soul, his immortality; he must live with himself for ever. He has a depth within him unfathomable, an infinite abyss of existence.[1]

This doctrine of the distinct individuality of the human soul is simply not understood, and so

> we class men in masses, as we might connect the stones of a building. Consider our common way of regarding history, politics, commerce, and the like and you will own that I speak truly. We generalise, and lay down laws, and then contemplate these creations of our own minds, and act upon and towards them, as if they were the real things, dropping what are more truly such ... we still think that this whole which we call the nation, is one and the same (i.e. over a period of time), and that the individuals who come and go, exist only in it and for it, and are but as the grains of a heap or the leaves of a tree.[2]

It is clear from a passage such as this that however idealist in some sense his general philosophy may be, it is advisable when dealing with Newman's politics to ignore the terms 'idealist' or 'collectivist'. There is a common prejudice that idealist notions in philosophy lend themselves to, or involve, totalitarian politics, and for the sake of truth Newman must be protected from the force of this prejudice. Although Newman was obviously no Benthamite individualist, he was an individualist of another important type, and at least as far away as Bentham from holding any totalitarian doctrines. When his fundamental ideas about the State have been discussed, it will be possible to go on to consider how far Newman can claim another label with which he is not generally credited, that of liberalism.

3. THE MAINTENANCE OF THE STATE

Self-interested individuals may form a State to enlarge and stabilise their area of personal freedom, but can these same individuals hope to maintain the State once it is formed? A contract

[1] *P.S.*, iv, 82–83.   [2] *ibid.*, pp. 81–82.

theory of government alone does not solve all the difficulties raised by the perennial questions, Why *should* I obey the law of the State? Why *do* I obey this law? Newman did not treat these problems exhaustively, but some light will nevertheless be shed on them in the course of the present discussion.

Although Newman had much to say about the law of the State, he can hardly be said to have reached a full grasp of the sense in which law and the State are the same thing. Yet he was careful to distinguish the nation from the State. There was, apart from any theoretical importance in the distinction, the practical point that he was thereby enabled to extol the virtues, the power and strength of the English as a nation, while pointing out that this did not mean the State was correspondingly strong, but could be, and indeed—as he thought the Crimean War made clear—certainly was, weak, at least as far as external affairs were concerned. The distinction, however, did not mean that the nation and the State were different things

> but one certain identical thing viewed in a different relation. When we speak of the Nation, we take into account its variety of local rights, interests, attachments, customs, opinions; the character of its people, and the history of that character's formation. On the other hand, when we speak of the State, we imply the notion of orders, ranks, and powers, of the legislative and executive departments and the like.[1]

Now, nearly twenty years later, Newman sees the political life of the British nation, the 'common possession' which makes it a State, in the supremacy of the law. It would not be very wide of the mark to say that he was feeling his way to that idea of the State as a nation organised for action under juridical rules, which is so well known today.

Perhaps Newman's idea of the law of the State will be shocking to some. It was not for him an abstract conception of order, putting everything in its correct place in accordance with the demands of true justice and right reason; it was concerned with

[1] *P.S.*, iii, 221–222.

the attaining of those objects which were actually desired by the people who constituted the State. In fact

> a nation's laws are a nation's property, and have their life in the nation's life, and their interpretation in the nation's sentiment; and where that living intelligence does not shine through them, they become worthless and are put aside, whether formally or on an understanding.[1]

It might be thought that the aim of English law, for example, is justice, but that is not quite true, nor can it ever be, at least, not as an ultimate and simple end. The aim must be 'such a justice . . . as may not be inconsistent with the interests of a large conservatism'.[2] An example of how this is necessary is seen in the jury system. In itself it is a question how far it is not absurdly unfitted for the achievement of the ends of the law, but Newman thinks two reasons can be brought forward in its defence. In the first place, it has a beneficial political effect on those classes liable to serve as jurymen, since it associates them with the established order of things and invests them with salutary responsibilities. The second point is for Newman the most important. He stresses

> the inexpediency of suffering the tradition of Law to flow separate from that of popular feeling, whereas there ought to be a continual influx of the national mind into the judicial conscience; and, unless there was this careful adjustment between law and politics, the standards of right and wrong, set up at Westminster, would diverge from those received by the community at large, and the Nation might some day find itself condemned and baffled by its own supreme oracle of truth. This would be gravely inconvenient; . . . so it is imperative . . . that Public Opinion should give the Law to Law, and should rule those questions which directly bear upon any matter of national concern . . . for better far is it that injustice should be done to a pack of individuals, than that the maxims of the Nation should at any time incur the animadversion of its own paid officials, and a deadlock in State matters should be the result of so unfortunate an antagonism. In short, the supreme end of the law is satisfaction, peace, liberty, conservative interests . . . and not mere raw justice as such.[3]

[1] *Diff.*, i, 20.   [2] *D.A.*, p. 350.   [3] *ibid.*, pp. 349–351.

All this may appear at first sight very far removed from the tradition of Aquinas, and to bear little resemblance to anything St. Augustine has said, but it is important not to misunderstand Newman here. Newman's ideas on law are not far removed from those of these two great Doctors of the Church, though it is on the points where he is in most agreement with them that he has little to say. Thus, though Newman recognises the Eternal Law of God, in the sense in which St. Augustine held it, and quotes St. Thomas to the effect that the Natural Law is the participation of rational creatures in the Eternal Law,[1] he never sets out his opinions on these subjects with any completeness. It is clear that he thought the moral law was, in the last resort, grounded not on the Will, but the Nature of God,[2] and this made a Natural Law doctrine possible; but it was not Natural Law in the social and legal sphere (*ius naturale*), but in the individual and moral (*lex naturalis*), which particularly interested him. Further, Newman was particularly concerned with the subjective apprehension of this law by the individual, which was for him conscience; and few can ever have had a more absolute idea of the authoritativeness of conscience than Newman.

The admissions which Newman makes show that however much the contrary appears, he is never far from the idea of law as a rational ordering of things. But as always, his treatment of every question has an individual stamp. The law of the State is not spoken of as being a particular disposition of Natural Law, but as superseding conscience, the form under which the individual apprehends the Natural Law. Before this, however, 'Influence' was all important in human society, which 'was the absence of rule, it was the action of personality, the intercourse of soul with soul, the play of mind on mind'.[3] Influence and law are together in God, but in human society they are separate and often out of joint with each other. Since law presupposes a law-giver, then historically influence must come first, but the other great principle

---
[1] *Diff.*, ii, 246–247.
[2] W. Ward, *W. G. Ward and the Catholic Revival* (London, 1893), pp. 216–217. cf. *Idea*, p. 191.
[3] *H.S.*, iii, 88.

of government, law, soon appears, because as man becomes cultivated he looks around for something to replace the conscience which he finds in himself. 'The most plausible and obvious and ordinary of these expedients, is the Law of the State, human law; the more plausible and ordinary, because it really comes to us with a divine sanction, and necessarily has a place in every society or community of men.'[1] The reason for the necessity of replacing conscience by law is not stressed, but it appears that it is not because conscience can thus be avoided, and wrong done with impunity, so much as that law gives a more certain and universal rule than a particular conscience; it can be viewed as a systemisation of the consciences of the members of the State. Law would not necessarily then reflect true morality, since the consciences of the people are not necessarily properly instructed, but the connexion of law and morals is nevertheless a direct one; Law is not simply expediency, as Newman explicitly states in the discussion from which the above passage was taken.

Force was not forgotten by Newman in his remarks about Influence and Law.

> 'First we have the *virum pietate gravem*, whose word "rules the spirit and soothes the breasts" of the multitude; or the warrior; or the mythologist and bard—then follow at length the dynasty and the constitution. Such is the history of society; it begins in the poet and ends in the policeman.' And end in the policeman it must, since 'in this world no one rules by mere love; if you are but amiable you are no hero; to be powerful, you must be strong, and to have dominion you must have a genius for organising'.[2]

Thus 'material force is the *ultima ratio* of political society everywhere',[3] and though the 'modern robber' may sometimes ask in

---
[1] *ibid.*, p. 79.
[2] *ibid.*, pp. 77, 85. See also *L.G.*, pp. 164-168, for a discussion on Influence and Law. The upshot of this discussion is that since law is not, nor can ever be, complete and all embracing, there is still a legitimate sphere for the exertion of Influence, if only in order to amend the law so as to cover *lacunae* which changing circumstances may have brought about. It is in this that the existence of political party is to be justified, and released from the reproach which has so long been attached to the term 'party'. Similarly the growing power of the Press can be justified.
[3] *D.A.*, p. 355.

novels why he should be amenable to laws he does not enact, 'the magistrate, relying on the power of the sword... hangs or transports dissenters from his authority'.[1]

But if the connexion of law with reason and morality was more real to Newman than at first sight is apparent, it is true that he sometimes seems much more impressed by the elements of will and force which accompany the idea of law for him. This gives rise to the question as to whose will he saw in the law of the State. Newman seems to think of these laws as being at one time the product of a general (though not transcendent) will, at another the product of a law-giver, that is, the will of a limited number of persons. This is a problem which Newman has to face, since it comes before him in the form of the old problem, '*Quis custodiet ipsos custodes?*', with which he found himself confronted when he had explained the origin of the State by the voluntary resignation of man's natural liberty.

Newman's solution of this latter problem, by having recourse to his idea of a constitution, is also the solution of the very closely associated problem which has been raised. He thought that it was obvious that there was needed some power above the people to enforce the law, and 'this living guardian of the laws is called the Government, and a governing power is thus involved in the very notion of Society',[2] so that it was possible to refer to the government as the seat of power in the State. But the two elements of the State must be power and liberty, 'for without power there is not protection, and without liberty there is nothing to protect'.[3] If the government is the seat of power in the State, then it is to the constitution to which one must refer to find the seat of liberty,

---

[1] *Dev.*, p. 232.

[2] *D.A.*, p. 314. This idea of a government being involved in the very notion of Society he found in Guizot's *History of Civilisation* (London, 1846), i, 88. It is possible to trace a resemblance between much of Newman's thought and Guizot's on society, and Newman explicitly acknowledges his debt to Guizot (*H.S.*, i, 167). Many of the points on which he agrees with Guizot, however, are points which are not particularly unusual or distinctive, and which he may have acquired in the first instance from a wide variety of sources other than Guizot.

Newman and Guizot had some things in common, such as an addiction to Gibbon in their younger days. Cf. E. L. Woodward, *Three Studies in European Conservatism* (London, 1929), p. 113; Ward, *Life*, i, 34.   [3] *ibid.*, pp. 317–318.

to find the means of solving the very ordinary but always perplexing problem of how to safeguard those purposes for which the State was established. Now it is obvious that the constitution cannot be a mere code of laws, for the problem at issue is how to confine power within the law. The British constitution, for example, by which the rulers of the British State are themselves ruled, does not consist in Acts of Parliament or in the whole array of constitutional documents.

Newman's account of a constitution is perhaps best quoted in its entirety. He begins by referring to his profound conviction, which few volumes from his pen have not enshrined, of the importance of national character, which is as marked for him as individual character. Different nations have, he thinks, different characters, with strong and weak points in each, and some points purely idiosyncratic.

> Moreover, growing out of these varieties or idiosyncrasies, and corresponding to them, will be found in these several races, and proper to each, a certain assemblage of beliefs, convictions, rules, usages, traditions, proverbs, and principles; some political, some social, some moral; and these tending to some definite form of government and *modus vivendi*, or polity, as their natural scope. And this being the case, when a given race has that polity which is intended for it by nature, it is in the same state of repose and contentment which an individual enjoys who has the food, or the comforts, the stimulants, sedatives, or restoratives, which are suited to his *diathesis* and his need. This then is the Constitution of a State: securing, as it does, the national unity by at once strengthening and controlling its governing power. It is something more than law; it is the embodiment of special ideas, ideas perhaps which have been held by a race for ages, which are of immemorial usage, which have fixed themselves in its innermost heart, which are in its eyes sacred to it, and have practically the force of eternal truths, whether they be such or not. These ideas are sometimes trivial, and, at first sight, even absurd: sometimes they are superstitious, sometimes they are great or beautiful; but to those to whom they belong they are first principles, watchwords, common property, natural ties; a cause to fight for, an occasion of self-sacrifice. They are the expression of

some other sentiment—of loyalty, of order, of duty, of honour, of faith, of justice, of glory. They are the creative and conservative influences of Society; they erect nations into States, and invest States with Constitutions. They inspire and sway, as well as restrain, the ruler of a people, for he himself is but one of that people to which they belong.[1]

Thus Newman goes behind the actual legal framework to the factors which ensure that the law will in fact be obeyed, which show that a 'State depends and rests, not simply on force of arms, not on logic, not on anything short of the sentiment and will of those governed'.[2] This is the sense in which government is founded on opinion, not an opinion about some momentary issue, but a deep, general, abiding opinion. The important thing is that unmitigated absolutism is simply impossible, as human nature does not allow of it. (For all Newman's disgust with facile optimism, the conditions of his century allowed him to be more optimistic than many now can feel.) Force by itself is not sufficient to gain its ends, and a general habit of law-abidingness is necessary if laws are to be obeyed, nor will this habit exist if in fact the laws are not appropriate to the national life. So all the force of the despot fails to make him absolute. In any case there is a real limit to his power, since the knife of the assassin brings, in certain rather primitive types of society, a 'constitutional' check. In his *Letter to the Duke of Norfolk*, Newman takes Gladstone to task for his exaggerated fears of the Pope's Infallibility and right to depose rulers. He pointed out that, after all, the primary point for the politician is the actual obedience which a given exercise of authority can claim, and that in any case a vast difference existed between the climate of opinion in which the Pope's deposing power formerly operated, and the contemporary climate. These were factors which Gladstone had ignored.

It is also now possible to see the sense in which the laws are a nation's property, while not in fact initiated by it. The laws depend on a general habit of law-abidingness, which will only be preserved if in fact the laws are an appropriate expression of

[1] *D.A.*, pp. 315–316.   [2] *ibid.*, p. 317.

national character. If certain laws are not such, then, if not formally dropped, they simply cease to be effectively operative, they are put aside 'on an understanding'.[1] It seems, however, that though the habit of law-abidingness is impossible without this condition, it does not follow that the fulfilment of this condition is the sole and sufficient explanation for the existence of this habit, of the great conservative power of habit in welding a community. This habit of law-abidingness is encouraged by two considerations. In the first place, to put it at its lowest expression, a certain trust is necessary between members of society. 'The most distressing event that can happen to a state is (we know) the spreading of a want of confidence between man and man. Distrust, want of faith, breaks the very bonds of human society.'[2]

This act of trust is purely rational. It is necessary for society, for if one does not trust others then one cannot expect others to trust oneself. But this is not sufficient, and Newman displays a great belief in the necessity of a more generous spirit for social life to be possible. In an address to the Birmingham Annual Catholic Reunion in 1880 he refers to those

> ordinary and visible traits of character, of what is human merely, what is social in personal bearing, which, as a moral magnetism, unites men to each other; ... those qualities which are the basis, the *sine qua non* of a political community; ... those qualities which may be expressed by the word 'neighbourly'.[3]

All this information about Newman's views on law is perhaps interesting in itself, and is indispensable in settling the problem, now much nearer a solution, of justice in the State. But it will be remembered that although the State took its origin from the needs and desires of individuals, yet its continued life depended on the existence of a common possession shared by its members.

---

[1] *Diff.*, i, 20.

[2] *P.S.*, i, 196. cf. *ibid.*, iv, 28, where Newman also refers to the rational good sense which ensures obedience to law.

[3] *Add.*, p. 241. It will be noted that Newman is here not far from the Thomist distinction between the two types of 'friendliness' in the social life, *amicitia utilis* and *amicitia honesta et delectabilis*. See T. Gilby, *Between Community and Society* (London, 1953), pp. 189–193.

There is no contradiction in saying that the State depends on this common possession, and that it is also maintained by law. For law, it has been seen, cannot be separated from national character; it is the nation's property, and reflects the nation's life. In each nation there is an array of social, political and moral ideas which determine the form of its social life, and one or more of these ideas can be the common possession of a State. Thus an idea shared by a nation is a guarantee of law.

If an idea were to become the principle of the political existence of a nation it would have to be, not so much a special kind of idea, but held in a very special way. It would have to be held, in Newman's terminology, with a 'Real Assent', which in turn is defined in terms of a profound impression made on the imagination.[1] It is interesting to observe here that Newman points to phenomena which are in the broad sense mental, and narrowly speaking, non-rational in his account of the bonds of the State. This non-rational element still remains whatever the particular idea might be which serves as a social bond.

There is no doubt that this was the type of social bond that really interested Newman. He did not care to deny that the 'conservative power of habit', in particular the law-abiding habit which has been discussed, was in fact a social bond, but he thought it was simply a necessary condition of political society arising from the existence of a common possession; while what really interested him was the particular bond of a particular State, that which gave to it its especial character. He was concerned with the objects in which he believed the common possession of the State consisted, and these objects he considered to be those either of sense or imagination. By reason of this distinction between objects of sense and objects of the imagination Newman was able to make a distinction between barbarian and civilised States, such that the common possession of the barbarian State was an object of the imagination, of the civilised, sense. An examination of what Newman meant by these terms is necessary, and should not be neglected through any cynical consideration that a prime object

[1] G.A., pp. 57–67. See especially p. 67.

of the distinction was to enable a classification of the Turks as a barbarian Power, in order to tell them that they were 'in the way of the progress of the nineteenth century'.[1]

The first point about barbarism as Newman explained it is that it is a principle of isolation, not a principle of society, so that a simply barbarous State was a contradiction in terms.[2] A barbarian was in 'a state of nature', but this was not a state of primitive innocence before the corruption of society; it was a sort of permanent childhood. In a state of nature man has reason, conscience, passions and affections, just as 'civilised' man has, but in the former state man is influenced by them almost capriciously; 'he does not put his impulses under the control of principle, or form his mind upon a rule'.[3] Thus the barbarian is very much the sport of circumstances, drawn irresistibly to whatever objects happen to be held before him, acting according to the moment, regardless of consequences. But if the barbarian cannot submit to himself, there is little hope that he can make the surrender which Newman believes to be involved in the formation of a State. Hence

> no polity can be simply barbarous; barbarians may indeed combine in small bodies, . . . from the gregariousness of our nature, from the fellowship of blood, from accidental neighbourhood, or for self-preservation; but such societies are not bodies or polities; they are but the chance result of an occasion and are destitute of a common life.[4]

Barbarian States must, then, 'be so far removed from the extreme of savageness . . . that they . . . recognise the ideas of government, property and law, however imperfectly',[5] and this recognition will only arise from the existence of a common possession. Such a social bond may appear in a barbarian community, among barbarians who have advanced so far beyond their former chaotic mental life, that 'just one idea or feeling occupies the narrow range of [their] thoughts, to the exclusion of others'.[6]

[1] *H.S.*, i, 222.
[2] This point is made by R. G. Collingwood in his discussion of the nature of civilisation. See *The New Leviathan* (London, 1942), 36.92. His discussion has some parallels with Newman's, though many differences.
[3] *H.S.*, i, 163.   [4] *ibid.*, pp. 166–167.   [5] *ibid.*   [6] *ibid.*, p. 164.

Thus, 'Religion, superstition, belief in persons and families, objects, not proveable but vivid and imposing, will be the bond which keeps its members together.'[1] Here a striking fact emerges, which has important bearings on much that is to follow in this study of Newman's political thought—that among the 'objects of the imagination' which constituted the life of the barbarian State for Newman, were included Toryism, the divine right of kings and the Pope's political power, all being principles of barbarism due to succumb to the advance of civilisation, nobler in idea than the barbarism it replaces.[2] But the advance to a civilised State can neither be quick nor easy, for, as in the case of the barbarian Power which Newman thought was typified by the Turks, 'They have a principle of union congenial to the state of their intellect, and they have not the ratiocinative habit to scrutinise and invalidate it.'[3] Inasmuch as the barbarian begins to make some mental progress, he will be led away from the object of imagination in which his social bond consists, because 'Ratiocination and its kindred processes, which are the necessary instruments of political progress, are, taking things as we find them, hostile to imagination and auxiliary to sense.'[4]

This idea that reason, in the narrow sense of ratiocination, is the prime instrument of political progress is fundamental to Newman's political thought, and it is surprising how many have failed to see this. It acts in this way because we cannot help, from the constitution of our nature, sifting and scrutinising the ideas on which our society is based. It is not so easy to understand in what way reason is hostile to imagination and auxiliary to sense. Perhaps Newman means that particular objects of the imagination are found not proved, or not proveable, and so inappropiate for thinking people as a social bond; and that reason is linked with

[1] *H.S.*, i, 171.
[2] *ibid.*, pp. 170 ff. The full justice of subsuming Toryism ('Loyalty to persons', *Diff.*, ii, 268), under the head of 'belief in persons' will later be seen to be amply justified.
[3] *H.S.*, i, 171–172. Of the Turkish Power, 'ignorantly holding in possession one half of the history of the whole world', he says, 'There it lies and will not die, and has not in itself the elements of death, for it has the life of a stone, and, unless pounded and pulverised, is indestructible' (*ibid.*, p. 220).
[4] *ibid.*, p. 170.

sense in that reason rejects undemonstrated premisses and bases itself on sensory evidence. Again, if reason is to be forced back to undemonstrable premisses, these will be so abstract that only by reference to sense experience can they be meaningfully used.

It cannot be said that Newman does much to clear up the obscurities which surround his idea of political progress being dependent on reason, and reason being allied particularly to sense, but the fact that he holds the view is extremely important. Thus it enables him to say:

> Hence it is that civilised states ever tend to substitute objects of sense for objects of the imagination as the basis of their existence. . . . At present, . . . our own political life . . . lies in the supremacy of the law; and that again is resolvable into the internal peace, and protection of life and property, and freedom of the individual, which are its result; and these I call objects of sense.[1]

It is likely that many would say that these particular objects of sense are not entirely unrelated to imagination;[2] but it is at any rate clear that freedom of property, for instance, is capable of reference to some sense experience, in a way that the theory of the divine right of kings is not, and so Newman's distinction may be allowed to have some foundation.

If barbarism is 'a state of nature', civilisation is a state of mental cultivation and discipline, as much above barbarism as that is from the state of the brutes. It is

> that state to which man's nature points and tends, it is the systematic use, improvement, and combination of those faculties which are his characteristic, and, viewed in its idea, it is the perfection, the happiness of our mortal state. . . . It is the due disposition of the various powers of the soul, each in its place, the subordination or subjection of the inferior, and the union of all into one whole. Aims, rules, views, habits, projects; prudence, foresight, observation, inquiry, invention, resource, resolution, perseverance, are its characteristics.

[1] *ibid.*
[2] One sense in which Newman admits that the object of sense is related to imagination can be gathered from G.A., pp. 57–62.

Justice, benevolence, expedience, propriety, religion, are its recognised, its motive principles. Supernatural truth is its sovereign law. Such is it, in its true idea, synonymous with Christianity.[1]

Here once again comes a striking resemblance to St. Augustine's thought. It seems very reasonable to argue that for Augustine, the State, far from being intrinsically evil, could, at least as a perfect limit, be completely good.[2]

So, for Newman, the State could be perfectly just, at least as long as it was a perfectly Christian State, in profession and practice. But if we would view things as they really are, although the Christian State is the best, the truly civilised one, that which has in its religion a principle of good fellowship such as the State requires, nevertheless a civilised State need not actually be Christian. It is possible

> to combine in some sort the other [than spiritual] faculties of man into one, and to progress forward, with the substitution of natural religion for faith, and a refined expediency or propriety for true morality, just as with practice a man might manage to run without an arm or without sight, and as the defect of one organ is sometimes supplied to a certain extent by the preternatural action of another.[3]

Even so, however, there is the likelihood of such a State disintegrating internally.

> Where thought is encouraged, too many will think, and will think too much. The sentiment of sacredness in institutions fades away, and the measure of truth or expedience is the private judgement of the individual, . . . at length the common bond of unity in the state consists in nothing really common, but simply in the unanimous wish of each member of it to secure his own interests.[4]

But the ideal State, which would be a perfectly Christian State, remains an ideal, never to be reached, limit. The purely self-interested State, which therefore ceases to be a State, must be

---

[1] H.S., i, 164–165. Newman owes much of his views on civilisation to Guizot, from whom, together with Schlegel, he gains support for his belief in the pre-eminence of modern, European civilisation—the civilisation *par excellence* for him.
[2] Ep., cxxxvii; cxxxviii (trans., Cunningham).
[3] H.S., i, 165.   [4] ibid., pp. 173–174.

viewed in very much the same light. Newman was prepared to face facts and be contented with a State coming between these limits. Thus, though convinced that the English State was cemented by 'self-interest', it was, he thought, at least 'in a large sense of the word'.[1] This broad self-interest, and the instinctive and characteristic English veneration of the law, were sufficient to ensure that England did not follow the cycle from worse to better, and then from better to worse. On the level of practical possibilities, Britain was Newman's ideal State.

4. JUSTICE AND THE STATE: SOME CONCLUSIONS

'That justice is a primary notion in our minds, and does not admit of resolution into other elements, may be argued from its connexion with [a] general love of order, congruity, and symmetry', said Newman,[2] thinking primarily of the sphere of individual morality. The connexion of Justice with the State is not stated by Newman with anything approaching this definiteness. Hints of his attitude to this question can be found in plenty, though they are generally missed. It has just been seen that Newman in his account of the ideal State, speaks of the 'due disposition of the various powers of the soul'; and this can be coupled with his remarks that 'the soul of man is intended to be a well ordered polity'.[3] The discussion on the nature of justice in Plato's *Republic* is called irresistibly to mind. Such hints help to confirm the present interpretation of Newman's thought.

It seems that, to say the least, Newman believed that justice was not an entirely alien principle to the State. It should be noted that law is obeyed because, and in so far as it is an adequate expression of national character, of national opinion, interests and sentiments. But the national opinion which is so closely related to law includes an opinion on what is just. Though true justice was not essential to the State, it seems that Newman must be interpreted, as St. Augustine has been, as holding that a relative justice is necessary. He was very much alive to the mass of

[1] *D.A.*, pp. 347-348.   [2] *U.S.*, p. 108.   [3] *P.S.*, v, 213.

interests and habits which were concerned in the life of the State, and the complexity of the order which resulted from them. Since it was the actual complex social order he had in mind, a product of past justice and injustice, of sinful and saintly minds, of beings partly instructed or wholly non-instructed in Eternal Wisdom, he did not expect this social order to be actually related properly to the demands of objective morality, while at the same time he was profoundly conscious of the difficulty with which a particular social order becomes established, and the ease with which a disturbance of that order can make things worse rather than better. It was for this reason that he was not scandalised by injustice to individuals which was nevertheless conservative of the social order.

If any proof of a fundamental conservatism in Newman is required, it can be found in this belief. It links him with the great conservatives, such as Burke, and it is significant that Lord Acton should link the names of Burke and Newman in order to condemn them both for divorcing morals from politics.[1] But whether or not Acton understood Burke, he certainly failed to understand Newman, as will be shown in due time. If we are to understand Newman aright, his acceptance of injustice to preserve social order does not mean simply that he preferred one sort of disorder to another. The disorder he was anxious to prevent was a real, present one, which by subverting the actual established order, however unsatisfactory this order might be, would effectively prevent the maintenance of those conditions which must be secured for the achievement of man's true end. Even if the justice of the State is a justice relative to the defects of sinful man, yet much of its actions may be the same as those that would follow from a more enlightened morality.

However, it cannot be disguised that there is a difficulty in holding this sort of view, since Newman has gone out of his way to make certain remarks about the evils of the State, and the bad principles in which its life is necessarily involved. These remarks seem so clear and forthright that the view might plausibly be

[1] *Letters of Lord Acton to M. Gladstone* (ed. H. Paul, London, 1913), p. 181.

maintained that Newman certainly believes the State in actual fact to be involved in injustice, even if in an ideal, never-to-be-realised world it could be just. Now it seems almost a pity to have to refuse to him the position which such outspoken utterances might have accorded him, thrusting him back into the ranks of those who say what others have said, but it really seems as though this must be done—it cannot be allowed that Newman means to assert in these passages what he appears to assert.

The fact that these remarks appear in Sermons may well be some explanation of an outspokenness and severity of tone which a different setting might not have evoked. Perhaps in his pulpit, he had dim memories before him of Augustine, who would not allow justice in a State which did not give God His due. Perhaps Newman had acquired a hostile attitude to the State from his reading of Church history, only to be reinforced by his own experiences of the struggle of Church and State, which had played such a part in his life. And if he did not mean to say as much as appears, he is surely not unlike that great medieval cleric who abused earthly rulers, on a famous occasion, in rounder terms than he might have found necessary had he sat down at a cooler hour.[1]

It is quite true that, however tempting a course it may be, Newman's express words cannot be dismissed as meaning no more than that the historical origins of a State are often morally doubtful, nor that the 'bold deeds and bad principles' in which he says the State must indulge, can be referred to dealings with external enemies of the State. The question, really, is whether the evil he speaks of in the State is evil according to objective, true morality; or, is not only evil in this sense, but evil in regard to the general moral standards of a political society. If he meant the former, then the remarks under consideration can be regarded as consistent

---

[1] Pope Gregory VII to Bishop Hermann of Metz (1081). 'Who does not know that kings and rulers took their beginnings from those who, being ignorant of God, have assumed, because of blind greed and intolerable presumption, to make themselves masters of their equals, namely men, by means of pride, violence, bad faith, murder, and nearly every kind of crime, being incited thereto by the prince of this world, the Devil?' Quoted by Carlyle, *op. cit.*, iii (1915), p. 94.

with the idea of a relative justice in the State; if he meant the latter, the difficulty remains. Assuming the truth of the first alternative, it can be seen that the bad principles of the State's life need not mean that all the principles are bad, but that its life could be endangered in particular circumstances if it completely renounced all bad principles entirely—much good could be mixed with some evil, though the permanent possibility of injustice would exist. Nor could the life of the State endure despite any evil, since some evils, such as the unlimited pursuit of self-interest by all its members, would, as we have seen, mean the extinction of the State.

It may be wise to consider here a discussion which Newman carries on in his *Stray Essays*, about his attitude to the 'World'. He realises the misunderstanding which can arise over his condemnations of the World—and from what he says it appears that the State can be included here—and he stresses that when he says the World is evil, he means to include therein the Church and all individuals under this heading. Here we have the distinction between the World of Newman and the *terrena civitas* of St. Augustine coming into the open. The State for Newman is evil, certainly, but then so would be a State composed completely of Christians.[1] There is a light and a dark side to everyone's nature, and no one would always be influenced by right motives; evil would ever float to the top. Thus when Newman denounces the life of the State as evil he is not merely denouncing an abstraction. The members of the State individually are at least partly evil, but their evil principles spread rapidly in social life. Thus the State's life is evil because its members' lives are evil.

But it is, after all, still possible that Newman meant what he appeared to mean—that the State was committed to maxims which were wrong by any standard of morality. If such is the case, it seems we must come to rest in a simple inconsistency, about which little more can be said.

Now it is sometimes thought that it smacks of inconsistency to affirm the radical injustice of States, while at the same time to

[1] S.E., pp. 79–80.

enlarge upon the divine origin of earthly power. If anyone should be open to such a charge it must surely be Newman. His views on justice have been set out, and yet, while holding them, he was not forgetful of those great Christian Scriptural texts which enjoin obedience to the powers that be. He was as willing, as a Protestant, to discourse upon the 'priestly nature' of those temporal powers who dispensed 'God's Eternal Justice'[1] on earth, as he was later, as a Catholic, to characterise the State as the representative and image on earth of God's justice.[2] It may well be asked: If justice is not necessary for the Ruler, how can he be the image of God's justice? If a State not built on Christian principles is scarcely more than a pack of robbers, are the robbers then ordained by God?

To these questions Newman gives no direct answer, for they were not questions which he himself ever posed. He did not appear to recognise any difficulty in the matter, but it is, perhaps, possible to see certain considerations which he might have put forward, if the difficulty of his situation had been urged to him. It is obvious, for instance, that in a perfectly Christian State the ruler would indeed be the image and representative of God's justice. In a State, however, which concretely falls short of this ideal, the ruler is still such an image, albeit a little blurred, because however much the idea of true justice is ignored or forgotten, the main fact is that the ruler is concerned to create or maintain a living order, which is the first essential for a human being. If the ruler is unrelievedly bad, however, his demands will often conflict with what are acknowledged to be ordinances of God, in which case the citizen must disobey his ruler, since he cannot commit sin under any excuse. But this implies that the command of the ruler, where it conflicts with the acknowledged word of God, cannot be itself an ordinance of God, for that would be to say that God ordered contradictory things, which is impossible. Therefore it is necessary to understand the divine origin of earthly power in a sense which will do justice to the complexity of the situation. And, at once, it is clear that though the gift of power

[1] *P.S.*, ii, 391.   [2] *Diff.*, i, 200.

be from God, this does not imply that the actual designation of the ruler be the act of God, nor therefore all the acts for which a particular ruler is responsible, even though all that he does, and all that flows from his actions, are in a sense included in God's Providence. It is clear that however unjust a ruler might be it does not prove that he is not in some way from God, though the limit of obedience to such a ruler is a vexed question. It is not profitable to discuss whether Newman believed the power of a robber band to come from God, since though he might think that certain rulers, in flouting Christianity, were scarcely more than such, all his thought on the State goes to show that there is far more difference between it and a robber band, or any other limited and particular group, than the scale of operations.

However sad a thought that the powers that be are from God, and are often evil; or however interesting a thought as demonstrating ways in which good can come out of evil, Newman simply saw no inconsistency in the thought; and on reflexion, it is hard to see why he should do so.

In his pessimism about the role of justice in the State Newman appears very close to Pascal, and correspondingly far from traditional Catholic Natural Law doctrine. But M. Jacques Maritain has shown that Pascal, who went much further than Newman in the dismissal of the very possibility of justice in human affairs, has certain ideas which limit the extent of his opposition to the Natural Law tradition.[1] It will be interesting to see how far Newman may be said to belong to this tradition. It is possibly because of the remoteness of much which Newman says from the traditional doctrines that no serious Catholic attempt to present his political thought has until now been made. Newman undoubtedly presents a problem to writers in the Catholic Natural Law tradition inasmuch as he is a great Catholic who appears to deviate from it, and also appears as a possible supporter of an unwelcome interpretation of St. Augustine on the position of justice in the State.

Of course, the divergence of Newman from this tradition

[1] 'Political Ideas of Pascal', *Redeeming the Time* (London, 1943), pp. 29-45.

cannot be absolute or complete. By the Catholic Natural Law tradition is meant that general system of ideas which perhaps first found a complete, coherent expression with St. Thomas Aquinas; though the ideas themselves were the products of classical antiquity and Christianity. Since Aquinas, the Natural Law doctrine has encountered some vicissitudes, but it is possible to point to a great revival of it in recent times. Now, since the great, fundamental Christian truths are accepted alike by any follower of Aquinas and by Newman certain limits are immediately imposed on any differences of opinion, though it is evident that although these differences are certainly likely to be small in the sphere of what ought to be, there is no reason why they should not be great in the region of what actually is, and such seems actually to be the case. But, at the outset, it must be emphasised that, in so far as Catholic Natural Law teaching rests on the metaphysics of Thomism, it cannot be accepted by Newman. It has been said that 'as St. Thomas was the embodiment of medieval deductive rationalism . . . so was Newman of the inductive temper of the nineteenth century'.[1] There is much truth in this, and though efforts have been made to reconcile Newman's thought with Thomism, they have not been entirely successful.[2] In the end it has always to be admitted that Newman may not have held certain vital doctrines of Thomism, such as that relating to abstractive intuition mentioned earlier in the chapter. He was no Scholastic. Knowing little of Thomism before becoming a Catholic, he learnt little afterwards, and what he learned he did not assimilate.[3] Even if it is true that some of Newman's political ideas correspond with Thomist and Natural Law ones, it is very important to note that his whole starting-point and approach is non-metaphysical.

It must not be supposed, of course, that all writers in the

[1] W. Ward, *Ten Personal Studies* (London, 1908), p. 252. cf. *H.S.*, i, 170.
[2] See M. D'Arcy, *Nature of Belief* (London, 1931), pp. 107–205; P. Flanagan, *Newman, Faith and the Believer* (no place, no date), *passim*. The differences between Newman and Thomism were strikingly brought out by T. Harper. See *Month* (1870), xii, 599–611 667–692; (1870), xiii, 31–59, 159–184, 663–684.
[3] See E. Przywara, *Einführung in Newman's Wesen und Werk*, p. 57. (Vol. IV of *Christentum*, Freiburg im Breisgau, 1922.)

Catholic Natural Law tradition are agreed on all details, but there is enough agreement to make a rapid survey of its leading ideas possible.[1] For all take as their point of departure the idea of man; and though the nature of man is a metaphysical concept, it is not one that is arrived at by exclusively *a priori* methods. They start from the empirical fact that man has many tendencies or impulses in his nature, and that these, such as the sex impulse for example, appear to have a definite goal or end, in this case, the procreation of the species. Now man is like an animal in having these impulses, but unlike them he has reason, such that he not only has the impulse but can also recognise the end to which it tends. With this recognition of ends, he finds himself not in a 'must' relationship to the attainment of them, like the animal, but in an 'ought' relationship,[2] in which he can act or not act. This is the basis of Natural Law, but it is evident that it is concerned with man as an individual as stated here; it is the moral law, which is termed *lex naturalis, loi naturelle,* or *Naturgesetz* by these writers.

Man then, in accordance with the Aristotelian terminology of form and matter, is a union of body (matter) and soul (form), which soul, the forming principle, is endowed with reason and free will. Now according to this theory of form and matter it is possible to achieve their union in two ways, either by an outside agent expressing the form in matter, or by an internal process, in which an internal moving principle forms the matter, and this latter is the way of the living substance, of organic growth. Thus the end of the process, in the latter, is the perfect expression of the form or nature, and so in the fourfold terminology of causation, the formal cause and final cause are the same. So to speak of the nature of man implies a reference to his end, and it becomes

---

[1] The best-known works in England dealing with this subject are as follows: H. Rommen, *State in Catholic Thought* (St. Louis, Mo., 1945); J. Messner, *Social Ethics* (London, 1949); the various works of J. Maritain and more recently a work by an English Dominican, T. Gilby, *Between Community and Society* (London, 1953).

[2] The grounds of this obligatoriness cannot be discussed here. It will be appreciated that this sketch of Natural Law theory is not intended to be exhaustive, but to enable certain parallels to be drawn. Thus the many difficulties raised by certain arguments of this theory must be ignored.

possible to say that the end of man's life is to perfect himself in a life corresponding to reason. But this end is simply impossible in isolation and therefore society is essential for the attainment of man's end, that is to say, for man's nature, and so man is called a social animal. Here the discussion moves into the sphere of *ius naturale, droit naturel*, or *Naturrecht*. The State is not the only necessary society, but it is the *societas perfecta*, a conception which is now emancipated from its connexion with the Greek idea of autarchy. It is a mistake to view the State exclusively from the point of view of its end, but at the very least it is evident that the State is more than a mere peaceful living together of persons, that its unity is not simply the unity of the herd, nor is its unity imposed from without like that of an army. The social unity of the State is in fact informed with an inner principle which makes for the co-ordination and self-determination of persons towards the common good.

Here we come across the conception of a common good which is looked at warily by many, with its claim to be prior to the good of the individual. However, it is apparent here that the common good is, using the terminology already adopted, the formal cause and the final cause of the State. It makes it both what it is and what it strives to be. Inasmuch as it is the '*forma*' of the State it is an order, it is the formal good order. It is prior to the individual good in the order of ends, but this does not make the State simply and solely prior to the individual, since the State is inferior in the order of being. It is an ontological accident (not logical, which would imply that it was not necessary) and it needs to be completed by its subject, man.

It is possible to see now the sense in which justice is essential to the State for this theory. Although much perhaps needs to be said about the idea of justice and its psychological grounds, for the purposes of this discussion it can be said that justice really involves the readiness to fulfil the juridical obligations of natural or positive law. It could be said that rules of co-ordination and subordination are necessary for any society, and that justice is concerned with these rules. However expressed, the idea of justice is driven back to the idea of rights, though this is not ultimate since rights only have meaning in society. The fact is that the rights are the correlatives of the duties which man must perform, and these duties depend on that human nature which has already been discussed. The *'justum'* then, for the modern Scholastic, is the conformity of social acts and relations to our human, social nature; and if a law ignores this human nature it is unjust. An unjust law, so far as this is not a contradiction in terms, by ignoring rights which correspond to the nature of human beings, upsets the *'ordo'* of the State, and contradicts its final cause. The more this situation develops, the less a State it would become, but there could not really be an unjust State simply so-called; it would be like asserting that it was a disordered order. Further, however much Natural Law must be associated with a certain type of Theism, it claims a sanction in this world, so that disregard of its claims brings in time its own inevitable punishment.

Such is, in outline, the basis of the Catholic Natural Law theory, at least as far as it bears on the present discussion, and one sees at once how much of what Newman says might pass as an echo of this. He refers to the social nature of man, he frequently refers to 'ends' in connexion with man and society, he thinks that 'there can be no community without order', that 'order is heaven's first law', that rights depend on duties;[1] a host of such remarks could be adduced.

But all these remarks are isolated and by themselves inconclusive, though they indicate the direction any attempt must take in making a full reconciliation between Newman's political thought and Natural Law doctrines. Such an attempt will not be made here. The important thing is that the vastly different approach of Newman to politics should be noted, and enough has been put forward to make this possible. It will be useful, however, before concluding this survey of Newman's views on the State, to examine in relation to Catholic politics what he has to say on the subject of authority. It is a subject on which he is

[1] *G.A.* (1887), p. 233; *H.S.*, i, 5; iii, 117; *P.S.*, iii, 217.

often misunderstood, and enough evidence has now emerged to make possible some clarification of his position.

The problem of authority might be taken as the same problem as that of political obligation—the famous question, 'Why should I obey the law?' Now this problem does not arise in Natural Law theory in the form it often does elsewhere. Man is not viewed as an abstract and isolated individual, but as in the midst of the cosmos, and authority is seen as a kind of relationship between men which is simply necessary for human culture. The problem of authority then becomes a problem of deciding who shall be the person to hold the necessary authority. Three broad solutions were possible for Newman. Firstly, authority could have been conferred by God on a certain person by a special act; secondly, it might be that at the time of the formation of the State one man might be so pre-eminent in many virtues that he could be considered as given by God as a ruler, but this means that a person has been designated to hold authority, and authority has not been transferred from the people, whose acceptance of or consent to the ruler is not the cause but a condition of his authority; thirdly, authority could be vested in the citizens, but formally or informally transferred to one man or a group of men.

If Newman has to be placed in these categories there is no doubt that he belongs in the third. His account of the origin of the State makes it quite clear that he thought that authority was vested in the people, before being transferred to the ruler. However, it was possible to believe with Bellarmine that such a transference was a moral necessity, and once made, lasting, or to hold with Suarez that the citizens are free to make this transference or not, and to decide the conditions on which it shall be made. If there is not enough evidence to commit Newman to one or the other view, there are some interesting pointers. It is easier to show evidence of Newman being influenced by Bellarmine rather than Suarez,[1] and Newman might even be said to be showing a tendency to go beyond Bellarmine back to designation theories in

[1] Newman had found a work of Bellarmine's 'extremely useful' in 1837. P.C., Christie, 14 June 1837.

the continued emphasis he puts on the role in public life of great men, natural rulers and the like. But it is revealing that in the discussion on constitutional principles in *Who's to Blame?*[1] a system of delegation of power for a certain period, and then bringing it to account, is put forward as the best of these principles. Perhaps from this work alone it is possible to assert in Newman a preference for the Suarez position to any of the others mentioned. At least it is clear that Newman is very far from the general anti-democratic views of a de Maistre or a Taparelli, with whom he was in such little sympathy. But a closer inspection of Newman's attitude to democracy must be delayed, and another aspect of the problem of authority be examined.

Although few have hitherto made any serious attempt to understand Newman's ideas on the problem of political authority, yet for long it has been widely felt that Newman must forfeit serious consideration of his ideas, since, it is imagined, he gloried in sacrificing the individual to authority in general. Through the years he has been presented as a convinced sceptic, profoundly pessimistic about man's capacity for attaining truth or practising virtue, and consequently giving all up in despair and resigning all to authority, leaving it to guarantee truth in religion and the inviolability of the social bond against the evil passions of individuals. Now it is more than a mere debating point to say that authority in religion does not necessarily have the same role as authority in politics, and it is easier to find direct reference in his work to the former, rather than the latter. It is well known, for instance, that Newman bitterly opposed the movement for the declaration of Papal Infallibility, and there are no grounds whatsoever for supposing that the approval he was willing to give to the eventual declaration could be turned into a defence of political authoritarianism. Yet, in the end it cannot be denied that the tone or temper of mind displayed in the one field might well operate in the other, so that a brief glance at what Newman says about authority in general must be made.

The Oxford Movement was based on 'submission to a definite,

[1] *D.A.*, pp. 320–324.

existing authority',[1] and as a Catholic Newman was able to extol the value of authority at least as much as formerly. Yet he was far from admitting that the Catholic Church excluded all Private Judgement. It was rather that the Catholic Church alone provided an arena for both principles.

Now authority in the Church, resting on infallibility, was not just one principle among others, it was 'not a naked or isolated fact, but the animating principle of a large scheme of doctrine'.[2] This means that it must not be viewed as simply external, as the imposition of an individual will upon another such will. It is concerned with the expression and completion of truth, as much as interfering to prevent error, and in doing this it is not simply external to the community in which it acts, but is in a sense the community acting on itself, since what is defined and enforced by the authoritative voice of the Church is only what in fact has been ever held by its members, though with increasing distinctness. Of course, to the individual heretic, for instance, the question of the exact location of the authority which faced him would not be of immediate import, and the tension between the individual and authority in the Church Newman did not deny; in the last resort the only solution for the individual was to entrust his cause to time.

> In reading ecclesiastical history, when I was an Anglican, [Newman remarks] it used to be forcibly brought home to me, how the initial error of what afterwards became heresy was the urging forward some truth against the prohibition of authority at an unseasonable time. There is a time for everything, and many a man desires a reformation of an abuse or the fuller development of a doctrine, or the adoption of a particular policy, but forgets to ask himself whether the right time for it is come; and, knowing that there is no one who will be doing anything towards its accomplishment in his own lifetime unless he does it himself, he will not listen to the voice of

---

[1] *Diff.*, i, 133. But W. Ward argues that Newman as an Anglican could not stress authority, since his Church sanctioned Protestantism and Latitudinarianism, and so he opposed liberalism in the name of minute, dogmatic formulae and ritualism, thus investing himself with a very reactionary appearance. *Life and Times of Cardinal Wiseman* (2nd ed., London, 1897), i, 296.   [2] *Dev.*, p. 91.

authority, and he spoils a good work in his own century, in order that another man as yet unborn, may not have the opportunity of bringing it happily to perfection in the next.... He may seem to the world to be nothing else than a bold champion for the truth and a martyr to free opinion, when he is just one of those persons whom the competent authority ought to silence.[1]

It might well seem from this that the role of Private Judgement is negligible after all, but it should be realised that this term is ambiguous. It can be used in a strict technical sense, while it can be used simply to refer to the duty of following conscience, and on this latter point Newman was as insistent as anyone. In his celebrated reply to Gladstone's charges about the unreliability of Catholics in their political allegiance, Newman stressed the practical and psychological limitations to which the Pope's political power was necessarily submitted, that a crucial point was not what the Pope ordered, but whether the Pope would be obeyed, and that this obedience could only be forthcoming as long as the Pope stayed within the moral framework to which in fact he appeals for the source of his power. Thus it is that Newman drinks first to Conscience, the aboriginal Vicar of Christ, and to the Pope afterwards.[2] This is a point which is brought out by a consideration of Newman's remarks about Keble, preeminently a man guided by authority, since on inquiring into the nature of this authority, it emerges that

> Conscience is an authority; the Bible is an authority; such is the Church; such is Antiquity; such are the words of the wise; such are hereditary lessons; such are ethical truths; such are historical memories; such are legal saws and state maxims; such are proverbs; such are sentiments, presages, and prepossessions.[3]

And so, after all, the traditions and the rest which at first seemed to need the validation of some authority turn out to be themselves authorities. It is not merely that Newman was using 'authority' in what he confessed was a very wide sense, but rather

---

[1] *Apo.*, p. 350. Perhaps Newman had Lamennais in mind here.
[2] *Diff.*, ii, 261; 248–249.   [3] *Apo.*, p. 495.

that he was making clear that any authority whatsoever presupposes a form of Private Judgement, that in the last resort the individual conscience is all important, since authority means rightful power, implying a duty on the part of the individual to respect it, and of this duty, in his own unique, individual case, the individual person must be the final judge. In truth no one set a higher value on conscience than Newman, and few can have been as willing to act on it, at whatever personal cost. It would in some ways be as easy to make Newman a champion of Private Judgement as of authority. He did nevertheless champion authority against religious liberalism, and this whole question of liberalism must soon be surveyed, but it can be fairly stated that there is nothing in his whole attitude to authority which can cause a liberal democrat of this day to question the value of Newman's political thought.

Perhaps it is now becoming apparent that Newman has much more to contribute to political thought than many have suspected. With the discussion on liberalism, to which the chapter on Church and State is a necessary introduction, his major political interests and most important message for the present day will have been reached. This discussion can be begun, now that it has been established that his profound conservatism, based on religious and philosophic conviction as it was, did not imply a pessimism about man and society which could lead him to despair of politics or the State. For all the Augustinianism which he displays, it might be as easy to compare Newman with John Locke as with St. Augustine. Indeed, all that has been said so far, while showing Newman to be in some ways unique, also goes to show that he was closer in many respects to the general political thought of his fellow countrymen at that age than he was to many great contemporary thinkers of his own Church.

III

CHURCH AND STATE

1. THE CHURCH AS A STATE

'NEWMAN, even apart from his theology, was an able political thinker who had devoted the twelve years of his connexion with the Oxford Movement to the study of the problem of sovereignty in its acutest phase—that of Church and State.'[1]

This judgement of the late Professor Laski can be accepted. The question of Church and State was always present in one shape or another for the leaders of the Oxford Movement. Three of the four volumes of the *Remains* of Hurrell Froude, an acknowledged driving force of the Movement, are devoted to this question. It was a problem with which Newman was inevitably faced, and it is precisely his merit that he did face it, and did not take refuge in the idea that if only the Church and the State could keep to their own proper sphere, no collision was possible. This was the easy view of Richard Whately,[2] to whom Newman owed not a little on this whole question; it was that of Hurrell Froude.[3] It was not Newman's view. For him there was no escape from the fact that the very same person and things belonged at once to two supreme jurisdictions, so that both Church and State, in legislating for their respective members, were necessarily at the same time affecting not only their own, but some of each other's members.[4]

Yet there can be no real problem of Church and State unless a sufficiently high view be taken of the nature and purposes of both institutions. A problem arose for Newman because his conception

[1] H. Laski, *Problem of Sovereignty* (London, 1917), p. 202.

[2] *Letters on the Church* by an Episcopalian (London, 1826), p. 191. The authorship of Whately, left doubtful by his biographer, is now generally accepted. It is interesting to note that the Preface to the *Letters* claims that an appeal to reason is to be made, not authority, a remark characteristic of an Oriel 'Noetic' such as Whately.

[3] *Remains* (Derby, 1839), iii, 393.

[4] Newman's most extended discussions on Church and State are to be found in the first volume of *Difficulties of Anglicans*. See particularly pp. 173-180, 198-203.

of the State was much more adequate than that, for instance, of Richard Whately, who had not flinched from comparing the State to an 'agricultural society'.[1] The State for Newman was not, of course, omnipotent, nor was it a moral organism in the sense that it creates its own morality, nor did the citizen belong to it entirely by all that he was, and all that he had in him. It was of limited functions and had a service character. Yet it was still the representative and instrument of the eternal law of God in its administration and organisation of a common life, so that treason against it might become rebellion against God. Further, Newman's strong conservatism led him to abhor any attempt to disturb the settled order of society. With these views, he could not escape the obvious conclusion that anyone setting up or supporting a rival society to the State, which might endanger or embarrass it, must accept the onus of proving the necessity for this society. But Newman did think he had a clear case to produce, and so it becomes necessary to examine that view of the Church which justified Newman raising the old, but ever-vexatious problem of the relations of Church and State.

Now it has been seen that Newman very soon began to lose his early Calvinism, and with it his notion of the Church as a Church of the Elect. He rapidly came to believe that only God knew who was elected to eternal glory, so that even if the Church could in a sense be said to exist for the sake of the Elect, yet it addressed itself to all men alike, and was itself composed of a very 'mixed multitude' of saints and sinners. Newman thus came to a more orthodox insistence on the Church as the actual existent visible body, rather than as an invisible group within this body.

But it was not only in the calmness of theological reflexion that Newman's ideas about the Church developed, but in the excited atmosphere of the period of the first Reform Bill of 1832. A general reforming spirit was abroad, and the torpid and worldly Church which had emerged from the eighteenth century presented an obvious target to reformers. Some reform the Church had indeed already undertaken before the nineteenth century was

---
[1] *Letters on the Church*, p. 155.

far advanced, but there was much which could still find little justification, in the eyes especially of an increasing group of Utilitarians. The Utilitarian attack was not perhaps so dangerous as it might have been, and the extravagant ideas of James Mill, with his 'grim joke' of a 'proposal for the transformation of the Church of England into a National Mechanics Institute',[1] show the failure that sometimes did exist to appreciate the reserves of strength of the Church of England. But the widespread hostility to the Church, not only from Philosophic but also the old-style Radicals, and the dislike of a large and increasingly powerful body of Dissenters, meant that the Established Church was in genuine danger.[2]

In 1832, Whately could write of it, 'I fear its days are numbered.'[3] Looking back on those days, William Palmer (of Worcester College) said, 'There was not a single stone of the sacred edifice of the Church which was not examined, shaken, undermined, by a meddling and ignorant curiosity.'[4]

Against all such interference Whately came out in 1826 with a powerful plea. 'LET US ALONE' were the final words of his *Letters on the Church* which so influenced Newman. From here Newman learnt that the Church is 'not merely a collective name for all who happen to agree in certain opinions; . . . but is a society, or body corporate . . . of divine institution'.[5] Thus was the disappearance of any tendency on Newman's part to speak of an invisible Church very much hastened.

But the book, though it influenced Newman greatly, nevertheless suffered in Newman's eyes from one fatal defect. It set up this divinely founded society in the State, and yet gave it nothing to do; or rather, nothing which needed for its performance a

---

[1] Dicey, *Law and Opinion* (2nd ed., London, 1914), pp. 321–322.
[2] J. Overton, *English Church in the Nineteenth Century* (London, 1894), p. 312. The same writer may be cited as sanctioning the view of a torpid and worldly Anglican Church in the eighteenth century. 'Church Abuses', Abbey and Overton, *English Church in the Eighteenth Century* (London, 1887), Vol. II, Ch. I.
[3] J. Whately, *Life of Whately* (London, 1886), i, 159.
[4] *Narrative of Events* (2nd ed., Oxford, 1843), p. 4.
[5] p. 63. Cf. *Apo.*, p. 115, where Newman says Whately taught him 'the existence of the Church, as a substantive body, or corporation'.

society with a divine charter. For all that Whately gave the Church to do Newman could see no reason 'why anyone who has his evenings to himself, and is of an active turn, should not do everything which he ascribes to his heaven-born society'.[1] This was a defect which was speedily remedied for Newman in his association with Hurrell Froude in the early stages of the Oxford Movement.

Froude emphasised the fact that the political and religious changes since Hooker's day meant that it was no longer possible to see the Church and the State as consisting of the same members, though in very different relations; that the position of the Church needed reformulating in the light of the conditions then obtaining. Consequently Froude stressed, as Whately had done, the divine institution of the Church, 'he delighted in the notion of an hierarchical system, of sacerdotal power and full ecclesiastical liberty'.[2] But the liberties of the Church were means to an all-important end for Froude, which only the Church, with its dogma and sacramental life, could achieve. Newman learnt from Froude and not Whately here, and in the period of the Oxford Movement Newman developed that more Catholic view of the Church and its functions which was to cause him to leave the Anglican Church in 1845.

It was not so much Newman's conception of the Church and its functions, so much as its relations to Rome which was the principal change in Newman's religious position after 1833. Newman had thought there were mainly three branches of the Church—Roman, Greek and Anglican—substantially agreed on fundamental doctrine.[3] The Anglican Church was a true portion of the Church though infected with some Protestantism, and he hoped to find a *Via Media* for it between Protestantism and the errors of Rome. But though the attempt to establish this *Via Media* failed, and the Roman became the only true Church for

---

[1] *Diff.*, i, 210. [2] *Apo.*, p. 125.
[3] Thus Newman's theory was not that of the typical Anglican Branch Church. The more typical Anglican theory exemplified by W. Palmer (of Worcester College) is that the link between the branches cannot be fundamental doctrine, but lies in the Apostolical Succession and the correspondence in the type of society. See *Ess.*, i, 134–185; also Newman's Preface to *Notes of a Visit to the Russian Church* (London, 1882), by W. Palmer (of Magdalen College).

Newman, it was not so much his idea of the Church which changed, as his opinion that this idea was concretely realised in the Anglican Church. Thus in dealing with the problem of Church and State, it is not misleading to treat the problem as one which basically remained for Newman always the same.

The mature view of Newman[1] was that the Church was founded by Christ, who dwelt on earth as Prophet, Priest, and King; and to these titles the Church, the Bride of Christ, succeeds. The three functions of the Church then are the prophetical, which is concerned with the safeguarding of true doctrine; the sacramental, which is concerned with safeguarding the sacramental system; and the regal function, the one which brings the Church into the political sphere. These three functions did not appear fully developed at the same time; at first Christianity was recognised as a worship, then it became a theology, and lastly the Church 'seated itself, as an ecclesiastical polity, among princes, and chose Rome for its centre'.[2] If the three functions did not emerge simultaneously, neither was the order of emergence the order of importance, since theology must be the regulating principle of the whole Church system. The political element needs to be kept subservient to the Prophetical Office, for the very good reason that it is far more congenial to the human mind, and ever struggling to free itself from its salutary restraints.[3]

The political function of the Church may be examined under two aspects. Internally the Church must be organised to secure her mission, to supervise the relations of part with part; externally, the Church must face the World, and more particularly the State, and for this it must be a body politic. It is the external aspect which concerns us here. Newman would say that the Church is a body politic because it is a visible society. It is a visible society since Scripture shows that 'only a visible Church can be a stay and maintenanace of the Truth'.[4] Thus the Church is 'not only a

---

[1] Best seen from the Preface to the third edition of *Via Media*, from which the ideas in the above passage are taken, unless otherwise stated.

[2] *V.M.*, i, p. xli.   [3] *ibid.*, p. xlviii.

[4] *ibid.*, pp. 193-194. Newman deals with the question of why the Church must be a visible Church in *Tract 11: The Visible Church*.

spiritual, but a visible body and as being a visible it is necessarily a political body. It becomes, and cannot but become, a temporal polity'.[1] Newman shows why this is so by referring to the act of the early Christians, who, by assembling for religious purposes were breaking a solemn law and violating a vital principle of the Roman Constitution.

> If Christianity were in its essence only private and personal ... there was no necessity for their meeting together at all. If, on the other hand, in assembling for worship and holy communion, they were fulfilling an indispensable observance, Christianity has imposed a social law on the world, and formally enters the field of politics.[2]

Late in his life Newman summed up his position very clearly.

> If the Church is to be regal, a witness for Heaven unchangeable amidst secular changes, if in every age she is to hold her own, and proclaim as well as profess the truth, if she is to thrive without or against the civil power, if she is to be resourceful and self-recuperative under all fortunes, she must be more than Holy and Apostolic; she must be Catholic. Hence it is that, first, she has ever from her beginning had a hierarchy and a head, with a strict unity of polity, the claim of an exclusive divine authority and blessing, the trusteeship of the gospel gifts, and the exercise over her members of an absolute and almost despotic rule. And next, as to her work, it is her special duty, as a sovereign State, to consolidate her several portions, to enlarge her territory, to keep up and to increase her various populations in this ever-dying, ever nascent world, in which to be stationary is to lose ground, and to repose is to fail.[3]

Thus Professor Laski says that Newman was driven back to the common medieval notion that the Church itself is a State, that the Tractarians had resort in some form to the theory of Aquinas, of the Church as a *societas perfecta*, a self-sufficient society.[4] But Newman's ideas on the Church seem to have owed little to the Middle Ages, although Froude brought him to have a high regard for the medieval Church. The language of Aquinas

---

[1] *Add.*, p. 174. cf. *Ari.*, p. 257; *Tract 11*, pp. 4, 5.   [2] *Dev.*, p. 236.
[3] *V.M.*, i, pp. lxxx-lxxxi.   [4] *Problem of Sovereignty*, p. 116.

on these questions will be sought in vain in Newman's writing. Yet it is possible to discover one occasion when Newman might seem to be echoing this language, and a consideration of this passage will lead to a clearer notion of the reasons which led to Newman's calling the Church a State. He says

> that the Church is a sovereign and self-sustaining power, in the same sense in which any temporal State is such. She is sufficient for herself; she is absolutely independent in her own sphere; she has irresponsible control over her subjects in religious matters; she makes laws for them of her own authority, and enforces obedience on them as the tenure of their membership, with her.[1]

The notion of law seems here all important. He says elsewhere:

> the Catholic Church is by its very structure and mission a political power, by which I mean a visible, substantive body of men, united together by common engagements and laws, and thereby necessarily having relations both towards its members and towards outsiders.[2]

A sense in which the Church can meaningfully be compared to a State is that its laws are, like the State's, subtly connected with its life. Now it has been seen that 'a nation's laws are a nation's property, and have their life in the nation's life, and their interpretation in the nation's sentiment'. Life, in this connexion, consisted in, or manifested itself in, activity of principle. There are various kinds of life, and each kind is the influence or operation in a body of those principles upon which the body is constituted. Thus though the principle of the Church is not the same as that of the State, and therefore their life is not the same, yet they are alike in that both are stamped with their own peculiar character, such that by a kind of secret instinct they expel any element which could endanger the vital principle of the institution. Laws are the Church's property then, in the same way that a nation's laws are its own property.

There are other resemblances. Perhaps the general habit of

[1] *Diff.*, i, 173.
[2] *V.M.*, i, 107. cf. *S.D.*, p. 220, where Newman says that the Church is 'a body politic, bound together by common laws, ruled by one head, holding intercourse part with part, acting together'.

law-abidingness which Newman postulated to explain obedience to the law of the State might be thought by him to be present also in the case of the Church. Again, the ultimate sanction of the Church is to cut off a member from communion, and to deprive him of the benefits which the Church provides. The State can deprive its members of its own peculiar advantages of the temporal sort; it deprives the criminal of some of the rights and benefits of political society. Even the use of physical force was not a monopoly of the State. The use of coercive force was allowable for the Church, though not necessary as for the State, and this force was to stop short of shedding blood.[1] Newman did not fail to note the early view that force might be used to gain supernatural ends (and in view of the Donatist history, possibly with some success), but thought that it would obviously only argue a lack of moral or rational grounds in its justification if used for a long time, or on a large scale. It would, at his own time, have so clearly defeated its own ends that he could scarcely conceive that anyone would be likely to advocate it.[2] Newman's lifelong opinion was that the use of force in religion, while not necessarily and in the abstract wrong, was useless or disastrous.

This general question is a part of the whole problem of the place of religion in the modern State, a problem which Newman did not shirk. In this connexion a series of unpublished letters of Newman to Lord Emly (Monsell Collection) on religious persecution in Spain are of great importance. The present inquiry, however, is into the reasons for Newman speaking of the Church as a State, and it is clear that the circumscribed use of force by the Church which Newman allows does not go much further than the other considerations to justify him in his use of language. He did not admit, or perhaps merely does not face the great differences which most would find between anything which could usefully and usually be considered a State and his most exalted idea of a Church.

[1] P.C., Ward, 6 January 1864.
[2] *St. Ath.*, ii, 123–126. For Newman's first published adverse reference to the use of force in religion, see *St. Bartholomew's Eve* (Oxford, 1821), p. 20, lines 343–346. Cf. *Ess.*, i, 278–279 n.

Indeed, the Church was at times more than a State for Newman —it was an Empire.

> It is the peculiarity of an imperial state to bear rule over other states; and it is another peculiarity, not indeed essential, but almost necessary, that it should be always in movement, advancing or retiring, never stationary, aggression being the condition of its existence. Conquest is almost of the essence of an empire, and when it ceases to conquer it ceases to be. Such is an empire of this world; . . . such also in its substance is the kingdom of Christ.[1]

The sermon from which this passage is taken, 'The Christian Church an Imperial Power', goes as far in extolling the right of the Church to sit in judgement on the nations as Newman ever went, though the view of the Church which is taken there is not substantially different from that which he elsewhere takes. It becomes necessary to examine Newman's account of the relations between such a Church and the State in which it dwells.

Now the State had a unique role to play, for Newman, in the organisation of a common life, and it could claim a divine sanction. Yet since there could be no clear division between spiritual and temporal affairs, as a given situation might present both aspects, the Church could scarcely fail to be at times at cross-purposes with the State. The State and the Church need not be always at odds, since they both are distinct societies with distinct aims. Again, since both the power of the magistrate and the priest are from God, then it is reasonable to suppose there will be a general coincidence in the principles on which the welfare of the State and the Church depend. But the possibility of a clash between Church and State in a particular case cannot be permanently avoided. This might remain a difference without serious results if the attitude of the State were that of the Church. For the Church 'upholds obedience to the magistrate; she recognises his office as from God; she is the preacher of peace, the sanction of law, the first element of order and the safeguard of morality, and that without possible vaccillation or failure; she

---

[1] S.D., pp. 228–229.

may be fully trusted; she is a sure friend for she is indefectible and undying'.¹

The attitude of the State is far from this. It is the ever-present tendency of the State to glorify itself, to make itself into a sovereign State in the Hobbesian mould. '*Aut Caesar aut nullus*' is the motto of the State, and double jurisdictions, a divided allegiance, an *imperium in imperio* are anathema to it. 'All power is founded ... on public opinion', Newman said, and for 'the State to allow the existence of a collateral and rival authority, is to weaken its own; ... even though that authority never showed its presence by collision. ...'²

But the claim to an absolute obedience could never be granted. This was what Newman thought Gladstone was demanding of Catholics in their controversy over the civil allegiance of Catholics.

> When, then, Mr. Gladstone asks Catholics how they can obey the Queen and yet obey the Pope, since it may happen that the command of the two authorities may clash, I answer, that it is my rule, both to obey the one and to obey the other, but that there is no rule in this world without exceptions, and if either the Pope or the Queen demanded of me an 'Absolute Obedience', he or she would be transgressing the laws of human society.³

Thus Newman rejects the concept of sovereignty, but he was well aware that it was an idea which had nevertheless a very strong hold on many. For this reason he did not think a merely national Church could ever hope to stand up against the State. As a Catholic Newman could see a possibility for the harmonious relationship between Church and State which before he had not been able to advance. The dualism of Church and State was workable since as the Church 'is everywhere, for that very reason it is in the fulness of her jurisdiction nowhere. Ten thousand subordinate authorities have been planted round, or have issued from, that venerable Chair where sits the plenitude of Apostolical power. Hence, when she would act, the blow is broken, and the

---

¹ *Diff.*, i, 175.   ² *ibid.*   ³ *ibid.*, ii, 243.

concussion avoided, by the innumerable springs, if I may use the word, on which the celestial machinery is hung.'¹

Thus as a matter of history has the problem been solved, and what might have seemed a dangerous dualism, fraught with grave perils for society, has proved in fact capable of working smoothly. But a real difficulty always remains, since there is an ever-present possibility of conflict, and the Church for Newman can never be quiescent or stationary, but ever seeking to extend its imperial sway. It was a sure instinct which made the Roman magistrate dread Christianity. 'It was a dangerous enemy to any power not built upon itself.'²

2. THE CHURCH AS AN ESTABLISHMENT

The mere existence of such a Church as Newman thought necessary poses its own problem in the State, but a further problem arises as to the particular relationship which must obtain between the Church and the State. The Church, if it is to be a self-sufficient society, does not need the State to help perform its mission, since it can do this even in active opposition to the State. How far the State needs the Church is a further question. It is clear that Newman from the first fully realised the extent to which the Church could be useful to the State. Yet he did not at once come to a full realisation of the danger to the Church from its very usefulness to the State, and the perils of allowing the State to enmesh the Church in its own network. That his attitude to the Establishment changed greatly is a fact of special importance on which much will turn in the rest of this account of Newman's political thought.

There is no need to emphasise the extent to which Newman and the Tractarians were prepared to go in defending the indefensible privileges of the Established Church. A touch of the hysterical can be detected in Newman's reproach to Grey on the Irish Church Reform Bill—'Well done! My blind Premier, confiscate and rob, till, like Samson, you pull down the Political Structure on your own head.'³ Even before 1833 Newman had

[1] *Diff.*, i, 180.   [2] *Dev.*, p. 232.   [3] *M.*, i, 353.

on one occasion appeared to be siding with the most conservative defenders of the Establishment. This was in the fight against Peel in his attempt at re-election for Oxford, when that statesman seemed, as it were, to be seeking a mandate from the University for the earlier change of view he had already undergone on the question of the practical necessity of Catholic Emancipation. But although the full motives for Newman's vigorous efforts against Peel are obscure, it should not be overlooked that he had himself hitherto been a petitioner for Emancipation, so that Newman's ranging of himself along with the 'two bottle orthodox' must not be taken for identity.[1] It is also significant that in the draft of instructions prepared by Newman for the propagandists of the Oxford Movement, he includes the following statement: 'We have nothing to do with maintaining the temporalities of the Church, much as we deprecate any undue influence with them by external authority.'[2] The High Churchmanship of Newman and the Tractarians was of a different calibre from that of some stout defenders of the Church.

Newman thought that the Tractarian was one of the three theological parties in the Church (the others were the liberal and the evangelical), but that in the bosom of the Church was

> a party more numerous by far than these three theological ones—a party which, created by the legal position of the Church, profiting by its riches and by the institutions of its creed, is the counter weight and the chain which secures the whole. It is the party of order, the party of Conservatives, or Tories, as they have hitherto been called. . . . It constitutes the mass of the Church. The clergy in particular —Bishops, Deans, Chapters, Rectors—are always distinguished by their Toryism on all English questions.[3]

Like the Tractarians this body asserted the prerogatives and authority of the Church as a visible body, and hence could claim

---

[1] *Apo.*, p. 117; p. 149.   [2] *M.*, ii, 4.
[3] *Apo.*, pp. xxv–xxvi. (This passage is from an Appendix to the French edition of the *Apologia*, in which Newman makes a very interesting summary of the constitution and history of the Church of England.) The question of how far Newman can be said to have been a Tory will be discussed in Chapter IV.

the title 'High Church', but, unlike the Tractarians, they were much 'more zealous for the preservation of a national Church than solicitous for the beliefs which that national Church professes'.[1] But since the temporal privileges of the Church depended on the civil power it happened accidentally 'that a partisan of the High Church is almost an Erastian; that is to say, a man who denies the spiritual power pertaining to the Church and maintains that the Church is one of the branches of the civil government'. But of the Tractarian movement Newman said in 1850, that its 'first principle was ecclesiastical liberty; the doctrine which it specially opposed was in ecclesiastical language, the heresy of Erastus, and in political, the Royal Supremacy. The object of its attack was the Establishment as such.'[2]

The attack on Erastianism was the 'form' of the Movement, and gave it shape and character, though Newman says of himself and his friends:

> They did not understand that the Established Religion was set up in Erastianism, that Erastianism was its essence, and that to destroy Erastianism was to destroy the religion. The movement then, and the Establishment, were in simple antagonism from the first, although neither party knew it; they were logical contradictories . . . experience was necessary to teach this to men who knew more of St. Athanasius than of the Privy Council or the Court of the Arches.[3]

But there were two types of Erastianism which Newman opposed. The first is typified in Archdeacon Froude, of whom his son said that 'The Church itself he regarded as part of the constitution; and the Prayer Book as an Act of Parliament which only folly or disloyalty could quarrel with.'[4] This was the genuine High Church Toryism of the old school; but there was an attitude to the Establishment which Newman found if anything even more distasteful, and this was especially typified by Thomas Arnold.

[1] *Apo.*, pp. xxv-xxvi. [2] *Diff.*, i, 101. [3] *ibid.*, pp. 105-106.
[4] J. A. Froude, *Short Studies on Great Subjects* (London, 1909), iv, 254. The last of the few letters from the Archdeacon to Newman characteristically dwells on a coming Conservative meeting in Totnes, and the local revival of Tory feeling. P.C., Froude, 23 January 1837.

Church and State

Arnold saw clearly that the Established Church was far from being truly national, and he thought the best defence of the Church was to make it so. 'Nothing, as it seems to me, can save the Church but an union with the Dissenters,' he said, and his *Principles of Church Reform* aimed to do just that. Now whatever the incidental though widespread annoyance which this book caused,[1] it struck at the roots of Newman's whole religious and political system. The basis of Arnold's position was that 'the pretended distinction between spiritual things and secular [is] a distinction utterly without foundation'.[2] But this was not intended by Arnold to suggest that what was generally considered spiritual was the less noble, but that temporal, and particularly political things, were much more so than was often thought. For him 'the desire of taking an active share in the great work of government' was 'the highest earthly desire of the ripened mind'.[3] But the great work of government needed the Church, and unless Church and State were combined they would both become corrupt, and each could only gain its utmost perfection by its union with the other.[4]

All this is the precise contrary to Newman's attitude, and the opposition between the two could scarcely be more complete. It was not only that Newman's whole conception of a dogmatic and sacramental Church was necessarily overthrown by these views, but that a denial of the very need for the institution of a Church of any sort was logically implied by Arnold. Nor was this conclusion merely implicit in Arnold's position. Arnold looked forward to the withering away of the external organisation of the Church and to its spirit somehow transforming the State into a

---

[1] The proposals to allow Dissenters' meetings in Anglican churches, and finally to embrace Roman Catholicism and Unitarianism within the Establishment were responsible for some of the more reasonable and practicable ideas being ignored. Stanley, *Life of Arnold* (9th ed., London, 1868), pp. 274-275.

On the other hand these proposals were good indications of Arnold's general position, and his inability to see others' points of view. See W. (Worcester) Palmer, *Remarks on Arnold's "Principles of Church Reform"* (London, 1833), p. 17.

[2] Arnold, *Fragment on the Church* (London, 1844), p. 12.

[3] Stanley, *op. cit.* (1844), i, 180.

[4] Arnold, *Fragments on Church and State* (London, 1845), p. 94.

Christian Kingdom.[1] It would be a mistake to confuse Arnold's ideal with the totalitarian ideas of modern times, but it seems nevertheless suspiciously reminiscent of those all-inclusive polities of the Ancient World which Arnold so much admired. It is not surprising that Arnold should come at last to the view that a non-Christian 'is most justly excluded from citizenship in a Christian State'; that, as for individuals, 'against society they have no rights whatsoever'.[2] It is easy to credit the evidence of W. G. Ward, that Arnold admitted being ready to 'give James Mill as much opportunity for advocating his opinion as is consistent with a voyage to Botany Bay'.[3]

Now it follows from what will be argued in this study that Newman would object to the political implications which Arnold's theory involved; but there were obvious ecclesiastical reasons for objection. Newman had imbibed from both Whately and Froude a general hatred of Erastianism, for all of them were reminded by those defending the civil duties of the clergy 'of the dog in the fable, who mistook the clog round his neck for a badge of honourable distinction'. But it was not the onerousness of any such duties in themselves which Newman detested. It was that they were a symbol of that desire of the State, which Whately had inveighed against, to use the Church for its own illegitimate ends; its desire 'to hurl against (its) enemies the terrors of the next world in addition to those of the sword'.[4] If this was not what Arnold was saying, it seems that Newman nevertheless believed that the grand aim and result of Arnold's teaching was no more than to make man a good member of society. Much of Newman's preaching is directed against this attitude which he saw in Arnold.[5] Froude was in constant warfare with Arnold here, even when the great Erastian's name is not mentioned. He took as one of the phrases against which he would especially struggle, 'resident gentleman'. This was Arnold's phrase. Arnold's ideal was that the clergyman's family should be: 'a little centre of civilisation,

---

[1] *Fragments on Church and State*, p. 49.   [2] *ibid.*, pp. 52–53.
[3] W. Ward, *W. G. Ward and the Catholic Revival* (London, 1893) pp. 458–459.
[4] *Letters on the Church*, p. 102; p. 128.
[5] e.g. *P.S.*, iii, 13; iv, 161. Also *H.S.*, i, 375–377.

from which gleams of refinement of manners, of neatness, of taste, as well as of science and general literature, are diffused through districts into which they would otherwise never penetrate'. The clergyman was a 'gentleman resident' in a parish to 'comfort affliction' and 'counsel ignorance'.[1]

This was a view of the Church and its role which came near to that which Coleridge had put forward in 1830 in his *Constitution of the Church and State*, in which the idea is expressed that the Church in England is only by a happy accident connected with Christianity at all, that its essential role is to act as the 'Clerisy' of the nation, maintaining and improving the intellectual and moral heritage of the nation.[2] Arnold by no means followed Coleridge on to the metaphysical heights to which the latter ascended, but he had much in common on this conception of the role of the Church. So, to some extent, had another renowned contemporary and author of a well-known book on Church and State—Gladstone.

The insertion of Gladstone's name here is not for the purpose of incidental comparisons of opinions on this subject. Newman came to change his mind about it, and it is in a discussion between these two great Victorians that the change can best be observed. Gladstone, of course, was never a Tractarian, although his religious development owed much to his friend, James Hope (afterwards Hope-Scott), who was himself much indebted to Newman.[3] By 1838, however, Gladstone felt able to assure England of her National Church that 'her character is legibly divine',[4] and to insist on the State establishing the Anglican Church, since the State could not perform its proper functions without a morality ultimately dependent on religion. Newman was not greatly impressed by Gladstone's book, though he

[1] 'Review of *Letters on the Church*', *Edinburgh Review* (1826), xliv, 501–502.
[2] (ed. H. N. Coleridge, London, 1839), p. 59, Chapter V, 45 ff.
It must be admitted that Coleridge distinguishes between the Church of Christ and the National Church, though as Crane Brinton says, 'not very satisfactorily'. *English Political Thought in the Nineteenth Century* (London, 1933), p. 78.
[3] D. C. Lathbury, *Letters on the Church and Religion of W. E. Gladstone* (London, 1910), i, 227; ii, 13.
[4] *State in its Relations with the Church* (4th ed., London, 1844), p. 14.

hoped it would do good, and this lack of enthusiasm can be attributed to the suspected presence in it of a smack of that Coleridgean attitude which emphasises too greatly the social value and purposes of the National Church.[1] But this may be to do Gladstone a slight injustice, since, as Macaulay said, Gladstone possessed 'a vast command of a kind of language, grave and majestic, but of vague and uncertain import',[2] and he may well not have meant quite what some had thought. It was Macaulay (in his celebrated article in the *Edinburgh Review*) who may reasonably be said to have destroyed the arguments of Gladstone, by his counter-arguments that though religion may be good the State is not fitted to propagate it, and his revival of Chillingworth's old arguments about the likelihood of a failure in the Apostolical Succession.

Gladstone's sad fall 'from principle to expediency' in Church matters may not[3] have been unconnected with Macaulay's review, though the 1844 edition of the statesman's book did not alter the main thesis which had invited attack. But Gladstone was re-thinking his position, and when Newman's *Sermons on Subjects of the Day* came out in that year Gladstone was quick to find something there with which to grapple. In September he wrote to Newman[4] that he was perturbed by a passage in which occurs the remark, referring to the political world: 'They are afraid to kindle their fire from the altar of God; they are afraid to acknowledge her through whom only they gain light and strength and salvation, the Mother of Saints.'[5] It had become visionary to expect that the Church should get anything like its due now, Gladstone argued, since less than half the population of the United Kingdom belonged to the Church of England, and some of these were disaffected to it. With the advent of democracy the disaffected moiety were the political equals of others, and in fact

---

[1] P.C., Hope-Scott, 1 March 1839. But see *M*., ii, 321. For possible Coleridge influence see Gladstone, *op. cit.*, pp. 6, 17, 18.

[2] 'Review of *Church and State*', *Edinburgh Review* (1839), lxix, 233.

[3] See Christopher Wordsworth's complaint to Hope-Scott, Lathbury, *Letters on the Church and Religion of W. E. Gladstone*, ii, 373.

[4] P.C., Gladstone, 3 September 1844.   [5] *S.D.*, p. 107.

generated more political excitement. The result was that the individual could do little for the Church cause in Parliament, since the Christianity of the State was the result and not the cause of the Christianity of the Nation. Altogether, Gladstone urged, it was 'no more possible to re-establish a national religion by enacting it than to change the wind by forcing round the weather-cock'.

Newman's reply to this letter[1] was evasive. He was then at Littlemore, and the days of his Anglican career were drawing to their painful close. Yet his reply is of the greatest importance nevertheless, since it confirms that Newman's political views were changing. He says: 'I have many difficulties in speaking—from the consciousness that I look on the facts of the ecclesiastical and political world in a point of view different from what I formerly did. . . .'

An indication of the way in which this change had gone was not long in coming. Gladstone was extremely anxious to find Newman's real opinion on the question so near and so perplexing to him—'Your passing thoughts attract anxious attention', he had told Newman in the letter just quoted. The occasion of his success in bringing Newman to speak out was the celebrated Maynooth controversy, in which Gladstone felt himself in an awkward position as a result of his known views on the Church.

The advice Newman gave Gladstone[2] was that the cessation of the conditions under which the State could be assumed to have a particular religious character did not imply a Christian's duty to retire from service of the State. Newman summarised the position as he saw it. 'Mr. Gladstone had said the State *ought* to have a conscience—but it has not a conscience. Can *he* give it a conscience? Is he to impose his own conscience on the State? . . . He must deal with facts. It has a thousand consciences, as being in its legislative and executive capacities, the aggregate of a hundred minds—that is, it has no conscience.'

Thus Newman recognised, 'in anything but a state of hopeless

---

[1] Dated Littlemore, 14 September 1844. British Museum, *Add. Mss.* 44361.
[2] *Keble Corr.*, pp. 375–377.

and helpless despair that the "old order" was not only passing, but had passed'.[1] But this letter points to a more interesting conclusion than that Newman clearly saw the old order had gone. In the early years of the Oxford Movement, he could still speak of the State's duty to support the Church,[2] but he had rapidly become hostile to the connexion of Church and State which actually existed. The connexion of the State with religion seemed too likely to lead to some form of Erastianism, and Erastianism was the parent and tool of another enemy, liberalism. Thus it was not only the concrete fact that an established religion or a State with a conscience was impossible, but the opinion that it was undesirable, which Newman seems to have been approaching in his Anglican days. When Newman refers to the change in his political standpoint it seems that this is what he must have meant. Again, in the later letter to Gladstone, this is surely involved in Newman's argument that Gladstone was giving 'that advice which facts made necessary, and which, if followed out, will, it is to be hoped, lead to some basis of principle which we do not see at present'.[3]

It will now be seen how far Newman can be said to have found a principle on which the non-religious State can be justified.

[1] *Keble Corr.*, p. 374.
[2] As late as 1836, for instance. See P.C., Rose, 20 May 1836.
[3] *Keble Corr.*, p. 377.

IV
LIBERALISM

1. NEWMAN'S OPPOSITION TO LIBERALISM

IT is a measure of the flexibility or vagueness of political terms that Newman can as easily and as truthfully be called either a liberal or an anti-liberal. As long as his political position is correctly understood, the choice of label to describe that position is unimportant. Unfortunately, Newman's politics have rarely been understood, and a great deal of the misunderstanding which has occurred has been due to a failure to clarify the notion of liberalism as it appeared to Newman. There is no one liberalism, and the common threads between different historic liberalisms, and different writers' interpretations of them is often hard to find. Even if it is agreed that there was an English nineteenth-century form of liberalism, distinctive enough for recognition and analysis, it would be a grave mistake to treat Newman's remarks on liberalism as referring to that phenomenon. It is necessary to examine first what Newman meant by the term, and to determine his attitude to liberalism defined in his own way, before venturing to comment on his attitude to it as it might be understood today by particular writers. This examination is necessary, firstly, merely for the sake of historical truth and understanding, in order to reconcile those two apparently antagonistic accounts of him, which show him on the one hand as a lifelong anti-liberal, Tory, conservative and traditionalist, and on the other as a 'romantic ally of the liberal spirit', as displaying an 'implicit liberalism' and undergoing a 'curious reversion to liberalism' as a Catholic.[1]

[1] The Tory and conservative interpretation of Newman is very common. The quotations indicating Newman's liberalism are to be found in the following places: Crane Brinton, *English Political Thought in the Nineteenth Century*, p. 164; Laski, *Problem of Sovereignty*, p. 174; S. Cadman Parkes, *Three Religious Leaders of Oxford* (London, 1916), p. 569.

Further, however, it may sometimes be necessary for more practical reasons to establish Newman's true position. Fifty years ago, for instance, in the heat of the Modernist controversy, Newman was stated by a writer in the *Dublin Review* to have been a Tory in politics, and therefore incapable of being a liberal in religion.[1] This attempt to drag Newman on to one side or another in any given question in some way involving politics has been made easy by the long confusion over his political position, and there has now been made an ingenious American attempt to press him into service as an example of the 'Conservative Mind'.[2] In this way Newman might seem to have a possible future as one of the inspirers of a new American conservatism. Unfortunately Newman is represented by the American author as putting forward views which it is very doubtful that he held. It could more easily be argued that Newman's ideas were in some ways precisely the reverse of those it is alleged that he held.

Since Mr. Russell Kirk's interpretation of Newman is parallel to that of many others, and yet manages to be more pithily and succinctly incorrect than others, it seems wise to quote here those views which it is hoped the rest of the chapter will refute. He says then that 'real conservatism ... transcends politics. Newman was a consistent Tory, devoted to the principle of aristocracy and the concept of loyalty to persons; yet this is not his important contribution to political thought.' The contribution this author has in mind soon becomes clear. 'Newman continues', he says, 'the philosophical chain of Hooker and Burke who knew that society is based on faith'; and later he states that Newman's bequest to a later age is that 'grim utilitarian expediency continues to be opposed by the ancient religious view of society'.[3]

It can scarcely be denied that Newman's attitude to liberalism and liberals, to Whiggery which had 'by degrees taken up all the filth that has been secreted in the fermentation of human thought',[4] and so in which liberalism had found a home, seems

---

[1] (1901), vol. 128, p. 302.   [2] R. Kirk, *The Conservative Mind* (Chicago, 1953).
[3] *ibid.*, pp. 244, 246, 256–257.
[4] Froude, *Remains*, i, 340. It seems reasonable to identify Newman with this remark of Froude's.

clear enough for anyone in its vigorous condemnation. He says of some unfortunate people—'they are Liberals, and in saying this I conceive I am saying almost as bad of them as can be said of anyone'.[1] Nor did he shrink from using language of Lord Grey and his party which seems reminiscent of contemporary politics, in calling them, in fact, 'vermin'.[2] The violence of this language must be traced not to any fierce hatred of an abstract liberalism, but to a very real fear for the safety of the Established Church at the hands of the Whigs. It is as well, in any effort to understand this whole question of liberalism here, to ignore at first these violent protests against particular men on particular measures, and to attempt to probe further to those ideas which Newman was concerned to combat.

It is best to examine Newman's conception of liberalism in two stages. First, his broad general notion of liberalism will be analysed, and the liberalism of this analysis will be seen to be wide enough to cover all the many and varied remarks on this subject which Newman uttered in his long life. But then, secondly, it will be necessary to examine a special aspect of this broader liberalism, an aspect which occupied Newman's attention a great deal, and about which he is least understood. There has been little misunderstanding about Newman's disgust with the shallow optimism about man and his capabilities which he thought ever more characteristic of his age. This 'imbecile' optimism underlay the whole general notion of liberalism for Newman, and he attacked it throughout his life. But with this as its basis, it is clear that liberalism can neither be an exclusively religious nor political idea. The optimism is judged to be absurd from the standpoint of the religious doctrine of the Fall, but the fact that men ignore the Fall has important political implications. Thus Newman thought that increasingly, and especially since 1688, 'men saw the good in themselves and not the evil, and consequently were puzzled by the failure of certain parts of the social system

---

[1] Letter of 13 March 1831, *M.*, i, 237.
[2] 'Those vile vermin in power are indeed exposing themselves,' P.C., Froude, 10 August 1831. This letter is partly to be found in *M.*, i, 245, though without the above sentence, which forms a postscript to it.

to work well, ascribing the failure to a lack of scientific knowledge, rather than of personal virtue'.[1] It cannot be said that the full implications of this statement were ever satisfactorily worked out, and it seems best to ignore them now.

Perhaps more important here is the conclusion that the same exaggerated optimism about men was seen by Newman to underlie the claims of 'rights' and 'liberty' made, for example, by the Whigs, the very incarnation of liberalism. It made possible the claim on behalf of man for an independence to which he can never attain. At the root of the plea for rights and liberty Newman saw the assertion of a 'free will' which refuses to be bound by anything outside itself. Those who make this plea 'set up some image of freedom in their minds, a freedom from the shackles of dependence, which they think their natural right, and which they aim to gain for themselves'.[2] But this is utterly unrealistic, since in any case human life has never known, nor can it ever know, such an independence. However, even if no one can ever be free from all external hindrances, it is still possible to hold that in a certain sphere man may do what he will, which for Newman means that 'it is the attribute of all rational beings to have a right to do wrong' (though he should rather speak of a power here, as he elsewhere does); 'but the first who exercised that right was the devil when he fell'.[3] Newman could well see the point of view of Dr. Johnson, who thought that 'the devil was the first Whig',[4] since the very principle of the Whigs was the selfish and proud one of standing on their own rights, which went with a forgetfulness of the duties which these rights implied. Newman here goes to the other extreme from his younger contemporary and fellow Churchman, Lord Acton, by his condemnation of the Whigs. 'Is not this the very spirit of Whiggery?' he asks. 'Opposition for its own sake, striving against the truth, because it happens to be commanded us; as if wisdom were less wise because it is less powerful.'[5] Behind Newman's argument can be seen the belief

---

[1] C.L., Wood, 4 September 1832. One of the most striking expressions of Newman' opposition to a highly optimistic view of human nature can be seen at U.S., p. 103.
[2] P.S., i, 199.   [3] ibid., iii, 218.
[4] P.P.C., p. 280.   [5] Letter of 25 July 1832, M., i, 269.

that liberty is captive by the truth,[1] that true liberty presupposes laws with which it must be in accordance—an idea with a long history, and much to commend it, although Newman does not attempt to develop it.

Liberalism, then, in the broad sense which has just been considered, can be seen very much as a mood or spirit, sometimes, though not necessarily, of a violent character,[2] which is based, however, on a definite but mistaken idea of man, and is associated with a false claim to human independence from any external will or guidance. It is not this broad use of the term liberalism which is the more interesting. It is not the way Newman defines it himself, in any of the incomplete definitions which he attempted. It might seem an obvious course to turn for a definition to the appendix 'Liberalism' in the *Apologia* of 1865, despite the fact that this appendix gives disappointingly little of Newman's complete position. Here it appears that liberalism 'is the mistake of subjecting to human judgement those revealed doctrines which are in their nature beyond and independent of it'.[3] This seems at first sight an exclusively religious conception, and many have always been, and are still, content to take the simple view that when Newman thought that he was attacking liberalism, he was attacking the anti-dogmatic principle. It is necessary not to contradict, but to amplify this view. When Newman, late in his life, was describing the religious liberalism he had for so long opposed, he stated as one of its principal tenets that 'Religion is in no sense the bond of society.'[4] It must not be supposed that these two quotations from Newman convey any separate or contradictory views. The views he expresses are so intimately bound up that they may be called the same, and together they form that special aspect of liberalism which can now be scrutinised.

It has just been seen that Newman at one time defines liberalism as the subjection of revealed doctrine to incompetent human

---

[1] *L.G.*, pp. 13–14. This is an echo of the traditional Catholic view set out in Leo XIII's encyclical, *Libertas*, 1888.

[2] *D.A.*, pp. 51, 59. Newman here seems to identify with liberalism a fierce spirit of lawlessness and rebellion against which many governments were struggling.

[3] *Apo.*, p. 493.   [4] Ward, *Life*, ii, 460.

judgement. Far from this being all that was comprised in the idea of liberalism, on some other of Newman's definitions it could even be denied the label, and called instead 'Rationalism'. This he defines, in words very close to the first definition of liberalism, as 'a certain abuse of Reason; that is, a use of it for purposes for which it was never intended, and is unfitted. To rationalise in matters of Revelation is to make our reason the standard and measure of the doctrines revealed.' This does not mean that rationalism and liberalism are synonymous; it means that 'Liberalism is the *development* of rationalism. It views faith as a mere natural gift, the like and consequence of reason—the moral sense; and by reason and the moral sense [the rationalist] estimates it and measures its objects. He soon comes to be satisfied with other men though they ignore faith and its objects, provided they recognise reason and the moral sense. This is Liberalism.'[1]

It now becomes possible to see the connexion for Newman between liberalism in politics and liberalism in religion. 'Liberalism in religion is the doctrine that there is no positive truth in religion, but that one creed is as good as another',[2] and since this must lead to a wide diversity of opinions on religious questions, it opens the way to the central tenet of political liberalism, that religion is in no sense the bond of society. The vigour and sincerity of Newman's attack on liberalism in religion can hardly be doubted, but it is a mistake to think that Newman was always opposed to liberalism in politics.

To prove this contention it is necessary first to consider in what way it is possible for Newman to speak of religion as a bond of society. It seems that religion could provide a social bond in two ways: firstly, as the earlier discussion on the State has shown, the all-important social bond for him was the common possession of the people of a State, and religion could be such a common possession; secondly, religion provided a social bond which taught 'to rule with sweetness and obey with dignity',[3] it made possible a solution for the problem of political obligation,

[1] C.L., Armstrong, 23 March 1887. [2] Ward, *Life*, ii, 460.
[3] Froude, 'Farewell to Toryism', *Remains* (London, 1838), i, 429.

preventing the naked struggle between the individual and external authority.

Now liberalism denied the need for religion as a social bond in this first sense, but Newman was quite realistic enough to see that, whether regrettably or not, religion no longer in fact was the common possession of the English State, nor was it likely in the foreseeable future ever to be so again. In his correspondence with Gladstone, which has already been mentioned, it was clear that Newman was searching for some rationalisation of the position to which religion in the State had been brought. This rationalisation, and further, justification, of the position of the State which no longer assumed Christianity to be the law of the land, was achieved by Newman partly through that conception of barbarism and civilisation which was discussed in connexion with the problem of justice in the State. It was seen that the processes of reason led to the barbarian States becoming civilised, and that this involved the change from a common possession which was an object of imagination to one which was an object of sense. But prominent among those objects of the imagination which formed the barbarian State was 'religion, true or false'.[1] Thus by the mere pejorative connotation of the term 'barbarian', Newman shows how far he was from those dreams of a Catholic Civilisation, of a Catholic theocracy, which were so powerful a factor in the political thought of some great thinkers of his Church in the period after the French Revolution. For Newman it seemed that 'certain ages, i.e. the ages of barbarism, are more susceptible of religious impressions than other ages; and call for, need, the visible rule of Religion; that, as every animal knows its own wants, and distinguishes by instinct between food and poison, so a ruder people asks for a strong form of religion, armed with temporal sanctions, and it is good for it; whereas other ages reject it, and it would be bad for them'. Thus 'a medieval system now would but foster the worst hypocrisy—not because this age is worse than that, but because imagination acts more powerfully upon barbarians, and reason on traders, *savants*,

[1] H.S., i, 162.

and newspaper readers'.[1] From all this Newman could not but be led to say: 'I do not see my way to hold that "Catholic Civilisation", as you describe it, is in *fact* (I do not say in the abstract), but in fact, has been, or shall be, or can be, a good, or *per se* desirable.'[2]

There is a curious fact here which seems never before to have been recognised. It is not so much that Newman rejected the ideal of a Catholic civilisation, as well as the opinion of its practicability, but that he came close on this point to the liberalism which he had so much opposed, for precisely the contrary reasons to those which might have been expected. It was seen that some have held that the gloomy view which Newman took of the evil of the world became brighter in his Catholic years, and with a more optimistic outlook on man it might seem likely that some approach would be made to the liberalism earlier abhorred. But this is to mistake the position. Newman changed his opinion on the role of religion in the State and drew to this extent nearer to the liberalism of his day, precisely because he did *not* lose his pessimistic outlook. In the discussion with Allies in which he put forward the fruits of his reflexion on this subject, the phrase, so familiar from his early sermons, reappears with a new significance—*Mundus totus in maligno positus est*, the whole world lieth in wickedness. The protagonists of a medieval political system seemed to forget this truth, and if the world is always evil, then even in the Middle Ages 'surely Christian society was the world, and nothing short of it'.[3] To say that this system was good in the abstract Newman would concede, but in doing so he rendered the concession nugatory. Such a system was intimately bound up *ab initio* with its own corruptions—nor would it be hoped that the system could be justified as a future ideal by the consideration that it was 'no reflexion on the *bonitas*

---

[1] M. Allies, *T. W. Allies* (London, 1907), pp. 113-114. The importance of the letters in chapter 6 of this work—'*The Formation of Christendom*' and Cardinal Newman' (pp. 105-146)—has been strangely overlooked.

[2] *ibid.*, p. 111. Allies had said 'Catholic Civilisation ... was the ideal which the Church aimed at in the Middle Ages, and which she worked into the laws, manners, institutions, public policy, or public opinion of Europe.'

[3] *ibid.*, p. 113.

of the *optimum*, that *corruptio optimi est pessima*' since 'the *corruptio* is coincident, synchronous, with the introduction of the *optimum*; so that in fact the *optimum* and *pessimum* always go together'.[1]

Thus Newman came to prefer the mediocre, neutral, tolerant State, and this correspondence with Allies shows that Newman's experience of the Erastianism which he had encountered in his Anglican career had deeply affected him.

It would seem that Newman found much more to oppose in the liberal rejection of the place of religion as a social bond in the second sense which has been laid down. In this way, religion relaxed the tension between authority and the individual by making a virtue of the individual's free acceptance of just authority, and by making authority more than mere arbitrary power, subjecting it in the last resort to a higher power than itself. Religion reinforced whatever other social bonds might exist by investing them with supernatural sanctions; and without these sanctions the problem of securing submission to law and order by the masses becomes crucial. Whatever replaces religion, then, must 'substitute first of all a universal and thoroughly secular education, calculated to bring home to every individual that to be orderly, industrious, and sober is his personal interest. Then, for great working principles to take the place of religion, for the use of the masses thus carefully educated, it provides the broad fundamental ethical truths, of justice, benevolence, veracity and the like; proved experience; and those natural laws which exist and act spontaneously in society. . . .'[2]

How far this liberal attempt to replace religion might be expected to be successful can be determined by returning once more to Newman's views about the State. It has been seen that the civilised State, in its perfect idea, was the Christian State, but that, in mere matter of fact, such was never the case; that, indeed, true morality was not essential to the State, which could exist by means of a refined expediency instead. If the 'broad ethical truths' which the liberals appeal to were more than, or only

[1] *ibid.*, pp. 120, 123. [2] Ward, *Life*, ii, 461.

equivalent to, this refined expediency, it might seem that the liberal State would be able to survive. But not indefinitely. Newman shows no confidence that 'broad ethical truths' will stand unassailed without religion, and in any case, although a State may endure for some time without true morality, yet, without it, its ultimate corruption is assured. How widespread Christian morality must be to influence the national character and thus ensure that the laws of the State are kept in some relation to true morality, and that, perhaps more importantly, the laws will be obeyed on a moral principle, how far all this must be so is not discussed by Newman; but it seems safe to say that unless Christianity or religion (which are of course largely synonymous for Newman) be almost universal, the ultimate downfall of the civilised State is assured. Outside Christianity is a world of cyclic recurrence; Christianity alone has brought a deliverance from this and made a genuine progress possible, a progress which can be conserved and built upon. In short, the liberal State, in so far as it uproots religion, cannot look for a continued existence, but its duration will vary according to its success in this uprooting, and according to the strength of the influence which religion has had in moulding national character.

It must be admitted that there has recently come to light evidence which might make necessary some qualification of this assessment of Newman's position. Among the unpublished material recently found at the Birmingham Oratory there is an interesting fragment, undated, but from the writing apparently dating from Newman's middle age, which he heads, 'The influence upon morality of a decline in religious belief.'[1] From this it appears that 'the decline of religious belief might never affect the morality even of a whole class of men or of a generation; long habit, conservatism, law, respect for each other's opinion, or personal convenience and interest, supplying as regards morality the place of religion'. The whole subject is recognised as being extremely complex, 'hardly admitting of scientific treatment', but enough is advanced to make it clear that Newman did not

[1] Box 2.

regard the rejection of religion as a social bond, in this second sense, as an immediate danger of any sort to the State.

Nevertheless, Newman was highly critical of certain positive liberal attempts to replace religion as a social bond, even though it was very largely on the score of the patent inadequacy of the suggested replacements. It will help illuminate Newman's position to examine the attack he directed on what he has listed as two such liberal propositions—that 'utility and expedience are the measure of political duty', and 'that virtue is the child of knowledge and vice of ignorance'.[1]

Benthamism was the dominating influence on legislation, according to Dicey, between the years 1825 and 1870, that is, in the years of Newman's most active life; and since Benthamism involved so much that was the complete contradictory of some of his leading ideas, it is not surprising that he reacted against it strongly. But it would be a mistake to suppose that he ever subjected Benthamite liberalism, in its early or in its later forms, to any very minute analysis. He had, indeed, as a young man, been approached with a view to his making it the special task of his life to fight the influence of Benthamism, to constructing a counter-philosophy to oppose it.[2] This would have been altogether outside his own conception of the needs of the case: the opposition which Newman thought was necessary, and which he in fact supplied, was the assertion of counter-principles, which he thought as justifiable, and more true, than those principles which he accused Benthamites (and liberals in general) of so arbitrarily assuming.[3]

From the outset Newman was necessarily opposed to Benthamism, since it involved that rosy view of human nature, the imbecility of which he thought hard facts must sooner or later

---

[1] *Apo.*, pp. 500–501.   [2] *M.*, ii, 155–156.
[3] C.L., Blachford, 22 February 1877.
  Till quite late in life Newman was increasingly vexed at the manner in which J. S. Mill and others assumed, as it seemed to him, first principles from the basis of which they were very contemptuous of much religious argument. He was very pleased when the rising A. J. Balfour undertook to grapple with this sort of assumption. See C.L., Blachford, 11 December 1877.

expose. This optimism was not the prerogative of Bentham, and seems essential to any form of Utilitarianism. John Stuart Mill, for example, was convinced that a life of happiness, with only a few transitory pains, was attainable for all, with only the existing 'wretched' education and social arrangements as a real hindrance. For Bentham himself, Newman had little admiration; and though he allowed him the merit of being clear, he was repelled by a disastrous narrowness in that great legal reformer. Bentham's system had no use but for the most palpable facts, and unless they were before his nose, 'and he is very short-sighted', they were simply ignored. In any case Bentham was too reminiscent of what Newman has called 'medieval deductive rationalism', so that 'with him to speak truth is to be ready with a definition'.[1]

Although Newman does not seem to recognise Bentham's very real merits, which, in view of the wide difference in standpoint between them is not a matter for surprise, these particular criticisms by Newman are not likely to be challenged. Nor, in view of the fact that the moral basis of Utilitarianism, as expounded by Bentham and later by J. S. Mill, was defectively set out, is it worth examining the scattered contributions of Newman to a criticism of it, which in any case do not go much beyond what his great master, Butler, had taught.[2] The important question is then, as to the validity of the principle of Utility as the end of government, with which perhaps Newman would have had little quarrel as a legislative criterion, since 'the aim of civil government is the well-being of the governed, and its object is expediency'.[3] But the well-being of the governed represented a wider idea than that of Utility for Newman, for Utility meant for him a well-being of a narrow materialistic kind, as when, in a sermon, he preaches against those who say 'that utility and expedience, or,

[1] *D.A.*, p. 269.
[2] Newman thought he went somewhat beyond Butler in one particular, see *M.*, i, 256–257. Newman deals with these questions in the sermon 'Justice, As a Principle of Divine Government', *U.S.*, pp. 99–119; and in *P.S.*, ii, 52–57; elsewhere can be found mainly only isolated remarks.
[3] *Ess.*, i, 29.

in other words, whatever tends to produce wealth, is the only rule on which laws should be framed'.¹ 'Expedience', as often used by Newman, is closely associated, if not synonymous, with Utility, and in this connexion it refers to the waiving aside of true morality to ensure temporal prosperity—so that that object is expedient which most conduces to the attainment of Utility. But expedience is not always seen by Newman in the unfavourable light with which its connexion with Utility has flooded it, and he elsewhere uses the term with no suspicion of disapprobation as referring to that which conduces to the well-being of a particular society, irrespective of the particular aim of the society, and even though the rules of an abstract justice might be ignored thereby.² This brings the discussion back to the question of justice in the State already examined. It is possible to say that in so far as expediency was unconnected with Utilitarianism, Newman was not prepared to denounce it, but the expedience of the Utilitarian was denounced because it was the Utilitarianism itself which was a false and pernicious theory.

However, Utility, even in the grossly materialistic sense, was not an immediately impossible principle in the life of the State—'Let Benthamism reign, if men have no aspirations'³—but it was an ultimately destructive principle, since it meant that 'the common bond of unity in the State consists in nothing really common, but simply in the unanimous wish of each member of it to secure his own interests'. Newman ignores the attempt to work the Utilitarian miracle, the transformation of egoism into altruism. The State, in fact, is doomed, 'but like some old arch, which, when its supports are crumbled away, stands by the force of cohesion, no one knows how'.⁴ Thus, when Newman rejects the rule of Utility for the rule of duty in a famous passage of his *Letter to the Duke of Norfolk*, he means that, whatever the role of religion as a bond of society, the pursuit of a utilitarian happiness cannot provide one, nor show the way to one, such

---

[1] *S.D.*, p. 86.   [2] *V.M.*, i, p. xli. See also *H.S.*, i, pp. xii, 156, 258.
[3] *D.A.*, p. 292. See also *Dev.*, p. 188.
[4] Newman is not speaking here of Benthamism in particular, but it seems reasonable to apply his words in this way.

as the pursuit of knowledge was at that time sometimes claimed to be.

> People say to me [said Newman] that it is but a dream to suppose that Christianity should regain the organic power in human society which once it possessed. I cannot help that; I never said it could. I am not a politician; I am proposing no measures, but exposing a fallacy and resisting a pretence. Let Benthamism reign, if men have no aspirations; but do not tell them to be romantic, and then solace them with glory; do not attempt by philosophy what once was done by religion. The ascendancy of Faith may be impracticable, but the reign of Knowledge is incomprehensible. The problem for statesmen of this age is how to educate the masses, and literature and science cannot give the solution.[1]

The attempt to make Knowledge a principle of social unity Newman associated largely with Brougham. However, it was a remark of Sir Robert Peel's, that Knowledge was 'binding men together by a *new* bond',[2] on which Newman fastened, taking it as an uncritical acceptance of Brougham's ideas, the significance of which Peel possibly failed to see. Of course the liberal principle that 'virtue is the child of knowledge, and vice of ignorance' was implicit in Benthamism. For Bentham 'the knowledge which carries virtue along with it, is the knowledge how to take care of number one—a clear appreciation of what is pleasurable, what painful, and what promotes the one and prevents the other;'[3] but as Newman goes on to explain, it would be a great injustice to Brougham and Peel to suppose that when they spoke of Knowledge being Virtue, they were Benthamising. However, Newman had little difficulty in showing that the fine oratory about the beauty of Knowledge in which they indulged was little more than empty words; that Knowledge can neither be the means nor the antecedent of moral improvement in the individual; ('Can the process be analysed and drawn out, or does it act like a dose or a charm which comes into use empirically?' he asks); that to bring men together in a reading room will not necessarily conduce to bringing them together in any more important social

[1] *D.A.*, p. 292.   [2] *ibid.*, p. 285.   [3] *ibid.*, p. 262.

sense; that to teach 'that grief, anger, cowardice, self-conceit, pride, or passion, can be subdued by an examination of shells or grasses, or inhaling of gases, or chipping of rocks, or calculating the longitude, is the veriest of pretences which sophist or mountebank ever professed to a gaping auditory'.[1]

'Broughamism', then, was a shallow impostor—'Such is this new art of living, offered to the labouring classes—we will say, for instance, in a severe winter, snow on the ground, glass falling, bread rising, coal at 20d. the cwt., and no work.'[2] In the last resort it was the offering of ' "charms and temptations" to allure them from sensuality and riot'; it was the attempt to provide a civilising function which religion could more satisfactorily provide. Yet though religion could provide this, it could only do so as a secondary and almost incidental task. If religion were to be regarded primarily as a device for the stability of the State, or the improvement of social life, Newman would be able to see little difference between this and liberalism.[3]

This is the clue to the understanding of Newman's attitude to Arnold, whom it would be difficult at first sight to see as a liberal on Newman's definitions, and yet who was the very personification of liberalism for him. The liberal rejected religion as a bond of society, but Arnold seemed to make religion the most important social bond in his ideal State. But the genuine liberal wanted to reject, as a social bond, religion as it has been known, and to replace it with broad ethical truths. This implied for most liberals the rejection of the Church, while Arnold, in Newman's eyes, wanted to make the Church the very mouthpiece of these ethical truths. Thus for Arnold, as it has already been seen, the organisation of the Church was only of value in so far as it succeeded so well in its task of making men good members of society that it deprived itself of its own *raison d'être*, and began to wither away.

If Arnold is to be considered a liberal for Newman, then, it is because he was in the first place a religious liberal in his rejection of dogma, and this led him to a political liberalism which held

[1] *ibid.*, p. 268.   [2] *ibid.*   [3] cf. 'Liberalism', *V.V.*, p. 122.

that religion, a supernatural and dogmatic religion such as has been known in the Christian world, is in no sense the bond of society.

But however Arnold's position fits the precise definition of liberalism made by Newman, he did not lack any of that spirit of liberalism, any of that facile optimism which Newman thought generally lay behind it. For Arnold 'all the world is by the very law of its creation in eternal progress';[1] thus his 'abhorrence of Conservatism [was] not because it checks liberty . . . but because it checks the growth of mankind in wisdom, goodness, and happiness';[2] this was why Conservatism was always wrong, 'so thoroughly wrong in principle that even when the particular reform proposed may be by no means the best possible, yet it is good as a triumph over Conservatism';[3] this was the spirit in which he could say of the bringing of the Birmingham railway to Rugby, 'I rejoice to see it, and think that feudality is gone for ever. It is so great a blessing to think that any one evil is really extinct.'[4]

It is difficult to imagine a greater contrast than that between Newman and Arnold—between Newman's dogmatic religion and Arnold's belief that his own liberal principles were, in perfect development, identical with Christianity itself; between the lover of chivalry and tradition, and the man who thought these things literally anti-Christian. Even when both were in agreement on any point, very different conclusions were the result. Thus both were of the opinion that the origin of many States lay in injustice. This meant for Newman that so, to some extent, they would always remain, and it has been seen how far he was tolerant of this injustice. Arnold, however, drew the conclusion that since the origin of most States was in injustice, the

---

[1] Stanley, *op. cit.*, i, 250.

[2] *ibid.*, p. 385. Cf. *ibid.*, p. 316, 'the wickedness of Toryism—of that spirit which has throughout the long experience of all history continually thwarted the cause of God and goodness'.

[3] *ibid.*, ii, 19. It is fair to say that Arnold could display a balanced and intelligent criticism of Conservatives and conservatism, as in *Letters to the 'Sheffield Courant', on the Social Distress of the Lower Orders* (1831–1832).

[4] Stanley, *op. cit.*, ii, 388.

presumption should always be in favour of change.¹ Again, Arnold shared Newman's dislike and distrust of continental liberals, who seemed sadly lacking in that high-mindedness of which he himself was the type—they seemed to him hardly worthy of the title 'liberal'—but their existence was after all historically inevitable; they were the outcome of 'Newmanism'; they were the other side of the coin.² For Arnold then, Newman is very much to be identified with the old order of things which the liberals were attacking; but this was not quite true in 1840, and twenty years later it was very far from being so. There is a great gulf between the Newman of 1829 who was alarmed at the prospect of the disestablishment of the English Church, and Newman of the correspondence with Allies in 1860. Yet any change which occurred in Newman's political attitude was a legitimate development from views which he had held from a very early period.

It should now be clear what Newman meant by liberalism, and why he opposed it. This interpretation of Newman's thought is not one which many have reached, but until now it does not seem that a serious attempt to understand it, making use of all the available material, has been made. But from the published material alone it is possible to grasp Newman's position. One reason why there has been confusion on this subject is that, on Newman's definitions, it may be very difficult to decide in any concrete situation who can actually be designated as a liberal. Thus Newman remarks to one of his numerous correspondents, 'you would call Gladstone a liberal, I, an anti-liberal'.³ The genuine liberal, starting from his anti-dogmatic principle, would be led to an attack on the presence of traditional religion in the political framework of the nation, but in any given political dispute arising out of this a dogmatist like Gladstone or Newman might

¹ Arnold, *The Christian Duty of Granting the Claims of the Roman Catholics* (Oxford, 1829), p. 9.
² Stanley, *op. cit.* (9th ed., London, 1868), ii, 374. (Letter of 23.7.40) 'for Newmanism leads to Socialism, and Socialism leads to Newmanism—the eternal oscillations of the drunken mime—the varying vices and vilenesses of the slave, and the slave broken loose'. By Socialism Arnold seems to mean here a revolutionary liberalism.
³ C.L., Clarke, 20 December 1868.

side with these genuine liberals. This was the point in the letter just quoted, since Newman was defending himself from the charge of liberalism which his correspondent had levelled at him on account of his agreement with a particular concrete liberal aim. But although in some cases an anti-liberal might have the same concrete political policy, Newman recognised a tendency for liberalism to go beyond an attack on any form of political institutionalising of religion, to a general attack on the social manifestation of religion in any form. Thus 'the effect . . . of the Liberal party all through Europe is to put down a clerical order as such'.[1]

Any doubt about what Newman meant by liberalism might have been avoided had Newman ever undertaken an extended discussion on the whole subject, but he did not set out systematically very much of his political thought. It is true that Newman entitles an Appendix to the *Apologia* 'Liberalism', but while these few pages are of unique importance here, it should be realised that they do not so much give a profound analysis of the concept of liberalism as an historical sketch of the liberalism at Oxford with which the Tractarian movement had grappled. It would be a mistake to rely on this Appendix alone for an understanding of Newman's true position, and indeed he explicitly pointed this out to his friend, R. H. Hutton.[2] It is not necessary, then, to examine separately and in detail the list of eighteen liberal propositions which Newman indicates as those most abhorrent to himself and his associates at that time. Those propositions which have any direct bearing on the subject of this book are dealt with in it in one form or another.[3] But it is now time to move away from explanations of what liberalism was, and why it was opposed, to certain more concrete considerations. It should be possible now to complete this whole account of liberalism, and at the same time resolve any remaining problems about the

---

[1] C.L., Blachford, 25 October 1874.   [2] C.L., Hutton, 3 June 1865.
[3] The eleventh proposition, that 'there is no such thing as a national or State conscience' is not elsewhere discussed. Newman's hostility to the proposition is best seen in an interesting sermon, 'On Our National Sins', preached in 1832 (Box 4. Oratory MSS.). It can be inferred that he lost much of this hostility. See P.C., Monsell, 27 January 1868.

extent of Newman's Toryism and conservatism, and this can best be done by reviewing briefly how far in practice Newman opposed the liberalism which he encountered.

2. HOW LIBERAL WAS NEWMAN?

It will be remembered that within a few years of his arrival in Oxford, Newman found himself 'drifting in the direction of the liberalism of the day',[1] but this is not necessarily in contradiction to the statement that from his arrival at Oxford he was led by his innate conservatism to imbibe the prevalent Toryism at Oxford. Newman specifically mentions in what way he was becoming liberal, by explaining that he was beginning to prefer intellectual excellence to moral. This was liberalism, which 'consists in looking at all conclusions ["in religion" inserted here in a later hand] in proportion to the strength of their premisses (*vid.* Locke) or resolving all beliefs into opinions. For this purpose it denies that a certain moral state of mind is necessary out of which the perception of first principles in religion comes to life and exercise.'[2]

It has been seen how religious liberalism of this type is connected with a form of political liberalism, but there is nothing to indicate that Newman was showing any signs of developing this incipient liberalism into the political variety.

The Tories at Oxford supported the Established Church, and so did Newman. As late as 1836 he could speak feelingly of 'the *duty* of a Christian Government' to uphold the Church,[3] though as early as 1833 it had first broken on him, 'that the Church is essentially a popular institution, and the past English union of it with the State has been a happy anomaly'.[4] By the last years of his stay in the Anglican Church, Newman had allowed the idea which had struck him in 1833 to oust the one expressed still in 1836. But even so Newman still purported to attack liberalism all the while he was at Oxford, and indeed long after. The liberalism

[1] *Apo.*, p. 116.
[2] C.C., A.463, p. 89.
[3] P.C., Rose, 20 May 1836.
[4] *M.*, i, 458. See also pp. 450, 454.

which he attacked so bitterly in the early years of the Oxford Movement after 1833 was in the first place liberalism in the sphere of religious doctrine. Outside this sphere, Newman attacked political liberalism, at least in his sense of the term. He certainly did not attack political liberalism of every and any sort. If by this term were meant for instance, a particular doctrine about the limits of State action and the role of individual freedoms, then it would not be possible to see Newman as an anti-liberal. The actual Liberal politicians whom Newman opposed so violently were seen and singled out for abuse inasmuch as they were the embodiment of a political liberalism in his broadest meaning of the term.

The difference in Newman's attitude to the Reform Bill of 1832 and the Irish Church Reform Bill of 1833 is instructive here. Tom Mozley tells us that Newman showed no hostility to what became the 1832 Act until the Reformed Parliament began to show its animus against the Church.[1] As the great majority of Bishops had voted against the Bill on its first appearance it might be thought that the Church had first shown its animus against Reform, and it must also be admitted that Mozley's memory was at fault in finding no evidence for Newman's hostility to Reform in 1832. Yet what Mozley says is very near the truth. The full account of Newman's attitude to the democracy to which he thought the Act of 1832 the first step will be given in the final chapter, but it is fair to identify him very closely with his friend Hurrell Froude, who 'was disgusted with the Toryism of the opponents of the Reform Bill', and who said in 1832, 'If it was not for a personal hatred of the Whigs I should care comparatively little for the Reform Bill.'[2] If Newman was worried about it, it was because he feared that the forces which carried it would make short work with orthodoxy. There is no doubt about the violence of Newman's opposition to the Irish Church Reform Bill of 1833, and here, as with Catholic Emancipation which he at once approved and condemned, it was mainly

---

[1] Mozley, *Reminiscences of Oriel* (2nd ed., London, 1882), i, 253.
[2] *Apo.*, p. 126; Froude, *Remains*, i, 250.

Liberalism

the motives and spirit which lay behind them which were for him so characteristically liberal. In 1868, after nearly a quarter of a century as a Catholic, Newman could not envisage the disestablishment of the Irish Church with enthusiasm, and for the same reasons. 'Changes, awful for their greatness, are coming on', he wrote. 'Perhaps they won't come in our time, for I am old enough to remember how much evil was expected from the first Reform Act, which did not come to pass. But, whether the evil comes sooner or later, it will come; and though as an act of justice, I can but rejoice that the Irish establishment is going, yet I am not sure that it will be on the whole a gain to the Catholic cause.'[1] This shows clearly that Newman can criticise liberalism, when thinking of its spirit and motives, while at the same time approving of its particular concrete results.

Now from his correspondence with Gladstone it is clear that Newman had by 1844 quite explicitly rejected his earlier belief in the duty of the State to uphold the Church, while from his correspondence with Allies it can be seen that by 1860 he not only recognised and allowed, but positively welcomed the new relationship of Church and State which his age had seen. There is nothing in the recital of these facts which can make it difficult to understand Newman's attitude to liberalism before his break with the Anglican Church in 1845. It is not so easy to fit into place all that he says as a Catholic on this subject. The difficulty is obvious. In one of his most well-known writings, *Letter to the Duke of Norfolk*, Newman defends the very Pope who went out of his way to condemn the secular, neutral, tolerant State of Newman's ideal. How can one explain the apologist of Papal Infallibility, the passing of which in 1870 was the death blow of that Liberal Catholic movement with which the same apologist must necessarily have been in great sympathy? It is necessary to probe this question a little further.

The decree of Papal Infallibility has little direct relation to politics, since the political implications of a change from the

[1] C.L., Bowles, Easter Monday, 1868. This copied letter includes an additional 'not' between 'will' and 'be' in the last sentence, presumably a mistake of the copyist as it alters the plain sense of the passage.

infallibility of the Church to that of the Pope are of minor importance. As far as the State is concerned, with its claim to sovereignty, it can make little difference whether a Pope or a Church introduces a divided allegiance into its dominions. It will be seen how effectively Newman demonstrated this to Gladstone. Yet the Infallibility Decree has an undoubted political significance, since it was carried at last after a struggle which caused bitter divisions in the Catholic Church, and these divisions in a great many cases were political in origin. The Church was apparently split, for the middle decades of the nineteenth century, into two warring factions—Liberal Catholics and Ultramontanes—and it would be difficult to say in which group the political element was more predominant.

Newman was born in 1801, the year which for some marks the commencement of the movement of events here in question, with the publication of Chateaubriand's romance *Atala*. It must be said that the Catholic revival of the nineteenth century was something wider than the Ultramontanism which accompanied it: this Ultramontanism was eminently political. Yet even this new political Ultramontanism, which replaced that of Fénelon and an earlier age, was always something more than a political creed in its stress on the infallibility and prerogatives of the Roman See. It was a new Ultramontanism, because the French Revolution had altered the whole context of many problems. And so while in France the Church, suffering from the past closing of its theological seminaries, was still fighting the ghost of Jansenism, still studying Church and State relations in the old Gallican context, there arose several great lay writers, and not only in France, who thought that a revived Ultramontanism could supply the wants of the age. The stability of the Church amidst the cataclysmic changes of the Revolution impressed these writers, and Catholicism, invigorated by their formulation of Ultramontanism, was to be the stable basis of future social order. Ultramontanism was widely received among Catholics everywhere, whose indignation at Pius VII's treatment at the hands of Napoleon reinforced the growing dissatisfaction with the old

Gallicanism, Josephism, Febronianism and Cisalpinism, so that Ultramontanism came as a breath of fresh air in a stuffy world. Again, whether its exponents were aware of it or not, the growth of nationalities had rendered the old state of affairs impossible if Rome were to continue as a Universal Church.

But Ultramontanism was never a single, united movement (nor is the term 'Ultramontane' always very informative when it can apply as much to Joseph Görres, the champion of liberty and nationality against absolutism, as to Joseph de Maistre, the very champion of absolutism). Ultramontanism was soon divided in France itself, and the name of Lamennais is for ever associated with the Liberal Catholic movement which can be said to have begun with the publication of *L'Avenir* in 1830.

The origins of Liberal Catholicism must be sought in the development of Lamennais's political views, but it seems a fair generalisation to say that Liberal Catholicism was only to become a force, and make a division in the Catholic body, because there was at the bottom a division already. There was a real difference between those who were prepared to inherit, and make the best of the Revolution, and those who reacted against it so strongly that they were blind to any genuine values it may have involved. This is not to say that de Maistre and Bonald, for instance, were simple reactionaries, who thought the past could be wiped clear and the old order restored; but they were far from the position of a Lacordaire. Lacordaire is perhaps the classic example of the Liberal Catholic, since his Catholicism was unquestioned, and his liberalism was the typically French, constitutional liberalism of his non-Catholic days.[1] Yet it was Lamennais who was nevertheless the leader of the Liberal Catholic movement in France which was brought to a sudden check by the encyclical *Mirari Vos* in 1834. If some of the more individual doctrines of Lamennais were not bequeathed to the remnant of his supporters, still his famous words, '*quand les Catholiques aussi crieront liberté bien des choses changeront*', were not forgotten. Montalembert and Lacordaire

---

[1] Montalembert, *Memoir of Abbé Lacordaire* (London, 1863), p. 20. Ward, *W. G. Ward and the Catholic Revival*, p. 106.

were not so committed to the fallen Lamennais that they could not later take up the cry.

The division among Catholics with regard to their attitude to the world which had been ushered in in 1789 could be seen clearly in the bitter arguments in France over the Falloux education law. This controversy pointed to a basic antagonism between, on the one hand, such men as Foisset and Montalembert in their attempt to baptise the principles of 1789, and on the other of Veuillot and his group, in their effort to withdraw Catholics from the world those principles had made into a compact, self-regarding and intransigeant body. The battle between the fanatical Ultramontanism of Veuillot in the *Univers* and the Liberal Catholics of the *Correspondant* was a feature of the years after the Revolution of 1848.

The Liberal Catholic movement was not only political in its aims, but had inherited that desire for intellectual reawakening which had been a feature of the early Ultramontanism of the century. These two aspects of Liberal Catholicism are visible in the year 1863, which was in some ways the high-water mark of the movement, when both were represented by the Malines and the Munich Congresses of that year. Now it was at the Malines Congress that Montalembert made his two famous speeches—on 'A Free Church in a Free State' (Cavour's formula of a few years before), and 'Liberty of Conscience'. These titles give the clue to the connexion of Liberal Catholicism with the liberalism which Newman speaks of. It was not the same as this liberalism, for it recognised the importance of a dogmatic religion, but it rejected religion as a bond of society in the sense of a legal or social establishment of it. Newman is here obviously at one with the Liberal Catholics in the desire for the free, secular State, though his connexion with them will soon be more closely examined.

The sequel to 1863 is well known. The *Syllabus* of 1864 was a blow for Montalembert and a triumph for Veuillot, however the document is properly to be understood. The Vatican Council in 1870 settled the struggle which had gone on over Infallibility by deciding for the Pope and the Ultramontanes, and against the

Inopportunists and Liberal Catholics. Of course many of the Liberal Catholics were Ultramontanes in the earlier sense of the term, even though they failed to go to the lengths of Veuillot in exalting the Pope's temporal and spiritual prerogatives. As a result, the Vatican Decrees are not in themselves a victory for Ultramontanism, as will be seen in the case of Newman in particular, yet undoubtedly the definition, when it came, was a mortal blow to Liberal Catholicism.

Now it is true that in the *Letter to the Duke of Norfolk* Newman gives what may be called a defence of the Infallibility decree, yet it is far from true to say that he ever had any sympathy with the Ultramontanism of Veuillot or W. G. Ward. His sympathies lay in quite the opposite direction. Döllinger he admired: in 1879 he had hoped that his own Cardinalate, giving as it were an imprimatur to views which were similar in both himself and Döllinger, would enable him to bring that great historian back to the Church. Veuillot he hated: in a celebrated letter Newman coupled the name of Veuillot with one Murphy, who was causing riots in England at that time by his No-Popery activities, which included hawking round prurient tracts on the Confessional.[1] Newman 'sympathised warmly with the general policy and sentiments of Lacordaire, and Montalembert, and still more of Dupanloup'.[2]

Neither can it be said that Newman can be identified with the older Ultramontanism of de Maistre. Newman rarely notices the work of that great papal champion, and there is little evidence that he had any but the most cursory knowledge about him. Nor should the similarity which may be detected in the general sense of the value of tradition felt by both Newman and Bonald be taken to imply any acquaintance with Bonald's work on his part, nor any but a superficial resemblance on their political standpoints.

If Newman's connexion with the political side of the revived

[1] Butler, *Life of Ullathorne* (London, 1926), ii, 58. When Veuillot became aware of Newman's opposition to him he began to make unpleasant suggestions about Newman's use of money collected by Veuillot and his paper for Newman's expenses in the Achilli Trial.   [2] Ward, *W. G. Ward and the Catholic Revival*, p. 194.

Catholicism of the Continent be sought, it is necessary to return to Lacordaire and Montalembert. Newman thought Lacordaire inconsistent in calling himself a 'Liberal', not in actually holding the views that he did, and it is obvious that this follows from the definition which it has been seen that Newman laid down.[1] As for Montalembert, Newman's approval of his views extended to the very speeches at Malines which had been the target of much Ultramontane abuse—'The word "democracy" was the only word which appeared to me unnecessary,' he wrote at the time.[2]

But a closer examination of Newman's relation to Liberal Catholicism abroad can be dispensed with, since he was much more intimately connected with a form of Liberal Catholicism at home. Perhaps many have been inclined to under-emphasise the extent of Newman's Liberal Catholicism here, to avoid creating the false impression that he was in some way implicated in, or in general sympathy with, the Modernist movement which was a source of alarm in the Church shortly after the turn of the century. Yet Newman was undoubtedly on the Liberal Catholic side on the questions which divided the Catholic body in England in his day.[3] As in France the education question was an issue which caused much bitterness, and as in France, two sides represented two attitudes to Catholic participation in the secular world. Newman chose the side which Montalembert had chosen. The differences between Newman and Manning stemmed largely from their opposite attitudes on the question of secular education, and it was not unconnected with this question that Newman increased the suspicion which his Liberal Catholicism had brought against him, with his *Rambler* article, 'On Consulting the Faithful in Matters of Doctrine'.[4] He was far in advance of his time in his

---

[1] *Apo.*, p. 492. Newman is in no way making any accusation against Lacordaire, but, while explicitly recognising that 'liberalism' is a term which can differ greatly in its meaning he yet keeps hold of his own definition in this discussion.

[2] P.C., Monsell, 8 October 1863. Quoted in Tristram, 'Newman and Montalembert', *Dublin Review*, vol. 222 (1949).

[3] Wilfrid Ward gives an account of some of these questions, and Newman's 'liberal' position with regard to them, in 'Newman and Liberal Catholicism', *W. G. Ward and the Catholic Revival*.

[4] (1859), pp. 198–230. Cf. Butler, *Ullathorne*, i, 309.

stress on the role of the laity in the Church. But his very connexion with the *Rambler* was a source of offence to many, and a sufficient badge of his Liberal Catholicism. It is not the case, however, that Newman could ever be completely identified with the views of Acton and Simpson, after Acton bought the *Rambler* in 1858. He regretted the annoyance the *Rambler* caused, the full extent of which can only be fully appreciated when the different elements which went to make up the rapidly reviving Catholic Church in this country are considered. Yet Newman felt as keenly as Acton and Simpson the need for a Catholic intellectual reawakening, nor did he object to the *Rambler*'s occupying itself with political matters—it was precisely politics on which he wanted the paper to concentrate. The fatal objection to the *Rambler* for Newman was its tone. It would not keep away from theology, and in any case failed to treat it in a careful enough manner. It laid itself open to an ecclesiastical censure which was not long in coming from ecclesiastics smarting from the attacks of the laymen of the *Rambler*.[1]

But if it is asserted that Newman was in almost full sympathy with the Liberal Catholicism of Acton's *Rambler*, it must be admitted that Acton thought there was a difference of opinion between Newman and himself on some important contemporary political questions.[2] He thought the differences were to be seen by a comparison between the two numbers of the *Rambler* which Newman edited in 1859, and those which followed his resignation of the editorship. It is not easy to trace fully the divergence of views on current politics between them, though it is clear that Newman was more friendly to Louis Napoleon and more hostile to Austria than was Acton.[3] Whatever the differences, in some ways Acton was not liberal enough for Newman, who

[1] D. Woodruff has pointed out that Acton's colleagues on the *Rambler* were convert clergymen, more convinced of the rights of the Church than the authority of the English hierarchy. *Acton on Church and State* (London, 1952), p. 5. The whole story of Newman's connexion with the *Rambler* has been told by Ward (*Life*, i, pp. xvi, xvii, xviii), and leaves little that could be added to this question.
[2] Gasquet, *Lord Acton and his Circle*, pp. 88, 162.
[3] For Newman's views see *Rambler* (May 1859), 'Prospects of War', pp. 109–114; (July 1859), 'Napoleonism not Impious', pp. 378–379. cf. Gasquet, *Lord Acton*, pp. 81, 162.

complained in 1860 of 'the foreign Toryism and the English anti-Toryism of the *Rambler*'.[1]

There was indeed a fundamental political difference between Acton and Newman, which goes to the roots of Newman's whole attitude on liberalism. It was not that both did not salute the primacy of conscience, though this led Newman more to considerations about the impossibility of absolute sovereignty than to assertions about an abstract liberty. It was that Acton failed to see the depth of Newman's political ideas, and mistook Newman's realism, his desire to see things as they really were, for a denial of the need for morality in politics.[2] Newman, as a professed ignoramus on political matters, was more prepared than the learned Acton to avoid abstract moral judgements in politics. It was Acton who put his finger on the difference between them, when (though not thinking of Newman at the time) he says that Augustinianism, a strong view of the corruption caused by original sin, is an impediment to his notion of conscience.[3] The Augustinianism of Newman meant that Newman was far from Acton's liberalism, though it was this very strong view of the World's evil which was responsible for bringing Newman to a liberalism of a kind. Newman's Liberal Catholicism was very individual; but that he went further than a desire for intellectual reawakening among Catholics, that he looked forward to the tolerant, secular State, without misgivings or regret, except about some of the motives which had helped to make it inevitable, is certain.

But if Newman was brought to a form of liberalism by what has been broadly called Augustinianism, it is noteworthy that this liberalism was also confirmed by the fact noted in the first chapter —that the parallel between Newman's Church and the World

---

[1] Ward, *Life*, i, 637.
[2] *Letters of Lord Acton to M. Gladstone* (ed. H. Paul, London, 1913), p. 181. Acton's appreciation of Newman's position with regard to Irish Disestablishment is not very great, and his account of a passage in Coleridge's *Memoir of Keble* (2nd ed., London, 1869), ii, 529, misleading. In any case Acton, especially with his peculiar background, was altogether unable to understand someone like Newman. See here D. Mathew, *Acton: The Formative Years* (London, 1946), pp. 114–122.
[3] G. E. Fasnacht, *Acton's Political Philosophy* (London, 1952), p. 187.

Liberalism

and the two cities of St. Augustine is not exact. Had Newman thought in terms of the Church as the Kingdom of God, and of an evil World outside and separate from it, then it is much more likely that he would have been on the reactionary flank of the Catholics of his day. It might then have seemed possible for him to hope to withdraw the Church from a wicked world, as the party represented by Veuillot and the *Univers* desired. This was contrary to the way in which Newman thought. The Church was in the World and not separate from it, as he so often stressed, and the idea of a withdrawal was unrealistic. Thus Newman could not simply turn his back on the society in which the Church was now placed, but had actively to face the situation and to come to terms with it.

This was far from the attitude of many in the Church of Newman's adoption, and his position in it was accordingly uncomfortable. In any case, sympathy with 'the founder of the modern Papacy', the beloved Pio Nono, in his political misfortunes, was great among Catholics, and indeed Newman himself had no small share in it.[1] The result was that there was little disposition to listen calmly to any attempt to limit the wide spiritual and temporal prerogatives claimed for the Pope by enthusiastic neo-Ultramontanes. Inasmuch as Newman was opposed to the agitation for the declaration of Papal Infallibility he incurred the same displeasure as that shown towards other Liberal Catholics.

But Newman's situation was always more complex than that of most Liberal Catholics at this time, and he cannot be regarded as being in complete sympathy with them. In the first place, he reserved most of his opposition to the Ultramontane group for his private letters, though, as with that letter which referred to these men as 'an aggressive and insolent faction',[2] his views often

[1] See 'The Pope and the Revolution', O.S.

[2] Ward, *Life*, ii, 288. Newman also kept for his private letters such reflexions as, 'Will not the next century demand Popes who are not Italians?' P.C., Monsell, 5 February 1865; and that 'the Jesuits (if I may use an undignified metaphor) tend to swamp the Church', that, 'with most other thinking men, I dread their unmitigated action on the Church'. S.S., Vatican Council, to Coleridge, 29 April 1869. This last letter was, in the end, not even sent.

became public. But in any case, Newman felt that the Liberal Catholics in England did not fully appreciate the actual difficulties in which the Church was placed, making it almost inevitable that its action in intellectual and political affairs would be widely misunderstood. In the preface to the third edition of the *Via Media* Newman stresses the implications of the fact that Christianity is at once a theological system, a religious rite and a political rule. 'Truth is the guiding policy of theology and theological inquiries; devotion and edification, of worship; and of government, expedience . . .' and he asks, 'What line of conduct, except on the long, the very long run, is at once edifying, expedient and true?'[1] From such considerations Newman was much more patient of the fact that the Church seemed to lag behind the political and intellectual advance which the century had witnessed. But it is now possible profitably to examine the defence Newman made of the instrument which was used against the Liberal Catholicism which he to some extent shared.

Although the *Syllabus of Modern Errors* and the encyclical *Quanta Cura* were more directly political, it is Papal Infallibility, because of its incontrovertible dogmatic status, which is usually regarded as the death blow of the Liberal Catholic movement. Now Newman it is clear enough, was an Inopportunist, although he accepted in advance the Papal Infallibility which was defined in 1870.[2] But it is also true that he was afraid of the far-reaching claims of a Veuillot or W. G. Ward, the latter of whom is credited with the humorous remark that he would like a new Papal Bull every morning with his *Times* at breakfast.[3] Newman feared, and what he feared came to pass, that if any definition at all were made, the fact of its being made would be rightly interpreted as a victory for the Veuillot school, but it would be wrongly believed

---

[1] *V.M.*, i, pp. xli–xlii.

[2] Ward, *Life*, ii, 310. Newman's views have often been misrepresented on this. An example is the recent publication of Salmon's *Infallibility of the Church* (ed. Woodhouse, London, 1952), which ignored evidence on this point easily ascertainable at the time it was written. Newman is adequately defended by B. C. Butler in *Church and Infallibility* (London, 1954), *passim*.

[3] Ward, *W. G. Ward and the Catholic Revival*, p. 14.

that the definition itself was in its terms in substance what Veuillot had wanted. This mistake was widely made at the time and is still made, though B. C. Butler's great work, *The Vatican Council*,[1] has had its effect in recent years in taking the whole Vatican Council history out of the realms of drama, if not melodrama, into more sober fields.

Newman's defence of the decree of 1870 was made in his *Letter to the Duke of Norfolk*, about which Professor Laski said that 'it is more than a piece of ephemeral argument. It remains with some remarks of Sir Henry Maine and a few brilliant dicta of F. W. Maitland as perhaps the profoundest discussion of sovereignty in the English language.'[2] The primary object of the work was to demonstrate that Gladstone had been unreasonable in questioning the political reliability of Catholics on the grounds that Papal Infallibility introduced a divided allegiance among them. Now Newman had little difficulty in showing that Gladstone was unreasonable here, that in the last resort Gladstone was demanding an impossible sovereignty of the State, while Newman stressed that he could give an absolute obedience neither to Pope nor Queen. Thus as already seen, he would 'drink—to the Pope, if you please—still, to Conscience first, and the Pope afterwards'. But the difficulty which must be faced does not lie in the question of sovereignty, but in the fact that the declaration of Infallibility may seem, as it seemed to Gladstone, to set the seal of authoritativeness on those very ideas which it has been claimed Newman had forsaken—yet Newman seems to defend the Decree which accomplishes this.

Now Newman admitted that the declaration of Infallibility was a victory for the centralising party in the Church, but he was far from admitting that this victory could in any way transform *Quanta Cura* and the *Syllabus* into part of the dogma of the Church. In any case, the 'modern civilisation' against which Pius IX had set his face was not something which could call for unqualified acceptance by all, as Newman, whose friend was shot

---

[1] London, 1930.
[2] *Problem of Sovereignty*, p. 202.

dead by the Liberals in Rome in 1848,[1] well knew. Perhaps there was more to condemn in that 'modern civilisation' than either Gladstone or Newman were aware in the middle of the nineteenth century. Newman insisted that, whatever the animus of the Pope, the Encyclical and the *Syllabus* were technical documents, not at all on a level with the uninstructed opinion of the chance newspaper reader, that they needed an understanding of the received rules of interpretation of such documents, which theologians alone generally possessed. Hence Newman claimed, what Manning and Ward in effect denied, that 'None but the *Schola Theologorum* is competent to determine the force of Papal and Synodal utterances, and the exact interpretation of them is a work of time.'[2] It is no recent English discovery that a word like 'liberty' is meaningless unless something is known about the way the word is being used. Thus Newman points out that to see the exact nature of the 'errors' which the *Syllabus* condemned, it was necessary to go from this index to the context in which the words occurred.[3] It is amusing that even today this obvious and necessary step is often missed.

As far as Gladstone's interpretation of the meaning and consequences of the Vatican Decrees was concerned, Newman had no difficulty in showing how ill-founded it was. In reality it was a grotesque absurdity that a statesman, whose country was gagging the Press in Ireland on the ground of its being seditious, should take the Pope to task for entering a decisive negative against the proposition that—'It is the liberty of *every* one to give public utterance, in *every* possible shape, by *every* possible channel, without any let or hindrance from God or man, to *all* his notions whatsoever.'[4]

---
[1] Ward, *Life*, i, 194. From the first Newman thought Pius duped by the Liberals (*ibid.*). A new assessment of the case for Pius is to be found in E. Y. Y. Hales's recent *Pio Nono* (London, 1954). This redresses the balance of opinion which has been reflected in the standard works of Nielsen and Bury on this period. [2] *Diff.*, ii, 176. [3] *ibid.*, p. 251.
[4] Newman argues that even in England such arguments are not unheard of—'are not the doctrines of even so grave and patient a thinker as the late J. S. Mill very much in that direction?' (*ibid.*, p. 363). Thus even 'the most revolting atrocities of heathen times and countries must for conscience sake be allowed free exercise in our great cities'. Though Mill 'had too much English common sense to carry out his principles to these legitimate but extreme conclusions' (*ibid.*, p. 364).

Liberalism

Yet despite all this, the difficulty still remains. The Infallibility Decree was passed in opposition to Newman and the Liberal Catholics, and if it did not increase it could not but underline the importance of obedience due to the Pope in particular commands, which were not infallible, and the general duty of 'thinking with the Pope'. Newman could not deny that the Pope was animated by a desire to keep as long as possible to the old world, and to hinder the growth of the modern secular State. He pointed out that even in his own lifetime the old idea of a Christian Polity had been still in force, and the Church of England established to the disadvantage of other religions. 'All this was called Toryism, and men gloried in the name; now it is called Popery and reviled.'[1] The modern world had made the existence of the State with a religious conscience impossible, and if the present Pope did not acknowledge this, Newman seems to say, future Popes would. He admits to a fondness for the old state of affairs himself—'All I know is, that Toryism, that is, loyalty to persons, springs immortal in the human breast.'[2]

But this admission must not be taken at more than its face value. Newman was too loyal a Catholic to attack openly the Pope if he did not agree with him, and it would have been fatal to the success of the *Letter to the Duke of Norfolk* to have aired the views which the correspondence with Allies has shown him to hold. What Gladstone had thought about Papal Infallibility was incorrect, and could be shown to be so, whatever Newman's own private opinion. And in fact Newman does not here deny these opinions, whatever his sentimental attachment to the past may have been. It is well to examine closely his words. He says 'Though I profess to be an admirer of the principles now superseded in themselves, mixed up as they were with the imperfections and evils incident to everything human, nevertheless I say frankly I do not see how they could possibly be maintained in the ascendant.'[3]

Newman admits the impossibility of a return to the past, but does not here imply that he would welcome a return if it were

[1] *ibid.*, p. 263.   [2] *ibid.*, p. 268.   [3] *ibid.*, p. 267.

possible. That he admired the 'principles' of the old world is true, though any religious man could not fail to do so. Yet they were mixed up with evils which he thought were inevitably a perversion of the principles themselves. If he does not stress these views, he certainly does not deny them, and it seems that in affirming the present impossibility of the political system desired by the Pope he had gone as far as was reasonable and necessary for him in the circumstances. Thus, despite the superficial impression which may easily be gained from the *Letter to the Duke of Norfolk*, the 'implicit liberalism' which Laski thought he saw in the first volume of *Difficulties of Anglicans* may still be detected in the second.

The evidence for Newman's rejection of Toryism as he knew it is overwhelming. It is true that a catalogue of strong Tory influences on him can be compiled. It is undeniable that in some ways he seems temperamentally a likely adherent of such views, as his romantic notions of chivalry and honour in the Scott mould,[1] and his well-known regard for personal loyalty help to suggest. But, for all this, Toryism as a political phenomenon was, in the last analysis, a thing of the past. It was an object of the imagination, and therefore a principle of barbarism, while the principle of the civilised State must be an object of sense. The bond of the barbarian State will be that of vivid and imposing objects, like 'Religion, superstition, belief in persons and families',[2] but the civilised State will leave these behind. This is why it is so misleading for Figgis to couple Newman's name with Filmer's.[3] It is not that Newman is alleged to share Filmer's patriarchalism, but the association of their names in the particular context might create an impression that they have more in common than is in fact the case. It is true that Newman might be said, like Filmer, to have had a deeper insight into the bonds of society than was common among his contemporaries. Yet Newman's position is far from that even of the rehabilitated Filmer of recent years. He consciously and carefully repudiated any form

---

[1] P.C., Nb. 2. [2] H.S., i, 174.
[3] J. N. Figgis, *Divine Rights of Kings* (2nd ed., Cambridge, 1914), p. 255.

Liberalism

of patriarchalism, as being inappropriate for the particular stage which human society had reached. The truth is that Toryism, Feudalism, Patriarchalism, were all connected by Newman, and they were all passing away. There is little suggestion of Patriarchalism in the letter of Newman to his friend Allies, which formed part of an interesting correspondence that took place between them on slavery, and of which correspondence only a part has hitherto appeared in print. Here Newman reports, 'I am tempted to call both slavery and despotism in their idea patriarchal power badly administered. Then: (1) Perhaps patriarchal power on a *large field* will *ever* be badly administered. (2) Perhaps a race in the course of centuries *outgrows* patriarchal power, which, *even were it well administered*, is inexpedient for it.'[1]

That patriarchal power, Toryism and Feudalism were closely associated for Newman and his intimate friend Froude comes out very clearly in Froude's poem which appeared under two different titles, in Froude's *Remains* as 'Farewell to Toryism', and in the *Lyra Apostolica* of later years as 'Farewell to Feudalism';[2] the text of the poem being in each case the same. The message of the poem was that though noble things, like the feudal court and the patriarchal sway of kings, were decaying, and the social 'bands' which taught to rule with gentleness and obey with dignity were fast disappearing, still, sad though this was, it was not the end of all things, and the Church had no need to fear for its position in the new world.

A view of Newman as a 'consistent Tory' was opposed at the beginning of this chapter, and its falsity has been demonstrated. Obviously Newman was in a very deep sense a conservative, and the first chapter of this book has shown in what way he is such. Indeed, it may well be argued that his conservatism is his main contribution to political thought. But it should be remembered that Newman was never a party man—'I have no great love for the Conservatives',[3] he wrote in 1866, in words which could be

[1] P.C., Allies, 10 November 1863. The published correspondence, of which this passage does not form a part, is at Allies, *op. cit.*, pp. 137–141.
[2] *Remains*, i, 429. *Lyra Apostolica* (London, 1879), p. 170. Newman took an active part in both these publications.   [3] C.L., de Lisle, 28 March 1866.

applied to almost any period of his life. Similarly with the label 'Tory'. If, after all, this label is still to be fastened on Newman, it is to be done in face of his own rejection of it. The Toryism of Cardinal Newman must be sought in those realms where 'a Tory philosopher cannot be wholly a Tory, but must often be a better Liberal than the Liberals themselves'.[1]

It would not have been altogether inappropiate if this whole book had been entitled 'The Liberalism of Cardinal Newman'. Any study of Newman's thought in general, or his political thought in particular must concern itself very much with this question of liberalism, an understanding of which helps to explain much else in Newman. It has been shown that, even on his own definitions, Newman was close to being a liberal on the question of the secular State. Again, if by liberalism is meant a doctrine which sets very narrow limits to the sphere of State action, then here again Newman must be considered a liberal. It was not that he denied that the State could do much efficiently if it were given the chance, but in extolling the virtues of private enterprise in *Who's to Blame?* Newman was consciously making a political and moral, and not an economic, choice.

There is a very real liberalism in Newman, in some ways almost individualistic, though of a very different temper from Benthamite individualism. It was based not on an abstract individual but on the individuality of the human soul. Indeed there is an ultimate individualism in Newman which can be traced back to the early vision of 'two and two only supreme and luminously self-evident beings, myself and my Creator'.[2] Yet this individualism is profoundly modified by other factors. Newman himself admitted that his Tractarian ideas 'elevate the Church, but they sink the individual'.[3] It is possible to argue that Newman's view of the Church as a kind of living organism is not entirely unconnected with the ideas of corporate personality which were current in England after his death. A great deal can be made out for the common judgement, first formulated by Dicey, that

[1] *Mill on Bentham and Coleridge* (ed. F. R. Leavis, London, 1950), p. 167.
[2] *Apo.*, p. 108.   [3] *Ess.*, i, 281.

Newman's criticism of Benthamite individualism in some way helped to clear a path for the more general acceptance of collectivist views at the end of the nineteenth century. This is not to assert any necessary logical affiliation of Newman's ideas to any form of collectivism, but merely to show that, in the concrete dialectic of history, whatsoever weakened the hold of Benthamism on the minds of men, at the same time to a great extent favoured the growth of collectivist ideas. It would not be fair to say that Newman was inconsistent in his attitude on the one hand to the rights and claims of the individual, and on the other to the needs and claims of the community. There is a certain tension between individualistic and collectivist views in Newman which was never quite resolved, but this was a result of an effort to do justice to the actual complex human situation as he found it, and any minimising of one element or another to achieve an artificial synthesis was out of the question for him.

Often, where Newman's position is ascertainable, and can be seen on close inspection to be both reasonable and consistent, a contradictory and confusing use of words can cause much obscurity. The term 'liberal' can of course be used in politics or religion with varying meanings, as already seen, but even when it is used in a more broad and general cultural sense it can refer to very different realities. Thus Matthew Arnold can look on Newman as one of the great influences which helped to sap the self-confidence of the harsh, vulgar Victorian liberalism which they both hated; and no doubt Newman may well have helped to soften the tone of contemporary liberalism, and have been partly responsible for the fact that liberalism in England never developed that anti-clerical spirit which so often accompanied it abroad. It is not always recognised how much Arnold thought that he owed to Newman. Indeed, he felt that only Newman, together with Goethe, Wordsworth and Sainte-Beuve, had really influenced him;[1] and to Newman himself he wrote, 'In all the conflicts I have with modern Liberalism and Dissent I recognise your work.'[2]

[1] P.C., Arnold, 28 May 1872.   [2] *ibid.*, 29 November 1871.

Yet it would be possible to speak of a cultural liberalism which Newman represented, in much the same way as Friedrich Schlegel did,[1] with whom Newman can in some ways be fruitfully compared. Schlegel was hostile to the popular education of the *Aufklärung*, again in much the same ways as Newman can be shown to be. For Schlegel liberalism was a cultured state, the illiberal man was the uncultured adorer of mediocrity. There is much that is obviously parallel in these views with those ideas already found expressed in Newman's earlier writings, but which receive their full expression in his great defence of the need for a liberal education which is made in the *Idea of a University*.

It will not be profitable to pursue further these particular senses in which Newman can be referred to as liberal or as an antiliberal. Yet it should finally be reiterated that fundamental to Newman's whole attitude on this question is his violent opposition to the shallow optimism with which he saw his contemporaries so deeply imbued. This was by no means an opposition to the excessive reliance on conscious reason which liberalism involved. While Newman stressed the importance of non-rational factors for the stability of social life, he yet placed a great reliance on reason in politics. The State was a unity of mind for him, and conscious reasoning was its method of advance. It existed below the level of conscious reason, but ratiocinative processes were involved in its progress to a more ideal form of civilisation. It was not simply the idea of progress which he attacked. There was no limit to the march of mind for Newman, and it has been seen that he was quite ready to accuse the Turks of standing in the way of the progress of the nineteenth century. It was not a vague and imprecise progress which was the target for criticism, so much as the belief in an automatic moral progress, gained as it seemed by time, without hard personal effort. It is true that there is no profound ultimate historical pessimism in Newman, but it is undeniable that his outlook on man and society is far from cheerful. The mass of men will always remain evil; the qualified

---

[1] A. Schlagdenhauffen, 'Le libéralisme Schlégelien', *Frédéric Schlegel et son groupe* (Paris, 1934), pp. 247 ff.

optimism which underlies the theory of a liberal education in the *Idea of a University* does not go very far. Few texts are more often repeated by Newman than that of St. John, 'The whole world lieth in wickedness.' If moral progress is to be made, it must be by dint of an internal moral struggle in the individual, and the ills of society can be cured in no other way.

But this is to raise an issue which so far has been ignored, yet which is for many absolutely vital to the appreciation, or dismissal, of Newman's social and political thought. For though it has been demonstrated that Newman had thought a great deal about politics, nevertheless it is a common reproach that he had no social conscience. Many contemptuously reject much of what he has to say largely because of this. It does not strike everyone today, nor did it half a century ago, that a preacher is entitled to stress the need for individual moral reform, while apparently ignoring vast social evils which even the most myopic could see. Much can be said in Newman's defence here, but what is advanced should be placed in the context of a final consideration of Newman's attitude to the modern democratic State, the final emergence of which he did not live to see.

V

NEWMAN AND THE MODERN DEMOCRATIC STATE

1. HAD NEWMAN A SOCIAL CONSCIENCE?

SOME sort of appraisal can now be made of what Newman has to offer to current political thinking, and not merely to the history of political thought. It cannot be held that his blunt remark, 'No one can dislike the democratic principle more than I do',[1] cuts him off from the serious and sympathetic consideration of present-day readers. For one thing the word democracy no longer has quite the same emotive force today for many English thinkers as hitherto, though of course it has by no means regained some earlier unpleasant associations. But this is not the real defence of so forthright a remark. It can be shown that a great deal of what Newman says is flatly contradictory to this remark, and there is good reason for putting very little weight on it.

There is a further problem which must first be solved. It has been stated by a great many students of Newman's works that he had no social conscience. If this is so, and both friend and foe alike have asserted it, it is bound to mean that his contribution to politics will be lessened in the eyes of very many people. For either Newman was aware of the great social problems of his age, or he was unaware of them. If he were unaware of them, it calls very much in question the value of the political thought of a man who was so very far from being grounded in the realities of his day. On the immediate and practical level alone little help in current predicaments would be sought from such a writer. If it is objected that Newman was aware of these problems, though he failed to dwell on them, the result is almost as damaging. At the present day a concern for social justice is much in evidence,

---

[1] *Diff.*, ii, 268.

and a writer who has a great deal to say about politics but takes no account of flagrant injustices will not arouse much sympathy. Indeed, it has seemed to many, and no doubt will continue to seem, particularly unfortunate that a priest should remain silent amidst so much in the nineteenth century which should surely have shocked the Christian soul.

To meet this difficulty it is necessary to decide how much, if anything, Newman says about social problems. It is obvious, since many have so concluded, that a superficial glance over Newman's published works reveals little reference to them, and it may not be so obvious, though it is just as true, that no amount of research will discover much crusading zeal displayed about them. Yet little as Newman says about social problems, it must be clearly understood that he was not unaware of them. It is of no avail to point out that a life spent in Oxford and Birmingham and the nature of his particular calling prevented Newman from coming into very close touch with some of the more unpleasant realities of the day. It will not do to explain away a great deal of the nineteenth century as no more than the product of distorted notions of the Hammonds. When all the exaggerations of emphasis of historians are taken into account, there still remains indisputable evidence of grave social problems and injustices, and Newman was aware of them. It had been a very real fear for him in 1835 that 'the vice, the ignorance, the wretchedness'[1] existing in the towns of England would lose their inhabitants to heathenism unless the Church of England were to waken up to the position. There are occasional sudden eruptions of feeling in his work as when 'the poor-houses, hospitals and prisons' of this country are condemned as 'dead men's sepulchres',[2] and it would be possible to make a list of similar references in his work, or to take into account the newspaper cuttings which he saved, displaying an interest in subjects as diverse as the conditions in Winson Green prison and the argument against vivisection. When all this is taken into account, however, it goes little further than to show that Newman was aware of some of the contemporary evils, and

[1] *V.M.*, ii, 69.   [2] *Diff.*, i, 253.

for an age like the present, when many popular and intelligent writers seem ready to blame the whole German nation for Buchenwald and Belsen, brushing aside all pleas of ignorance. Newman might seem to stand in need of some defence.

It is indeed curious that a man who can preach the need for the individual Christian to take a stand on social matters[1] should himself fail to go far in this direction in practice. There are, of course, some obvious explanations. In the first place, there is no doubt that Newman was absolutely engrossed in the intellectual problems of recommending Christianity to an increasingly scientific and irreligious age. Not only was Newman himself more interested in intellectual than social problems, and perhaps more usefully employed in dealing with the former, but he erects this disparagement of the social at the expense of the intellectual into a kind of general principle. Thus he writes to Allies that 'the noblest aspect of man is not the social, but the intellectual',[2] and to the end of his days seems never to have wavered in his belief that the chief problems of his own age were not social but intellectual. It is not difficult to see why the names of Bagshawe and Manning, two Catholic prelates who took a very different line from Newman here, should quite oust the name of their great contemporary from Catholic writing on social and political thought. But at least it has been shown that Newman was not ignoring social injustice from a preoccupation with his own livelihood or for any trivial reasons. The hold of Christianity on the nation was fast weakening, and unless the intellectual adequacy of its defence were improved much harm would be done The decline of religious belief was a social problem of the first order, and there is a sense in which all religious people must hold it as more important than any other social problem.

This line of argument may seem to go some way to acquitting Newman of a lack of public spirit and regard for the welfare of his fellow men, but in doing so it opens up a new direction for criticism. Obviously a decline in religious belief was deplorable for him, but why should the intellectual factor figure so

[1] *P.S.*, iii, 212–213.   [2] M. Allies, *T. W. Allies* (London, 1907), p. 113.

prominently in this? It may well have been that the intellectual inadequacy of some traditional defences of Christianity had driven away some inquiring minds, but it can as easily be said that the real scandal of the nineteenth century was that the Church lost its hold on the working classes, who were interested in more practical matters than intellectual problems. The criticism against Newman which this involves is that he did not seem to envisage the possibility that it was as important to keep the poor in the Church as the rich. It seems probable that this was wholly due to the enormous importance which Newman attributed to intellectual factors, although his enemies may prefer to see here some tinge of a class attitude from which he never quite freed himself.

If Newman was concerned with the rich, it was not because they were rich but because they were educated. He conceived that he had a mission to the gentlemen of the country, because they formed the educated classes.[1] It is true that generally speaking the rich were educated and the poor uneducated at that time, and Newman often uses the words poor and uneducated as quite synonymous. There was, indeed, for Newman 'a strongly marked line dividing the educated and illiterate classes, which not even the closest proximity tends to obliterate'.[2] It never seems to have occurred to him that there was any possibility of intellectual development among some of the poor and uneducated, and consequently he was hostile to Manning's plans to educate the Catholic poor and to Manning's apparent lack of concern for the education of the rich. Newman was sceptical about the possibility of a return to the age of poor scholars, but he did not foresee the rapid emergence of a society in which educational opportunities for all would be plentiful, though the scholars, while certainly not quite poor, are not far removed from a working-class wage. Again, it is only now, as a result of these new conditions, that the working and lower classes can be expected to be anything like uniformly of a low educational level.

[1] *Add.*, p. 125. But see p. 153, where the C.Y.M.S. remind Newman that he has always had a deep interest in the working class.   [2] *H.S.*, iii, 280.

None of this Newman seems to have appreciated, so that he looked to the education of the gentlemen of the country, as at his own Oratory School, to help solve those intellectual problems he found so pressing. It does not then seem necessary to invoke any actual dislike or fear on Newman's part of the working classes, though it is as well to examine this possibility. At the outset it should be made clear that Newman did not advocate a social hierarchy or a fixed status in any medieval sense. The term 'lower orders' was not in his vocabulary. The basis of his position appears in a remarkable letter to his brother Frank. He says 'Everyone has his place in society—there is a difference of duties and of persons fitted to them. "High" and "low" are mere names, and invidious ones. I would rather speak, if I could, of right hand and left hand ranks, all being on a level.'[1] It is a pity that Newman never developed these views. But there has never been any question that Newman did not make clear that rich and poor were on a level in the Church, and no one can question the practical effect of this in his personal relations with the poor in his parish life.[2] Basically his position needs no defence today, though it is hard to deny a certain less defensible attitude in his remarks in the *Idea of a University* about the 'condescension' of his lecturers in spending time on their more humble listeners, and in his hope that the knowledge gained would not make them forget their station.[3] It is amusing to note such discussions as that with Lady Georgiana Fullerton, in which Newman carefully considers whether Oscott might not prove too little refined for someone of such good family as her son.[4] Again, Sean O'Faolain's recent *Newman's Way* has made clear the abnormal sensitivity which Newman felt all his life about the humble origins of his family, and his father's chequered career.[5]

A modern politician might boast of such a background, but Newman was not prophetic in his attitude here. He assumed

---

[1] M. Ward, *The Young Mr. Newman* (London, 1948), p. 268.
[2] For his dislike of the pew system, see P.C., Bowden, 29 December 1842.
[3] pp. 487, 503.
[4] Augustus Craven, *Lady Georgiana Fullerton* (Paris, 1889), p. 217.
[5] See e.g. p. 68.

complacently a rigidity of class structure which did not exist, and he wanted to influence the upper and educated classes to which he would like himself thought to belong. He was not far in feeling from his contemporary, Ambrose Phillipps de Lisle, who once bitterly complained, 'Rome neither knows nor cares for the Position I hold among the Landed Aristocracy of England or its most ancient Feudal Families.'[1] It was not that he felt any hatred, dislike or contempt for the poor, but he seemed to look on them as inevitably fixed in their state. He did not assume any responsibility for attempting to alter what seemed to be unalterable, but, in a country where the executive was subordinate to class interests, as he himself observed,[2] he was content to look upon the poor as an object of charity rather than a challenge to social thinking and purpose.

Whatever substance there may be in criticisms of Newman's attitude to class, not many even of his admirers are likely to be satisfied with this sole explanation of his ignoring social problems that he was engrossed in intellectual ones. Few have even advanced this much, but have excused him on the grounds that he was a genius, and therefore exempt from the sort of criticism to which ordinary mortals are subject; or they have pointed out that it is too much to expect a man of such great spiritual force and concentration to be able to contemplate more practical matters. Altogether, however, a certain uneasiness seems to accompany most attempts to explain Newman's lack of a social conscience.[3] Yet there has all along been a further reason for this lack which seems never to have been brought forward. It is convenient here to pick out one social problem of the day, the then very real one of Temperance, and to examine Newman's attitude to the question. From published sources two contradictory accounts could be made out. On the one hand it is possible to emphasise the notion of Newman's lack of concern for these sort of questions by referring to the indignant story of his brother Frank, who,

[1] E. S. Purcell, *Life of de Lisle* (London, 1900), ii, 61.
[2] *D.A.*, pp. 351–352.
[3] See e.g. G. E. McEntee, *Social Catholic Movement in Great Britain* (New York, 1927), p. 16; *Newman Centennial Essays* (ed. Benard and Ryan, Washington, 1947), p. 66.

pleased that certain prominent Catholics joined him in advocating Temperance, was astounded to hear brother John assert that for his part he did not know whether there were too many drink shops or too few.[1] Brother John is in fact accused of not so much ignoring as attacking temperance societies. But, on the other hand, it is clear from an address of Newman's to a Catholic Total Abstinence League in 1879[2] that a quite opposite impression of his attitude could be made out. The contradiction is only apparent. There is a letter at the Oratory which explains and resolves it, and in doing so helps to explain Newman's whole attitude to social problems. It is as well to give the letter in full.[3]

Oratory 28 May '78.

My dear Canon Longman,

Fr. Ryder tells me you have asked him to a meeting of the mission clergy with a view to considering the expedience of their taking part in the Temperance Movement here, and he has urged me to state to you my own opinion about it. I have certainly a strong opinion on the subject, though from my want of mission experience, one-sided.

The question is, I believe, whether in October next the clergy should take any part, formal or informal, contemporaneous, collateral, or sympathetic, whether in recognition of, or in understanding with, the Alliance; and I wish I could in a few words which alone are possible in a letter, do justice to what seems to me the gravity of the question.

For the last fifty years, since 1827, there has been a formidable movement among us towards assigning in the national life political or civil motives for social and personal duties, and thereby withdrawing matters of conduct from the jurisdiction of religion. Men are to be made virtuous, and to do good works, to become good members of society, good husbands and fathers, on purely secular motives. We are having a wedge thrust into us which tends to the destruction of religion altogether; and this is our misery that there is no definite point at which we can logically take our stand, and resist encroachment on principle. Such is the workhouse system, such

---

[1] F. W. Newman, *Contributions to Early History of Cardinal Newman* (London, 1891), p. 110.   [2] *Add.*, p. 162.   [3] C.L.

was the civil marriage act. On this account I looked with jealousy even on Dr. Miller's October Hospital Collections; yet it was impossible to refuse to take part in them. The proceedings of the School Board are only a more pronounced form of what really is the Pelagian heresy. As I have said, the misery is that the wedge works its way. Plausible innovations introduced serious ones. I never should be surprised if we are forced to give in on this Alliance question, as we may perhaps be forced to make terms with the School Board; but I do not see that we are obliged yet; and we may gain experience of the necessary safeguards by waiting.

This letter is vital for the explanation of Newman's social attitude, though it does not provide an excuse for it to those who are critical of him here. How Pelagian were Bagshawe and Manning, it may well be asked? It should nevertheless by now have appeared that there is not sufficient in the constant accusation about Newman's lack of a social conscience to disqualify his political thought in general from serious consideration. It may well be that Newman has something to offer contemporary political thought, and to see in what way this is so it is necessary now to consider Newman's views on the democracy which he is often supposed to have disliked and rejected.

2. WAS NEWMAN A DEMOCRAT?

Even though some English writers can now bring themselves to raise no more than two cheers for democracy, democratic values are as yet scarcely in need of defence, if the adjective 'liberal' is also to be brought into use. A reasoned criticism of democracy is now acceptable, but the hostile, unreasoning and short-sighted attitude to it of many people in the nineteenth century does not merit serious attention. It is necessary to show that Newman's attitude to democracy was neither particularly hostile nor unintelligent, and like some of the better thinkers of the nineteenth century he saw the practical inevitability of its triumph, and strove to come to terms with it. This is not the current conception of his position. Readers of Ward's *Life of*

Newman will form the impression that he stayed all his life in irreconcilable opposition to democratic ideas. This is because Ward did not print, and in some cases did not know the existence of, certain letters which would have given a different impression, and furthermore Ward was himself not in sympathy with democratic ideas, and did not seem able to view his hero in an unwelcome light. His daughter, Maisie Ward, has reinforced all this by apparently assuming an identity of political views between Newman and the two Wards, W. G. and Wilfrid, which did not exist.[1]

Since Newman's views about democracy were not static, it is best to study them in their development, and to begin with a consideration of his attitude at the time of the Reform Bill of 1832. The Reform Bill which became law on 7 June 1832 was, of course, scarcely democratic in aim. It had been shaped by the most aristocratic Cabinet of the century as a measure on which a stand could be made, beyond which they thought it obviously unreasonable to go. But the Whigs had done more than they had intended, or were aware, and the way to universal suffrage was cleared by the Act of 1832. The results of the Act were not immediately startling, however, although many of the anomalies of the old electoral system were swept away, and although all those entitled to vote did not at once get on to the register, by 1839 just over 100,000, or over twice as many as before, were able to vote.

Opposition to the Reform Bill could be due to many other reasons than a dislike of democracy, but it is nevertheless instructive to examine Newman's attitude to it. If it were possible to take Tom Mozley's evidence uncritically it would indeed appear that Newman did not in fact oppose the Bill, and had no fear of democracy at this time but reserved his distaste for oligarchy.[2] Apart from any possible objection to the democratic consequences of the Act, however, Newman had reason to dislike it. It might be possible to maintain that Newman disliked the

[1] *Insurrection versus Resurection* (London, 1937), pp. 361–364. She establishes the anti-democratic nature of Wilfrid Ward's opinion at *ibid.*, pp. 363, 382–411.
[2] *Reminiscences of Oriel* (2nd ed., London, 1882), i, 253.

Bill because it owed its inception to those false views on liberty which the Whigs fostered, but that like many Tory die-hards of the time would not engage in opposition to it as the Tory leaders had forfeited their right to receive support by their abandonment of the Church over Catholic Emancipation in 1829. There is one letter of Newman's which seems to be saying something very like this.[1] It is certain, however, that Newman disliked the Bill, even though he said little at the time, because he thought its effect would be to give political power to those very classes who were least favourable to the Church; he thought that the cause which carried the Reform Bill would make short work with orthodoxy, and he feared for the Church, dreading 'above all things the pollution of such men as Lord Brougham, affecting to lay a friendly hand on it'.[2] It should be admitted, however, that in 1832 Newman had declared himself ready to allow 'all that any sensible well judging man may believe on the question of reforms',[3] and it is highly significant that his friend Hurrell Froude was disgusted by Tory attacks on the Reform Bill, in which he himself would by no means join.[4] Thus, apart from any question of democracy, Newman entertained certain doubts about the Reform Bill, but he was never outspoken against it as his colleague Keble had been.

But Newman by no means ignored the political and constitutional questions which the Act of 1832 involved. It does not seem generally known that the 'Contemporary Events' section of the *Rambler* of 1859, which Newman edited, was written by Newman himself, and contains his most considered opinions on the 1832 Act. He thought that 'a question of *principle* was then on trial, which can never be decided more than once. The principle of the admissibility of great fundamental changes in the constitution was acknowledged once for all. Never was a greater mistake committed by a clever man than by Lord John Russell when he spoke of *finality*. On the contrary, the originality and unprecedentedness of the measure of 1832 made it a *beginning*, whether

[1] *M.*, i, 236-237.   [2] *ibid.*, p. 237.
[3] C.L., Wood, 4 October 1832; also see P.C., Family Letters, 14 April 1833.
[4] *Apo.*, p. 126; Froude, *Remains*, i, 250.

the beginning of the end is yet to be seen.'[1] Newman states the case of the opponents of Reform, with their trust in the 'gnarled oak' of the constitution, and sums up with their claim that even if the existing state of things ought not to work, nevertheless it did. But he does not seem able to accept this claim. He was more inclined to believe that in 1832 'the British Constitution and polity would have come to a violent end, unless such violent measures had been taken by its political physicians ... the real state of the case is, that the nation outgrew its framework from no one's fault, and the framework had not been elastic enough to expand gradually and insensibly with its growth, and therefore had to be experimented on, or tinkered, that it might do its work anyhow. And now it will have to be tinkered again; and further tinkerings are below the horizon.'[2]

The real trouble about the Act of 1832 was that it had made democracy inevitable. At the end of his life Newman could still speak feelingly about it. 'I wonder you don't go back further for our present leap in the dark,' he wrote to Blachford in 1885, 'a leap which, coinciding with our foreign difficulties is a most grave event. Why don't you go back to 1832? since which I personally have not felt that I was clever enough to have any politics. That so-called Reform (though a Reform was necessary) was a party move in favour of Whiggism, and has not Reform been shamefully used, or shamelessly, by both parties as a party weapon ever since? Some years, I think, before Disraeli's and Gladstone's handling of it, I recollect an occasion when Lord John shed tears in the House, when he found his Bill was not to pass, he who had indirectly called the Act of 1832 scarcely less than a Revolution. Disraeli in 1865 [*sic* in copied letter] had this excuse, that he with many Tories thought that to lower the Franchise would be to increase the Aristocratic Power, but what excuse has poor Gladstone for helping on the Radicals?'[3] Part of the annoyance with Gladstone was due to a bitterness of feeling over the plight of 'the poor fellows in the Soudan',[4] but he was in any

[1] *Rambler*, i (1859), p. 128.   [2] *ibid.*, p. 130.   [3] C.L., Blachford, 19 May 1885.
[4] *ibid.*, 23 May 1885. Here Newman repeats that a Reform was necessary in 1832.

case at odds with him. 'I am deeply pained to think that Gladstone is the author of this revolution', he wrote. 'What a sad ending to a great career!'¹

It seems from all this that Newman was critical of the 1832 Reform Act for the whole of his life, and it was chiefly the problem of democracy that it involved which most worried him. It can be shown, however, that the difficulties and doubts which he always entertained about democracy were related to practical considerations, while his views on democracy as an ideal or value changed considerably. On the practical side, it should be noted that Newman did not deny the need for Reform, even in 1832, but he condemned an unprincipled Parliamentary attitude to further Reform, an attitude which he considered was a hindrance to responsible government. In this Newman is representative of a great deal of Tory opinion in England after 1832, which followed the Duke of Wellington in his belief that the Reform Act had made the task of responsible government quite impossible.

On the question of the democratic principles which Newman once confessed to dislike, a development of views is clearly apparent. Although Tom Mozley gives contrary evidence, it is clear that Newman in the days of the Reform Bill was to some extent an opponent of democratic ideas. In 1838 it is very seriously considered whether democracy and Anti-Christ are not in some way specially connected.² In the previous year Newman had written about Lamennais, and had found fault with him for his democratic tendencies. It was also a mark of reproach that Lamennais blamed the ruler for the excesses of 'the masses'; that he was committed to some sort of theory of development which made the resistance on principle of an innovation impossible; that this 'powerful, original, and instructive writer' did not even contemplate the idea that rebellion was a sin.³

But it is clear from this article on Lamennais that some of Newman's reasons for dislike of democracy would disappear when he took the faith which Lamennais rejected. Even in that same article he finds himself bound to admit that 'it is a matter of history

---

¹ *ibid.*, 28 December 1885.   ² *D.A.*, pp. 72 ff.   ³ *Ess.*, i, 120-124.

then, that the Latin Church rose to power, not by favour of princes, but of people'.[1] After 1845 Newman put aside the view that democracy and Anti-Christ were connected as firmly as he put aside the view that Rome and Anti-Christ were connected. Lamennais had been committed to some sort of theory of development, but Newman signalised his entry to the Church of Rome with the publication of a book containing a powerful and original theory of development. No less a person than the great Lord Acton considered that Newman's theory involved the old maxim that the voice of the people was the voice of God.[2] In other ways Newman takes over the ideas of Lamennais which he had earlier strictured, and where before he was ready to blame the masses for their errors and excuse the rulers, by 1853 he now asserts that 'it seldom happens that the people go wrong, without the rulers being somewhere in fault'.[3]

There is a real change of opinion here, though it should be kept in perspective. The fear of certain aspects of democracy remained. The best picture of Newman's attitude to democracy in the ten to fifteen years which followed his entry into the Catholic Church can be gained by studying his opinions on the British constitution at that time. It would be hard to find a more enthusiastic champion of its excellence. 'It is one of the greatest of human works,' he says, '... it soars, in its majesty, far above the opinions of men, and will be a marvel, almost a portent, to the end of time.'[4] In glorifying the constitution there was no forgetfulness of the idea that a nation's constitution was in effect the form of government which grew out of its beliefs and customs, out of its particular character. This was why it was absurd to imagine that the British constitution could be 'fitted upon every people under heaven, from the Blacks to the Italians'.[5] When the British constitution was glorified, it was the English national character which was extolled, the Englishman with 'that instinctive veneration for the law, that he can worship it even in the abstract, and thus is fitted to go shares with others all around him

---

[1] *Ess.*, i, 114. [2] Fasnacht, *Acton's Political Philosophy*, p. 106.
[3] *H.S.*, i, 142. [4] *P.P.C.*, p. 297. [5] *H.S.*, i, 180.

in that political sovereignty, which other races are obliged to concentrate in one ruler . . . [he is] inquisitive, acquisitive, enterprising, aspiring, progressive, without encroaching on his next neighbour's right to be the same'.[1] The Englishman was prepared to live and let live, and on the whole Catholicism was not intolerantly treated, so that Newman in later life was not sure that he had been grateful enough to the liberals who had helped to secure this.[2]

But whatever the liberality of the national character, the system which reflected it in England was not democratic. It was not democratic in the sense that the bulk of the population was not enfranchised when Newman wrote his *Who's to Blame?* in 1855; but if the unenfranchised part of the population were left out of consideration, in the way that the slave population of the Athenian democracy is sometimes left out of account in discussing the merits of that form of government, then the British constitution might seem to have much in common with this most famous of the ancient democracies, and Newman explicitly compares the British and Athenian national character.[3] He thinks the Athenian and the Englishman alike have an 'inward spring of restless independence'. Again, out of the variety of constitutional principles the British are to be identified with that 'by which a People would leave nothing to its rulers, but has itself, or by its immediate instruments, a concurrent part in everything that is done'.[4] It was Newman's argument that because of this the nation was strong and great, but the State weak. In *Who's to Blame?* Newman is not behind the most ardent liberal in attempting to circumscribe the activity of the State, and extolling free enterprise, though he is quite ready to concede that the State could run much more than it did of national affairs, and quite effectively, if it were only given the chance. But although Newman thought that the Nation limited the sphere of the Government, and made sure it had a real share in what Government there actually was, he did not consider this as particularly democratic, despite the

[1] *D.A.*, p. 335.
[2] C.L., Jenkins, 2 February 1880.
[3] *D.A.*, pp. 326–330.
[4] *Ibid.*, p. 323.

comparison with Athens. He was prepared to accept the mediocrity and the malevolence towards the great which he thought general in 1855; the inefficiency of Government, with 'boards and officers, engaged in checking each other, with a second apparatus to check the first apparatus, and other functionaries to keep an eye on both of them—Tom helping Jack, and Jack waiting for Bill, till the end is lost in the means';[1] he was prepared to accept this precisely because it was not democratic. He was prepared to accept the prevalent bribery: 'from the time of Sir Robert Walpole, bribes, to use an uncivil word, have been necessary to our Constitutional regime—visions of a higher but impracticable system having died away with Bolingbroke's "Patriot King". This is but one instance of what is seen in so many and various, that our Executive is on principle subordinate to class interests.'[2] Newman was prepared to defend all this.

> It is not a high system, but no human system is such. The knout and the tar-barrel aforementioned are not more defensible modes of proceeding, and are less pleasant than ours. Under ours, the individual is consulted far more carefully than under despotism or democracy.[3]

Who's to Blame? was not so much a plea for an eternal bourgeois ascendancy as a demonstration that the measures necessary to conduct such a war as the Crimean were not in harmony with the genius of the constitution. The Crimean War itself Newman thought stupid and unnecessary, and he was very much afraid that it was a portent of what the approach of democracy might bring. Thus when Bright asserted that aristocracies were bad, because among other reasons they involved countries in useless wars, Newman thought that the experience of the previous years should have shown that this could as easily be said of democracies.[4] Nevertheless, in the course of this very discussion, Newman

---

[1] *D.A.*, p. 323. Among other things Newman points out the weakness of the Army that arose from the current belief that 'no soldier must rise from the ranks, because he is not company for gentlemen' (*ibid.*, p. 360).   [2] *ibid.*, pp. 351-352.   [3] *ibid.*

[4] *Rambler*, i (1859), p. 129. In the same number of the *Rambler*, Newman repeats with alarm the words of Louis-Philippe, '*Il n'y a jamais eu chez les peuples libres de gouvernement assez fort pour réprimer longtemps la liberté à l'intérieur sans donner la gloire au dehors*' (*ibid.*, pp. 109–110).

recognises that the Reform Bill of 1832 had made the advance to democracy inevitable, and certain letters of his have been seen already in which he admits that the Bill had opened a door which could never again be shut. And so, in his *Who's to Blame?* of 1855, where Newman appears to entertain the hope of resisting the approach of democracy, he was already well aware that there was nothing sacrosanct about the £10 Householder, and he was, despite his scare over the Crimean War, losing some of the fear with which he had at one time viewed the advent of democratic government.

It is too little realised that Newman, as a Catholic, came to praise the 'beautiful idea', 'that profession of philosophical democracy' which is for ever associated with the name of Pericles. The Athenian democracy was never in fact what it was claimed to be, but Newman does not hesitate to assert that the idea which it strove to realise must look for an expression in Christianity. He is able to see much further than the 'democratical license' in which the Athenians indulged, and goes on to claim that the type of Athens in the modern world was his own Oratory of St. Philip.[1] For this reason alone it is impossible to take literally Newman's professed detestation of democratic principles. It is clear that it was not so much the principle but what he feared was the practice of democracy which he disliked. This was the real fear: 'When was a *demos* other than a tyrant?'[2] The problem of democratic tyranny is still with us, in the form particularly of strong pressure to social conformity, and Newman's doubts and fears were far from groundless. It is interesting to note that Newman seems to have been in much sympathy with John Stuart Mill, who saw more clearly than some writers of his day the future threats to liberty involved in the progress of democracy.[3]

It is not enough to recommend Newman to the present age

---

[1] *H.S.*, iii, 86.   [2] *C.L.*, Blachford, 28 December 1885.
[3] Newman pressed on Acton an article about Mill's *Liberty* for the *Rambler*. (See Gasquet, *Lord Acton*, p. 81.) This article by T. Arnold, son of Arnold of Rugby, made a wholehearted acceptance of Mill's general thesis. (See *Rambler*, vol. ii, part iv, 1859, pp. 62–75.)

that he praised the idea of democracy but was afraid of it in practice. Looking back now, the coming of democracy seems to have been inevitable, and it is not surprising that those nineteenth-century figures who saw its inevitability and strove to come to some sort of terms with it are the writers who attract our interest today. Thus de Tocqueville is read as carefully today as he was one hundred years ago. Newman had by no means the political insight of de Tocqueville, but he went further than an acceptance of the basic values of democracy, and soon did not offer resistance to what he saw to be historically inevitable. He was concerned to protect the liberty which democracy could endanger, and this explains his worry about Reform in 1885. 'What means the infatuation of educated men, who understanding that autocrats, kings, republics and other forms of power all require a drag or regulator, think that a *demos* can do without one?' he asks.[1]

During his life Newman moved a long way from the querulous complaint of his Anglican days that everyone now had to have an opinion, often on things about which they were quite incapable of judging.[2] Before 1845 he had seen that the problem of the day was 'how to educate the masses', and in 1887 he writes,[3] what must often have been repeated by others since, 'Wasn't Lowe right in saying, "We must educate our masters"?' But though the advent of democratic government was accepted as inevitable this did not preclude Newman from speculating on its drawbacks. 'I am not speaking against democracy as such,' he writes in 1868, 'but I should like to see the contrast of the virtues of a people of large inequality and a people of equality in wealth, worked out',[4] and he wonders especially if the result would be to rule out certain cultural benefits to which the former system can give rise. But in any case, Newman had come to think that 'nothing great or living can be done except when men are self-governed and independent',[5] and though he never came to idealise the French Revolution he lost the bitterness against it which he had formerly displayed. In 1870 he writes to Lord

[1] C.L., Blachford, 28 December 1885.   [2] *P.S.*, v, 36–37.
[3] C.L. (probably to Blachford), 18 July 1887.   [4] *ibid.*, Blachford, 23 January 1868.
[5] *ibid.*, Ornsby, 2 December 1864.

Blachford, 'The history of France is, I suppose, as you say, a history of great crimes—but not of crimes only. It is the grandest, most romantic history of Modern Times—perhaps great crimes are necessary for its being that.'[1]

Newman's mature attitude to this whole question is best seen in a letter to Matthew Arnold, who had asked him if he did not consider the Tory, anti-democratic, squirearchical character of the English Church its especial danger, a danger from which the Catholic Church is essentially free. Newman replied:

> ... as to your question, I agree with what you say about the Anglican and Catholic Churches relatively to democratic ideas. It was one of Hurrell Froude's main views that the Church must alter her position in the political world—and when he heard of Lamennais, he took up his views with great eagerness. I have said the same in the beginning of the *Church of the Fathers*—'I shall offend many men when I say, we must look to the people', & c. & c. I said this *apropos* of St. Ambrose, and based my view upon the Fathers. Froude had seized upon it from the intuitive apprehension he had of what was coming, and of what was fitting. We both hated the notion of rebellion and thought that the Church must bide her time. This idea is expressed several times in the *Lyra Apostolica*. It often happens that those who will not bide their time fail, not because they are not substantially right, but because they are thus impatient. I used to say that Montanus, Tertullian, Novatian, & c. were instances in point. Their ideas were eventually carried out. Perhaps Lamennais will be a true prophet after all. It is curious to see the minute tokens which are showing themselves of the drawings of the Papal policy just now in the direction of the democracy. Of course the present Papacy is (humanly speaking) quite unequal to such a line of action —but it was the policy of Gregory VII—and, though we may have a season of depression, as there was a hideous degradation, yet it may be in the counsels of Providence that the Catholic Church may at length come out unexpectedly as a popular power. Of course, the existence of the Communists makes the state of things now vastly different from what it was in the Middle Ages.[2]

[1] *ibid.*, Blachford, 18 September 1870.
[2] Letter of 3 December 1871, *The Times Lit. Sup.*, 10 March 1921. Reprinted in *Some Unpublished Letters of M. Arnold* (ed. A. Whitridge, Yale Univ. Press, 1923).

Since Newman did not set out to be a political philosopher, he did not scrutinise the concept of democracy closely and systematically, any more than he did any other political concept. But certain broad conclusions emerge from a consideration of the scattered comments and discussions, some of which have been given here. Firstly, it should be emphasised that Newman is fundamentally in agreement with those apologists of democracy who rest their case ultimately on the unique value of individual human personality. It was seen, in the chapter on the State, the enormous importance Newman attached to the recognition of the individuality of the human soul, to the unfathomable depths of human personality. Further, the democrat seems committed to a view of the State as in some sense a mechanism or device, and here again it is clear that Newman is in agreement, as evidenced from his own account of the State, and also from the significant absence from his work of the organic analogies so popular with Catholic writers on politics. The State must rest on consent for the democrat, and it certainly does for Newman. His account of the origin of the State in consent seems hardly meant to be historical, and it is probably fair to say that consent was looked on not as an historical fact, but a moral value. There are, of course, numerous difficulties in the idea of the State as a mechanism, and in the idea of government by consent, and Newman did not remove these, but at least his position is more tenable than that of some democrats. He was realistic about the place of force in politics, and in his emphasis on consent he gave full scope to the rational and non-rational factors which are involved in the life of the State.

Perhaps the operative ideal which is most highly prized in the modern democratic State of the West, the liberal democratic State, is that of liberty, and it is one which Newman shared. Indeed, it would be possible to go on to show how Newman shared the other ideals of the Revolution he once detested—fraternity and equality: fraternity, in his condemnation of the State which was composed of discrete individuals, each only intent on securing his own personal good; equality, in his claim for the fundamental equality of the individual personality, or at least, in the equality of consent by each individual to the State. It is the ideal of liberty which deserves the most attention, however, if only because it figures more prominently in his work. There is full recognition of the fact that this liberty involves freedom of discussion, and that the decisions which are made after full discussion must in a democracy be a majority-minority compromise, with all the possible disadvantages of this. At times Newman was annoyed by this necessity, but he had a sure grasp of its importance when he spoke of 'the new and true philosophy of compromise'.[1] Nor did he restrict the scope of political liberty in general as soon as the question of religion was raised, but instead he rejected the religious State as an ideal for a civilised society in the modern world, nor did he compensate this by any idealisation of the religious State in the past.

If it is now clear that Newman accepted the values of democracy, is it possible to argue as it has been done that it was not its principles but its practice of which he was dubious? Does this mean no more than that he liked some principles of democracy, and disliked others? It is true that a distinction of this sort which would quite fit Newman's case would be very hard to formulate, but there is a sense in which the statement is meaningful. For some of the difficulties of democracy which worried Newman were practical in the sense that only democracy itself could cure them. This applies to all those questions of the political responsibility of the people, such as the possibility of a foolish and thoughtless war which worried Newman, where political responsibility can only be developed by actually having it.

If Newman is still to be accused however of rejecting not only the possible practice but also a very principle of democracy, the principle in question must be that of equality. Of course, it follows from the high view of liberty which Newman holds that equality must to some extent suffer, for equality and liberty are not entirely compatible ideals. He was worried, as de Tocqueville had been, about the envy and malevolence of a democracy

[1] *Diff.*, ii, 239.

towards the great, and the danger of general mediocrity. It may well be that it is here that certain ideas which have been viewed suspiciously in this book might prove their value. In his concern for the 'educated classes', in his scepticism about the powers of attention of young men and would-be students who had been all day in the shops, he was no doubt making some sort of plea against the dangers of a general mediocrity and a false egalitarianism. This is where Newman's appreciation of leaders and great men is of great importance (though in most of his general remarks on the subject he seems to the end to have the Duke of Wellington in the background of his mind), for a democracy must value and know how to use them. For all his firm hold on the fact of fundamental human equality, there is no sign of that search of an abstract and mathematical equality which seems as likely to end in the totalitarian State as in the hoped for fuller and more human life.

Yet even if the possible dangers of the ideal of equality worried Newman, it is clear that he accepted them as the necessary price of a great good. This emerges very clearly from *Who's to Blame?* which contains a thorough-going acceptance of the British constitution and its attendant evils and scandals, in terms which are realistic enough to shock some readers, and make others even doubt if he is serious. But he is serious enough, and it is precisely the democratic difficulties which he accepts, summed up in the opinion that England is the paradise of little men and the purgatory of great ones. The fact remains that many would not now think of Britain at that day as democratic, since universal suffrage was still in the future, and it is another fact that Newman was unhappy about the extensions of suffrage in his own lifetime, though he was particularly worried about the way in which they were brought about. There is not enough evidence about Newman's views on this question to warrant any further remarks here, but it should perhaps be remembered that there is more to democracy than universal suffrage, and that it is not wise to judge nineteenth-century thinkers on our twentieth-century practice.

Newman was not a great theoretician of democracy, but by character, training and environment he can have had little disposition to it at all. Yet he rose above these limitations to an intelligent awareness of it. It was partly that he saw its practical inevitability—it was a great idea in the minds of men and was certain of development. But it was partly also that he saw that it was a true idea, and not a false one. This is to use language which many supporters of the modern democratic State will not use, so let it be said that he approved of the ideals of the democratic State, or at least, that he preferred the modern, liberal democratic State to any other in the past or present. Even at this level, there is a fact which has an importance beyond the mere effort to understand the life and work of Cardinal Newman.

3. NEWMAN'S POLITICAL INFLUENCE TODAY

It may well be claimed that the life and work of Cardinal Newman cannot be properly understood without some study of his political thought, and this means to say that a great many writers on Newman have not fully succeeded in their aims. Newman thought that social and political affairs were not his 'line', but this does not mean that what he has to say about these matters, nor indeed, what he fails to say, can be ignored. Of course, despite the revelation here of much which has perhaps been unsuspected before, it is plain that Newman is not a political thinker of the front rank. It would be absurd to place him in importance alongside J. S. Mill or T. H. Green, or even alongside Bradley and Bosanquet. Yet, both on account of the intrinsic worth of what he has to say and because of the tremendous position and reputation among his fellow Catholics which he has enjoyed, and never more than at the present moment, his influence has not been negligible and may yet be greater.

During the nineteenth century this influence was none the less great because it was not always acknowledged, apparent or direct. From his early sermons, his many books and his vast personal correspondence Newman had the means of gaining a strong influence over large numbers of people, who in turn were the means of influencing others. It is significant that Matthew Arnold says that Newman is one of the only four people who had profoundly influenced him, and tells him that 'In all the conflicts I have with modern Liberalism and Dissent I recognise your work.'[1] This statement alone might be sufficient proof of Newman's influence in the nineteenth century, but it is not only the influence exerted through a great writer such as this which must be borne in mind, but that through countless others whose names are now largely forgotten.

It is often plausibly stated that the strong reaction of the Tractarians to Benthamite liberalism helped to weaken it, and to set in motion one current of thought which made for the general acceptance of collectivist views about the State towards the end of the nineteenth century. One modern writer, as we have seen, goes so far as to talk of Newman's 'profound collectivism'. However much Newman may have reacted against a false individualism, it is highly misleading to attribute collectivist views to him, or even to say his ideas led to collectivism in any but an unintentional, indirect and illogical way. The Tractarian ideas elevated the Church, and sank the individual, in one particular sphere and from a particular point of view, but it is hard to imagine anyone in the last resort more individualistic than Newman. From an examination of the history of his life, apart from the views which he expressed, this basic individualism appears so strongly that it is not likely to be long denied. Perhaps until the last he rested in 'the thought of two and two only supreme and luminously self-evident beings, myself and my Creator'.[2] Again, it is sometimes thought that Newman's view of the Church as a kind of living organism were not unconnected with the ideas of corporate personality which were current in England after his death. Although a connexion could be argued and established here, it would hardly be direct enough to merit consideration, and the argument would soon have to go far beyond what Newman actually said, or could be credited with meaning to say. It is clear enough, however, that Newman's idea of a Church as a kind of

---

[1] P.C., Arnold, 29 November 1871. [2] *Apo.*, p. 108.

living thing, with a long tradition and developing purposes, may have remained in many minds when after his death the Courts seemed to challenge this view.

Interesting though it would be to examine closely the possible influence of Newman in the past, it seems more important now to examine the influence he might have on the present and the future. In some ways Newman has much to offer to all who are concerned with politics, but it is obviously likely that it is his fellow Catholics who will be most influenced by him. To them he has a great deal to say which may yet have good effect. Not the least of the contributions in this direction may be that Newman has demonstrated that it is possible for a Catholic to say a great deal about politics without using the language of Thomism. In some ways Newman himself was not using contemporary language in dealing with philosophy and politics, and much of his terminology is reminiscent of Locke and an earlier age. But at least the language was English, and was understood and is understandable, whereas the terminology of Thomism is not understood at all in England today outside the seminaries. As a result, the influence a Catholic writer using this terminology can expect to have on the thought of the day is very small. If Newman has shown that it is quite orthodox and sensible to use a different language it will be no slight result of his work.

It is not merely that Newman avoids the Thomist terminology but also, since he does not base his politics on Thomist metaphysics and keeps close instead to a native British empiricism, he retains the possibility of influencing those to whom Thomist metaphysics are unacceptable. It may be possible with some contrivance to show that much of Newman's philosophy will fit into a Thomist framework, and certainly much of the substance of his political thought can be shown to be similar to that of thinkers in the Thomist tradition. But Newman was no Thomist, and was received into the Catholic Church before the great Thomist revival of the nineteenth century began. The fact that Newman is widely considered among Catholics today to rank among the great doctors of the Church, even, some would say, to be of the stature of St. Augustine and St. Thomas Aquinas himself, gives a special importance to Newman's demonstration that Catholic discussion on politics need not start from Thomist metaphysics, nor proceed along the very often unrealistic Thomist lines, nor use that Thomist terminology which is so little understood today.

It is also of great interest to note that Newman avoids some well-worn paths of Catholic writers on politics, which paths do not lead as a rule to anything of great value. He does not trace all our present-day political and social evils to Luther and Protestantism and the Reformation, and is willing to go further back in history to find, not an idealised medieval society, but a world where political and social evils are already in existence. It is a world to which he has no desire to return. On no account must Newman be confounded with the other great Catholic thinkers of or near his times—with de Maistre, Bonald, Schlegel, Donoso Cortes, Balmes and the rest. These thinkers, powerful though they were within certain limits, were quite blind to much of the changes which had occurred since 1789, and are poor guides for Catholic political thinkers today. The fact that Newman is so far from the general climate and feeling of these reactionary writers is of the first importance. It is interesting to observe that Newman can carry on a correspondence about secret societies,[1] before the publication in the *Rambler* of an article by Simpson about sixteenth-century secret societies, without displaying any of that unbalanced attitude towards the role of these societies at and after the French Revolution which has characterised so many European Catholic political writers.

If Newman's position is very different from the romanticism of the anti-democratic type with which those writers are imbued, he is also far from the romanticism of a democrat like G. K. Chesterton. This is seen not only in their attitude to the Middle Ages, but in many other instances. Particularly is it noticeable that Newman had none of that romantic attachment to the small nation which Chesterton showed. Newman was nearly what

---

[1] Letter to Simpson, 3 April 1859. *Rambler Collection*, Oratory, p. 55.

Chesterton most hated—an imperialist—and the only occasions when Newman seems to be able to speak well of Disraeli are when that statesman's policy is forwarding imperialism.[1] It is difficult to decide how much stress to put on Newman's imperialistic leanings, but there was at least more to it than a mere imbibing of the atmosphere Joe Chamberlain created in the Birmingham where Newman lived for over forty years, and a difference in general attitude here from that of Chesterton is very clear.

In fact, Newman is different from a great many Catholic writers by his resolute realism, and avoidance of all types of romanticism. This realism was shown very clearly in Newman's acceptance of the modern democratic, secular, tolerant State, and it is here that Newman may yet have considerable influence amongst those Catholics who have yet to accept it as anything more than an unfortunate temporary necessity. It may be thought that the Papal Allocution of December 1953, which went far to allow what Newman has put forward on all this, may well have made Newman's contribution less necessary. But Newman's stature is great, and he had taken up his position on the secular State a hundred years before the Papal Allocution. If there is little need for Newman's influence on this point in Britain, it is obvious that there are still parts of the world which can learn much from him here. Nor can it be stated that Newman did not appreciate the difficulties in the way of complete religious freedom in certain countries. He could see that the position in Spain was such that no political enactment would be sufficient to obtain it, till much in Spanish society had changed. He thought that much the same was true of Sweden at that time.[2] But, whatever the difficulties, Newman made clear enough his view that the tolerant State not only might allowably come, but must come and ought to come in a civilised society.

It may be hoped that Newman's political ideas will be studied

---

[1] M. Church, *Life of Dean Church* (London, 1894), p. 269. This whole letter is to be found at C.L., Blachford, 22 July 1878. For dislike of Disraeli, see E. Bellasis, *Coram Cardinali* (London, 1916), p. 89. For an interesting link between Disraeli and the Oxford Movement, see Dawson, *Spirit of the Oxford Movement*, p. 107.

[2] P.C., Monsell, 17 June 1863.

by, and bear fruit with, many others than Catholics. Perhaps for these Newman's conservatism will still be thought to be his most important contribution to political thought. He has indeed given incomparable expression to the plea for the value of tradition, for the preference for the wisdom of the ages over the wisdom of the day.

Yet in allowing the reasonableness of this stress on his conservatism, it must once more be emphasised that this did not exclude a large measure of a kind of liberalism, which was ultimately made necessary by the very theory of development which is at the basis of his conservatism. It is true that Newman opposed the political liberalism of his day, but it was not because it was rationalistic, for Newman himself laid great stress on the role of conscious reason in politics; it was not because it was imbued with the general idea of progress, for Newman had something of this himself, nor was it because of liberal attacks on religion in the State. At the root of Newman's objection to political liberalism was the belief that 'the whole world lieth in wickedness'. Thus although he thought men's reason made a sort of progress possible, and did not deny some sort of moral progress might also be possible, he was violently opposed to any notion of automatic moral progress, achieved almost by passage of time and without enormous personal effort. He was completely at odds with what he took to be the spirit of the times. 'The country seems to me to be in a dream,' he said, 'being drugged with this fallacious notion of its superiority to other countries and other times.'[1] All around him Newman found a deep assumption that the Englishman was improving materially and morally with almost inevitable ease, and throughout his life he vigorously attacked this mood. This sort of mood is now gone, and it was events and not words which helped to dispatch it, but in any future settled times when men forget the evil of which man is always capable, Newman's words may well be needed again.

There is a great deal which he might have contributed to political thought which now has come from other sources. In

[1] C.L., Wood, 4 September 1832.

particular, it is strange that although the concept of myth in politics is now part of the general intellectual currency of the country, very few of the people who use the term are aware of the fact that Newman used the concept over one hundred years ago. It is curious that it should be left to Sorel in France to salute Newman for this, and that our native writers on politics should have ignored what all now see to be a very fruitful idea.

But more than any particular ideas, interesting and useful though they may be, it may well be that in the end it is the realistic and practical approach of Cardinal Newman to politics which will have the greatest effect. For the political problem of the day has been said to be that of 'getting down to essentials. What, in the present environment makes for survival? What for death?'[1] If Catholic political thinkers can learn from Newman, they will the better be able to help in meeting the situation with which the world is now faced, while other thinkers may be encouraged by the fact of his efforts and his influence to collaborate with them in the search for the politics of survival.

[1] J. Bowle, *Politics and Opinion in the Nineteenth Century* (London, 1954), p. 481.

A SELECT BIBLIOGRAPHY

I NEWMAN'S WRITINGS

(i) Those works abbreviations for which are to be found at the front of this study form the main source of information on Newman's political thought.

(ii) Letters of Newman are to be found in the volumes listed at the front of this book, while some important ones are also to be found in those works listed below.

ALLIES, MARY H. *T. W. Allies* (London, 1907).
BLACHFORD, F. LORD. *Letters*, ed. G. E. Marindin (London, 1896).
GLADSTONE, W. E. *Letters on the Church and Religion*, ed. D. C. Lathbury, 2 vols. (London, 1910).
ORNSBY, R. *Memoirs of J. R. Hope-Scott*, 2 vols. (London, 1884).
WARD, M. *Young Mr. Newman* (London, 1948).
WARD, W. *W. G. Ward and the Catholic Revival* (London, 1893).

(iii) Other important published writings of Newman are to be found in the following:

NEWMAN, J. H. 'Contemporary Events', *Rambler*, I, May 1859, July 1859.
PALMER, W. *Notes of a Visit to the Russian Church*, ed. Newman with Preface (London, 1882).

II BIOGRAPHICAL AND CRITICAL WORKS

ABBOT, E. A. *Anglican Career of Cardinal Newman*. 2 vols. (London, 1892). *Philomythus* (London, 1891).
ATKINS, G. G. *Life of Cardinal Newman* (New York, 1931).
BARRY, W. *Newman* (New York, 1905).
BELLASIS, E. *Coram Cardinali* (London, 1916).
BENARD, E. D. *Preface to Newman's Theology* (St. Louis, Mo., 1945).
BONNEGENT, C. *Théorie de la certitude dans Newman* (Paris, 1920).
BOUYER, L. *Newman* (Paris, 1952).
BREMOND, H. *Mystery of Newman* (London, 1907).
BRINTON, CRANE. *English Political Thought in the Nineteenth Century* (London, 1933).

CECIL, A. *Six Oxford Thinkers* (London, 1909).
CHURCH, R. W. *Occasional Papers*, ii, 379-482 (London, 1897).
CORCORAN, T. *Newman's Theory of a Liberal Education* (Dublin, 1929).
CROSS, F. L. *John Henry Newman* (London, 1933).
D'ARCY, M. C. *Nature of Belief* (London, 1931).
DARK, S. *Newman* (London, 1934).
D'CRUZ, F. A. *Cardinal Newman* (Madras, 1935).
DELATTRE, F. *Pensée de Newman: extraits* (Paris, 1906).
FABER, G. *Oxford Apostles* (London, 1933).
FAIRBAIRN, A. M. *Catholicism: Roman and Anglican* (London, 1889).
FEILING, K. *Sketches in Nineteenth Century Biography* (London, 1930).
FLANAGAN, P. *Newman, Faith and the Believer.* (No place, no date.)
GLADEN, K. *Die Erkenntnisphilosophie J. H. Kardinal Newmans* (Paderborn, 1933).
GORCE, D. *Newman et les Pères* (Paris, 1933).
GUITTON, J. *Philosophie de Newman* (Paris, 1933).
  Renan et Newman (Paris, 1938).
  Portrait de M. Pouget (Paris, 1941).
HAECKER, T. *Christentum und Kultur* (Munich, 1927).
HARPER, G. H. *Cardinal Newman and W. Froude* (Baltimore, 1933).
HARROLD, C. F. *John Henry Newman* (London and New York, 1945).
HUTTON, R. H. *Cardinal Newman* (London, 1891).
  Criticism on Contempory Thought and Thinkers, ii, 270-278 (London, 1894).
INGE, W. R. *Outspoken Essays.* First Series (London, 1919).
JUERGENS, S. P. *Newman on the Psychology of Faith in the Individual* (New York, 1928).
LASKI, H. *Problem of Sovereignty* (London, 1917).
LOCKHART, W. *Cardinal Newman: Reminiscences of Fifty Years Since* (London, 1891).
MCGRATH, F. *Newman's University: Idea and Reality* (London, 1951).
MEYNELL, W. *Cardinal Newman* (London, 1930).
MOZLEY, J. B. *Theory of Development* (London, 1878).
MOZLEY, T. *Reminiscences of Oriel.* 2 vols. (London, 1882).
NEWMAN, B. *Newman* (London, 1925).
O'FAOLAIN, S. *Newman's Way* (London, 1952).
PRZYWARA, E. *Einführung in Newmans Wesen und Werk.* Vol. IV of *Christentum* (Freiburg im Breisgau, 1922).
RICKABY, J. *Index to Works of Cardinal Newman* (London, 1914).

Ross, J. E. *John Henry Newman* (New York, 1933).
Sarolea, C. *Cardinal Newman and his Religious Life and Thought* (Edinburgh, 1908).
Stephen, L. *Agnostic's Apology* (London, 1893).
Thureau-Dangin, P. *Newman Catholique* (Paris, 1912).
Toohey, J. J. *An Indexed Synopsis of the Grammar of Assent* (New York, 1906).
Tristram, H., and Bacchus, F. 'John Henry Newman', Vacant-Mangenot-Amann, *Dictionnaire de Théologie Catholique XI* (Paris, 1931).
Various Authors. *Newman Centenary Essays*. Intro. H. Tristram (London, 1945).
    Tribute to Newman, ed. M. Tierney (Dublin, 1945).
    Newman and Littlemore (Oxford, 1945).
    Newman Centennial Essays (Washington, 1947).
    Newman: Studien. 2 vols. (Nürnberg, 1948 and 1954).
Ward, W. *Life of Cardinal Newman.* 2 vols. (London, 1912).
    Problems and Persons (London, 1903).
    Ten Personal Studies (London, 1908).
    Last Lectures (London, 1918).
Williams, W. J. *Newman, Pascal, Loisy and the Catholic Church* (London, 1906).

III PERIODICAL LITERATURE

Here an even more drastic pruning of the extensive list of works on Newman is required than in the previous section, especially as a great deal of it seems to be of no great value. This applies in particular to the French and American periodical literature.

Barry, W. 'The Turks, Cardinal Newman and the Council of Ten.' *Nineteenth Century*, August 1919.
Bouyer, L. 'Newman et le platonisme de l'âme anglaise.' *Revue de Philosophie*, XXXVI, 1936.
    'Newman's Influence in France.' *Dublin Review*, October 1945.
Byrne, J. J. 'The Notion of Doctrinal Development in the Anglican Writing of J. H. Newman.' *Ephemerides theologicae Lovanienses*, XV, 1937.

CROSS, F. L. 'Newman and the Doctrine of Development.' *Church Quarterly Review*, CXV, 1933.
GRANDMAISON, L. DE. 'J. H. Newman considéré comme maître.' *Etudes*, CX, 1907.
FROUDE, J. A. 'Newman and the Grammar of Assent.' *Edinburgh Review*, CXXXII, 1870.
HARROLD, C. F. 'Newman and the Alexandrian Platonists.' *Modern Philology*, XXXVII, 1940.
KENNY, T. 'Newman and Politics.' *Blackfriars*, XXXV, June 1954.
LYNCH, J. (ed.). 'The Newman-Perrone Paper on Development.' *Gregorianum*, XVI, fasc. iii, 1935.
RYAN, A. S. 'The Development of Newman's Political Thought.' *Review of Politics*, VII, 1945.
TRISTRAM, H. 'Newman and Carlyle.' *Cornhill Mag.*, LXV, 1928.
 'Newman and M. Arnold.' *Cornhill Mag.*, LX, 1926.
 'The Wilfrid Wards.' *Dublin Review*, April 1935.
 'J. A. Moehler et Newman.' *Revue des sciences philosophiques et théologiques*, XXVII, 1938.
WARD, W. 'Functions of Prejudice.' *Dublin Review*, 138, 1906.

IV OTHER WORKS

ACTON, LORD. *Letters to Mary Gladstone*, ed. A. Paul (London, 1904).
 Lord Acton and his Circle, ed. Gasquet (London, 1906).
 Selections from the Correspondence of the First Lord Acton, ed. Figgis and Laurence (London, 1917).
 Acton on Church and State, ed. D. Woodruff (London, 1952).
ALLIES, T. W. *Formation of Christendom*, vol. I (London, 1865).
ARNOLD, M. *Culture and Anarchy*, 3rd ed. (London, 1882).
 Some Unpublished Letters of M. Arnold, ed. A. Whitridge (Yale University Press, 1923).
ARNOLD, T. *Christian Duty of granting the claims of Roman Catholics* (Oxford, 1829).
 'Review of *Letters on the Church*.' *Edinburgh Review*, XLIV, 1826.
 Principles of Church Reform (London, 1833).
 Fragment on the Church (London, 1844).
 Fragments on Church and State (London, 1845).
ASHWELL, A. R. *Life of Samuel Wilberforce*, vol. I (London, 1880).
AUBERT, R. *Pontificate de Pie IX* (Paris, 1952).

AUGUSTINE, ST. *City of God*. Introduction by E. Barker, Everyman ed., 1945.
BRILIOTH, Y. *Anglican Revival* (London, 1925).
BURGON, DEAN. *Twelve Good Men*, 2 vols., 2nd ed. (London, 1888).
BURY, J. B. *History of Papacy in the Nineteenth Century*, ed. R. Murray (London, 1930).
BUTLER, E. C. *The Vatican Council* (London, 1930).
  Life of Bishop Ullathorne, 2 vols. (London, 1926).
BUTLER, J. *Analogy of Religion*, Bohn ed. (London, 1856).
CHURCH, R. W. *Life and Letters*, ed. M. Church (London, 1894).
  Oxford Movement (London, 1894).
CLOUGH, A. H. *Writing and Memoirs*, vol. I, ed. by his Wife (London, 1869).
COLERIDGE, J. T. *Memoir of J. Keble*, 2 vols., 2nd ed. (London, 1869).
COLERIDGE, S. T. *Constitution of Church and State*, ed. H. Coleridge (London, 1839).
CROLY, D. *Index to Tracts for the Times* (Oxford, 1842).
DAWSON, C. 'City of God', *Monument to St. Augustine* (London, 1930).
  Spirit of the Oxford Movement (London, 1933).
DEVAS, C. S. *Key to the World's Progress*, 2nd ed. (London, 1908).
DICEY, A. V. *Law and Opinion in England*, 2nd ed. (London, 1914).
FASNACHT, G. E. *Acton's Political Philosophy* (London, 1952).
FEILING, K. *The Second Tory Party, 1714–1832* (London, 1938).
FIGGIS, J. N. *Fellowship of Mystery* (London, 1914).
FROUDE, J. A. 'Oxford Counter Reformation', *Short Studies on Great Subjects*, vol. IV (London, 1909).
FROUDE, R. H. *Remains*. 4 vols., ed. Newman and Keble (London and Derby, 1838–1839).
GIBSON, W. *Abbé de Lamennais and the Liberal Catholic Movement in France* (London, 1896).
GLADSTONE, W. E. *State in its Relations with the Church*, 4th ed. (London, 1841).
  Church Principles considered in their Results (London, 1840).
GUIZOT, F. P. G. *History of Civilisation*, vol. I. Trans. W. Haxlitt (London, 1846).
HALES, E. Y. Y. *Pio Nono* (London, 1954).
HAWKINS, E. *A Dissertation on . . . Unauthoritative Tradition* (Oxford, 1819).

A Select Bibliography

HOCEDEZ, E. *Histoire de Théologie au XIX Siècle*, 3 vols. (Brussels, 1947-1952).
HODDER, E. *Life of Shaftesbury*, 3 vols. (London, 1887).
HOLLOWAY, J. *The Victorian Sage* (London, 1953).
JORDAN, J. *Review of Tradition as taught by the Writers of 'Tracts for the Times'* (London, 1840).
KEBLE, J. *National Apostasy* (London, 1931).
  Christian Year, 2 vols. (Oxford, 1827). (O.U.P. ed., 1914.)
  State in its relations with the Church, reprinted from *British Critic*, with Preface by H. P. Liddon (Oxford, 1869).
KNOX, E. A. *Tractarian Movement: 1833-1845* (London, 1933).
LECANUET, J. *L'Église de France sous la troisième république* (Paris, 1930).
LESLIE, S. *Life of Manning*, 2nd ed. (London, 1921).
  'Manning and Newman', *Manning: Anglican and Catholic* (London, 1951).
LIDDON, H. P. *Life of E. B. Pusey*, 4 vols. (London, 1893-1897).
LOCK, W. *John Keble* (London, 1893).
MARITAIN, J. *Redeeming the Time* (London, 1943).
MCENTEE, G. P. *Social Catholic Movement in Great Britain* (New York, 1927).
MCGRATH, F. *Newman's University: Idea and Reality* (London, 1951).
MANNING, H. E. *Caesarism and Ultramontanism* (London, 1877).
MATHEW, D. *Acton: The Formative Years* (London, 1946).
MIDDLETON, R. D. *Newman at Oxford: His Religious Development* (London, 1950).
  Dr. Routh (O.U.P., 1938).
MORLEY, J. *Life of Gladstone*, 3 vols. (London, 1903).
MOZLEY, J. B. *Letters*, ed. A. Mozley (London, 1885).
MOZLEY, J. K. *Some Tendencies in British Theology* (London, 1925).
NEWMAN, F. *Contributions Chiefly to the Early History of Cardinal Newman* (London, 1891).
O'DWYER, E. T. *Cardinal Newman and the Encyclical 'Pascendi'* (London, 1908).
OVERTON, J. H. *Non-Jurors* (London, 1902).
  English Church in the Nineteenth Century (London, 1894).
PALMER, W. *Narrative of Events Connected with 'Tracts for the Times'* (London, 1883).
PAPAL ALLOCUTION, to National Convention of Italian Catholic Jurists (December 1953).

PATTISON, M. *Memoirs* (London, 1885).
    Tendencies of Religious Thought in England, vol. I (London, 1860).
PECK, W. G. *Social Implications of the Oxford Movement* (London, 1933).
PRZYWARA, E. *Ringen der Gegenwart*, vol. II (Augsburg, 1929).
    Religionsbegründung (Freiburg im Breisgau, 1923).
    'St. Augustine in the Modern World', *Monument to St. Augustine* (London, 1930).
PURCELL, E. S. *Life of Cardinal Manning*, 2 vols. (London, 1896).
    Life of A. P. de Lisle, 2 vols. (London, 1900).
RUGGIERO, G. DE. *History of European Liberalism*. Trans. R. G. Collingwood (London, 1927).
SCHLEGEL, F. *Philosophy of History*. Trans. J. B. Robertson, 2nd ed. (London, 1846).
SIEVEKING, I. GIBERNE. *Memoir and Letters of F. W. Newman* (London, 1909).
SNEAD-COX, G. J. *Life of Cardinal Vaughan*, 2 vols. (London, 1910).
SPENCER, P. *Politics of Belief in Nineteenth Century France* (London, 1954).
STANLEY, DEAN. *Life of Arnold*, 2 vols. (London, 1844).
STORR, V. F. *Development of English Theology in the Nineteenth Century* (London, 1913).
THUREAU-DANGIN, P. *English Catholic Revival in the Nineteenth Century*, 2 vols. Trans. W. Wilberforce (London, 1914).
TUCKWELL, W. *Reminiscences of Oxford*, 2nd ed. (London, 1907).
    Pre-tractarian Oxford (London, 1909).
VARIOUS AUTHORS. *Monument to St. Augustine* (London, 1930).
    Manning: Anglican and Catholic, ed. J. Fitzsimons (London, 1942).
    Tolérance et Communauté Humaine. Cahiers de l'Actualité Réligieuse (Paris, 1953).
VAUGHAN, CARDINAL. *Letters to Lady Herbert of Lea*, ed. S. Leslie (London, 1942).
VIDLER, A. R. *Prophecy and Papacy* (London, 1954).
WANINGER, K. *Der soziale Katholismus in England* (München-Gladbach, 1914).
WARD, B. *Sequel to Catholic Emancipation*, 2 vols. (London, 1915).
WARD, M. *Wilfrid Wards and the Transition* (London, 1934).
    Insurrection versus Resurrection (London, 1937).
WARD, W. *Life of Cardinal Wiseman*, 2 vols., 2nd ed. (London, 1897).
    W. G. Ward and the Oxford Movement (London, 1889).

WARD, W. G. *Ideal of a Christian Church* (London, 1844).
WHATELY, J. *Life of Whately*, 2 vols. (London, 1866).
WHATELY, R. *Letters on the Church, by an Episcopalian* (London, 1826).
WHITRIDGE, A. *Dr. Arnold of Rugby* (London, 1928).
WILLEY, B. *Nineteenth Century Studies* (London, 1949).
WOODWARD, E. L. *Three Studies in European Conservatism* (London, 1929).

INDEX

Absolutism, 86
Abstractive intuition, 75
Achilli Trial, 151
Acton, Lord, 17, 26, 94, 153-154, 178, 181
Allies, M., 134, 168
Allies, T. W., 37, 134, 159, 161, 168
Anti-Christ, 177
Apostolical Succession, 124
Aquinas, St. Thomas, 82, 99, 113, 190
Aristocracy, 128, 176, 180
Aristotle, 100
Army, 180
Arnold, M., 163, 183, 187-188
Arnold, T. (junior), 181
Arnold, T. (senior), 121-123, 141-143, 181
Aufklärung, 164
Augustine, St., 22, 34, 43, 63-72, 78, 82, 92, 93, 107, 155, 190
   on philosophy of history, 36-38
Augustinianism, 154
Authority, 61-62, 103, 133
   and the individual, 135

Bagshawe, Bishop, 168, 173
Balfour, A. J., 137
Balmes, J., 190
Barbarism, 41, 54, 59, 88-91, 133, 160
Barker, E., 58, 65, 72
Barrow, R. H., 71
Barry, W., 42
Bellarmine, St. Robert, 65, 103
Bellasis, E., 191
Bentham, J., 77, 79, 138
Benthamism, 29, 137-139, 162-163, 188
Bergson, H., 50
Birmingham, 87, 191
Blachford, Lord, 176, 183
Blackstone, Sir W., 8
Bolingbroke, Henry, Viscount, 180

Bonald, Vicomte de, 149, 151, 190
Bosanquet, B., 193
Bouyer, L., 64
Bowle, J., 193
Bradley, F. H., 193
Bright, J., 180
Brilioth, Y., 65
Brinton, C., 1, 123, 127
Brougham, Lord, 140, 175
Burke, E., 1, 34-35, 56, 62, 94, 128
Bury, J. B., 158
Butler, Bishop, 33, 34, 48, 138
Butler, B. C., 156, 157
Butler, E. C., 151
Butler, W. A., 56

Calvinism, 10, 64, 109
Carlyle, A. J., 71
Catholic Emancipation, 5, 15, 119, 146, 175
Catholic Revival, 29, 148
Causation, 39, 100
Cavour, Count, 150
Chamberlain, Joe, 16, 191
Chateaubriand, F. R. de, 148
Chesterton, G. K., 12, 190-191
Chillingworth, W., 124
Chivalry, 142, 160
Church, 21, 109, 141, 161, 162, 188-189
   Anglican, 11-12, 111-112, 123-124, 143, 175, 183
   Established, 13, 24, 118-126, 129, 145
   Roman Catholic, 13, 15, 111-112, 148, 183
   and State, 2, 21-22, 54, 108-126, 148, 150
   and World, 43, 64-74, 96
Church, Dean, 5, 191
Church, M., 191
Cicero, 70

Index

Cisalpine Club, 15
Cisalpinism, 149
City of God, 34, 43, 63
Civilisation, 41, 54, 59, 88–92, 133, 158, 164
Civil marriages, 173
Civitas Dei, 65–66
Clement, 33
Coleridge, S. T., 27, 123
Collectivism, 21, 78–79, 163, 188
Collingwood, R. G., 59, 89
Colonies, 19
Common good, 77, 101
Common possession, 77–78, 87–88, 132–133
Compromise, 185
Conscience, 82, 106–107, 125–126, 144, 154, 157
Conservatism, 7, 20–21, 24–62, 119, 127, 136, 142, 145, 161, 192
　religious, 26, 29–30
Constitution, 85–86
　British, 8, 59, 85, 175–176, 178, 186
Contract theory, 21
Corn Laws, 6
Corporate personality, 162, 188–189
Correspondant, 150
Cortes, Juan Donoso, 190
Craven, A., 170
Croce, B., 50
Cullen, Cardinal, 17

D'Arcy, M. C., 30, 99
Davis, H. F., 27
Dawson, C., 12, 26, 65, 71, 191
Democracy, 19, 22, 146, 152, 166, 173–187
　Athenian, 181
Despotism, 161, 180
Development of Christian Doctrine, 14–15, 31–32
Development theory, 43–44, 48–56, 177, 192
　tests of, 54–56
Dicey, A. V., 110, 137

Digby, Kenelm, 15
Disraeli, B., 176, 191
Dissent, 13, 121, 163, 188
Divine Kingdom, 67
Divine Right of Kings, 90
Dogma, 30
Döllinger, J. J. I. von, 151
Donatists, 115
Droit naturel, 101
Dupanloup, Mgr. F., 151

Earthly city, 43, 65–66
Egalitarianism, 186
Eldon, Lord, 8
Elect, 64–65
Emly, Lord, 115
Empire, 116
Empiricism, 23, 189
Enclosures, 6
Equality, 184–186
Erastianism, 120, 122, 126, 135
Evangelicalism, 10, 64–65
Expedience, 139

Faber, F. W., 16
Fairbairn, A. M., 55
Fall (see original sin)
Falloux, Comte de, 150
Fasnacht, G. E., 154, 178
Febronianism, 149
Feiling, K., 3
Fénelon, F. de, 148
Feudalism, 142, 161
Fichte, J. G., 33
Figgis, J. N., 64, 160
Filmer, Sir R., 76, 160
First principles, 55
Flanagan, P., 99
Foisset, T., 150
Force, 83, 86, 115
France, 183
Fraternity, 184
Freedom of property, 91
Free will, 45
French Revolution, 42, 77, 148, 149, 182–183, 184, 190

Index

Froude, Archdeacon, 120
Froude, J. A., 5, 120
Froude, R. H., 11, 12, 25, 108, 111, 113, 122, 129, 132, 146, 161, 175, 183
Fullerton, Lady G., 170

Gallicanism, 18, 148–149
Gasquet, Cardinal, 153, 181
Genius loci, 60
Gilby, T., 100
Gladstone, W. E., 86, 117, 123–125, 143, 147–148, 157–159, 176–177
Goethe, J. W. von, 163
Görres, J., 149
Green, T. H., 1, 187
Gregory VII, 95, 183
Grey, Lord, 118, 129
Guiccardini, F., 46
Guitton, J., 43–44, 56
Guizot, F. P. G., 92

Habit, 87, 136
Hales, E. Y. Y., 158
Hammond, J. L. and B., 6, 167
Harnack, A. von, 65
Harper, T., 99
Hawkins, Provost, 9
Hegel, G. W. F., 33, 62
Herder, J. G., 59
High Church, 119, 120
History, 41
 cycles in, 36, 45–46, 136
 science of, 42
Hobbes, T., 117
Home & Foreign Review, 17
Honour, 160
Hooker, R., 128
Hope-Scott, J., 123
Hulme, T. E., 50
Hutton, R. H., 144

Idealism, 78–79
Illative sense, 49, 57
Imagination objects, 88, 133, 160

Individualism, 21, 76, 78–79, 162, 184, 188
Influence, 82
Inopportunists, 151, 156
Irish Church, disestablishment of, 147, 154
Irish University, 17
Ius naturale, 82, 101

Jacobitism, 7
Jansenism, 148
Jesuits, 155
Johnson, Dr., 130
Josephism, 149
Jury system, 81
Justice, 81, 135

Keble, J., 10, 12, 25, 27, 48, 106, 175
Kirk, R., 128
Knowledge, 140

Lacordaire, H., 149, 152
Laity, 153
Lamennais, F. R. de, 18, 106, 149, 150, 177–178, 183
Laski, H., 1, 21, 108, 113, 127, 157, 160
Lathbury, D. C., 123
L'Avenir, 149
Law, 34–35, 74, 76, 88, 104, 134–135
 abidingness, 86–87, 88, 115
 and justice, 47
 English, 81
 eternal, 82, 109
 historical, 40–42, 45
 moral, 45
 natural, 82, 98–102
 of State, 76, 80–87
 physical, 44, 45
 positive, 101
 social, 38, 44, 45
Leavis, F. R., 27
Leo XIII, 131
Leslie, S., 19
Lex naturalis, 82, 100

Index

Liberal Catholicism, 17–19, 148–156, 159
Liberalism, 10, 20, 25, 31, 126, 127–165, 188, 192
   political and religious, connexion of, 132
Liberty, 154, 158, 175, 184–185
Lisle, A. P. de, 15, 171
Littlemore, 14
Locke, J., 22, 54, 76, 107, 189
Logic, 9
Loi naturelle, 100
Longman, Canon, 172
Louis-Philippe, 180
Lowe, R., 182
Luke, Sir H., 42
Luther, M., 190

Macaulay, T. B., 124
McEntee, G. E., 171
Machiavelli, N., 46, 71
Maine, Sir H., 157
Maitland, F. W., 157
Maistre, J. de, 77, 104, 149, 151, 190
Malines Congress, 150, 152
Manichaeism, 43
Manning, Cardinal, 7, 16, 19, 152, 158, 168, 169, 173
Maritain, J., 98, 100
Marx, Karl, 50
Mathew, D., 154
Messner, J., 100
Mill, James, 110, 122
Mill, John Stuart, 1, 27, 137–138, 158, 181, 187
Mirari Vos, 149
Modernism, 32, 128, 152
Moehler, J. A., 56, 58–59
Montalembert, C. F. R. de, 149–150, 152
Morality, and politics, 154
   and religion, 136
Mozley, T., 6, 12, 146
Munich Congress, 155
Mussolini, B., 50
Myth, 49–52, 193

Napoleon Bonaparte, 148
Napoleon III, Louis, 153
Nation, and State, 80
   British, 80, 179
National Character, 58, 59, 87, 136
   English, 178–179
Nationalism, 59
Natural liberty, 84
Naturgesetz, 100
Naturrecht, 101
Newman, Charles, 4
Newman, Frank, 4, 170, 171–172
Newman, John (senior), 4
Nicholas of Cusa, 34
Nielsen, F., 158
Noetics, 8
Non-Jurors, 7

O'Connell, D., 13, 15
O'Faolain, S., 4, 170
Oligarchy, 174
Optimism, 129, 134, 142, 164
Oratory, 16, 136, 181
Oriel College, 8
Origen, 33
Original sin, 30, 63, 64, 129–130, 154
Oscott College, 15, 170
Overton, J., 110
Owen, R., 4
Oxford Movement, 11, 12, 13, 27, 104, 108, 111, 113, 119, 145, 162, 188

Palmer, W., of Magdalen, 111
Palmer, W., of Worcester, 13, 55, 111, 121
Papacy, 106, 148, 155, 159
   deposing power of, 86
   infallibility of, 17, 19, 55, 85, 104, 148, 150, 156–159
   temporal power of, 16, 19
Papal Allocution, 191
Parkes, S. C., 127
Pascal, B., 98
Patriarchalism, 160–161
Peel, Sir R., 5, 119, 140

Pelagian heresy, 173
Perfectibility, 30
Pericles, 181
Pessimism, 134, 164
Philosophy, of history, 36–47
   of Newman, 32–34
Pio Nono, 16, 155, 157
Pius VII, 148
Plato, 93
Platonism, 78
   Christian, 33, 78
   Neo-, 33
Plotinus, 34
Political parties, 51, 83
   science, 44
Power, 84
Predestination, 64
Prejudice, 57
Press, 83, 158
Private judgement, 106
Progress, 46, 64, 136, 164, 192
Przywara, E., 99
Public opinion, 81, 86, 117
Pugin, A. W. N., 16

Quanta Cura, 156, 157

Radicals, 13, 110, 176
   philosophic, 13, 110
Rambler, 17, 152–154, 175
Rationalism, 28, 132
Reade, F. V., 3
Real assent, 88
Realism, 154, 193
Reason, 46, 164
   corporate, 78
   explicit, 49
   implicit, 49
   individual, 78
Reformation, 190
Reform Bills, 109, 118, 146–147, 174–177
Religious persecution, 115
Revolution, 1688, 54, 129
   1848, 150

Rights, 102
   natural, 130
   of man, 53
Romanticism, 26, 77, 190
Rommen, H., 100
Rousseau, J. J., 26
Russell, Lord John, 175, 176
Ryder, Father, 172

Sainte-Beuve, C. A., 163
Salmon, G., 156
Schelling, F. W. J. von, 33
Schlagdenhauffen, A., 164
Schlegel, F., 37, 38, 43, 59, 92, 164, 190
Schleiermacher, F. D. E., 31
School Boards, 173
Scott, Sir W., 27
Secret societies, 190
Sense objects, 88, 133, 160
Simpson, R., 17, 153
Slavery, 161
Social bonds, 135, 137, 139, 141, 150
   class, 35, 169–171
   conscience, 22, 165, 166–173
   contract, 76, 77, 79–80
   justice, 166
   nature, 75
   study, 46
Socialism, 143
Societas perfecta, 101, 113
Society, 76, 77, 84
Sorel, G., 1, 20, 50–52, 193
Sovereignty, 21, 117–118, 148, 154, 157
Spain, 191
Spencer, H., 39
Stanley, Dean, 5, 121
Stark, W., 60, 78
State, 21, 44–45, 63–107, 109, 139, 141, 148, 162, 164, 179, 184, 187
   and justice, 63, 70–74, 93–107, 142–143
   and nation, 80
   Christian, 92–93, 135–137
   ideal, 92–93

State (contd.)
  secular, 18, 132–135, 148, 150, 159, 162, 191
Suarez, F., 103
Sudan, 176
Suffrage, 186
  universal, 174, 186
Sweden, 191
Syllabus of Modern Errors, 17, 150, 156, 157

Taparelli (S.J.), 104
Temperance, 171–172
Terrena civitas, 65–66, 96
Theology, and politics, 46–47
Thirty-nine Articles, 14
Thomism, 23, 75, 99–102, 189–190
Tocqueville, A. de, 182, 185
Toryism, 7–8, 11, 24–25, 52, 55, 90, 119, 127, 128, 142, 145–146, 154, 159–162, 175, 177
  Old, 8
Totalitarianism, 79, 186
Tract 90, 14
Tracts for the Times, 11, 13
Tractarian movement (see Oxford Movement)
Tradition, 57–58, 61–62, 142, 151, 192
Trinity College, 5, 8
Tristram, H., 56, 69, 152
Turkey, 41
Turks, 89, 90

Ultramontanism, 17–19, 148–152, 155
Unitarianism, 121
Univers, 150, 155

Universals, 75
Utilitarianism, 53, 110, 137–139

Vatican Council, 150, 157
Vatican Decrees, 151, 158–159
Veuillot, L., 150, 151, 155, 156
Via Media, 12, 14, 111
Vico, G. B., 50
Vivisection, 167

Walpole, Sir R., 180
Ward, M., 35, 170, 174
Ward, Wilfrid, 57, 105, 173–174
Ward, W. G., 122, 151, 156, 158, 174
Wars, Crimean, 80, 180–1
  Napoleonic, 3
Wellington, Duke of, 177, 186
Whately, Archbishop R., 9, 108, 110, 122
Whigs, 55, 128–129, 130, 146, 174–175, 176
White, R. J., 27
Whitridge, A., 183
Will, 84
  general, 84
Williams, W. G., 55
Winson Green Prison, 167
Wiseman, Cardinal, 15
Woodruff, D., 153
Wordsworth, C., 124
Wordsworth, W., 163
Workhouses, 172
Working class, 169
World, 63–64
  and Church, 96, 154–155
  different senses of, 67–70

Young Ireland, 17

DATE DUE

GAYLORD			PRINTED IN U.S.A.